Elements of Old Testament Theology

Elements

of

Old Testament
Theology

CLAUS WESTERMANN

Translated by
Douglas W. Stott

John Knox Press
ATLANTA

Library of Congress Cataloging in Publication Data

Westermann, Claus.
    Elements of Old Testament theology.

    Translation of: Theologie des Alten Testaments in
Grundzugen.
    Bibliography: p.
    Includes indexes.
    1. Bible. O.T.—Theology. I. Title.
BS1192.5.W4713   230   81-13752
ISBN 0-8042-0191-9   AACR2

©Vandenhoeck & Ruprecht, Göttingen 1978
English translation © copyright John Knox Press 1982
10 9 8 7 6 5 4 3 2 1
Printed in the United States of America
John Knox Press
Atlanta, Georgia 30365

To the Emeriti, Colleagues, and
Students of
the Heidelberg Theological
Faculty

Contents

What Does the Old Testament Say About God?

Preliminary Methodological Considerations

The answer to this question must be given by the entire Old Testament. A theology of the Old Testament has the task of summarizing and viewing together what the Old Testament as a whole, in all its sections, says about God. This task is not correctly understood if one declares one part of the Old Testament to be the most important and gives it prominence over the others; or if one regards the whole as determined by one concept such as convenant, election, or salvation; or if one asks beforehand what the center of the Old Testament is. The New Testament clearly has its center in the suffering, death, and resurrection of Christ, to which the Gospels are directed and which the Epistles take as their starting point. The Old Testament, however, bears no similarity at all to this structure, and it is thus not possible to transfer the question of a theological center from the New to the Old Testament.[1]

If we wish to describe what the Old Testament as a whole says about God, we must start by looking at the way the Old Testament presents itself, something everyone can recognize: "The Old Testament tells a story" (G. von Rad). With that statement we have reached our first decision about the form of an Old Testament theology: If the Old Testament narrates what it has to say about God in the form of a story (understood here in the broader sense of event), then the structure of an Old Testament theology must be based on events rather than concepts.

But how can we define this structure of events more exactly? There seems to be an obvious answer to this question. The task of a theology of the Old Testament could simply consist of re-narrating the story of the Old

Testament in an abbreviated and summarized form. This was certainly how Gerhard von Rad understood it: "Re-telling the story is therefore still the most legitimate way for theology to speak about the Old Testament." This would be possible if the whole of the Old Testament consisted of a continuous story from the first to the last chapter. However, this is not the case.

The Old Testament has come down to us in a threefold structure in which it also originated: the Torah, the Prophets, and the Writings; or the historical, prophetic, and didactic books, the nucleus of which is the Psalms. According to the traditionists' conception here, the Bible of the Old Testament includes the story narrated, but also the word of God inhering in the story and humanity's response in calling to God. The narrative of the historical books from Genesis to Chronicles does contain texts in which the word of God enters the action, and texts which contain the response of praise or lament; but the structure of the Old Testament in its three parts indicates that the narrative in the Old Testament is determined by the word of God occurring in it and by the response of those for whom and with whom this story unfolds.

It is therefore the canon of the Old Testament itself which shows us the structure of what happens in the Old Testament in its decisive elements. We have thus found an objective starting point for an Old Testament theology which is independent of any preconceptions about what the most important thing in the Old Testament is and independent of any other prior theological decisions. If one asks what the Old Testament says about God, this threefold structure shows us the way.[2]

But how can what the Old Testament says about God be viewed and described together in its many and diverse forms? How can it be expressed along broad and simple lines? In previous Old Testament theologies, this has been attempted predominantly by reducing what the Old Testament says about God to comprehensive terms such as *salvation, election, covenant, faith, kerygma, revelation, redemption, soteriology, eschatology,* etc. By using these noun concepts scholars moved away from the language of the Old Testament, which is overwhelmingly dominated by verbs. In addition, this meant a loss of the diversity in which the Old Testament speaks of God.[3]

If we wish to inquire concerning these broad lines determining the whole way in which the Old Testament speaks about God and yet not overlook the many forms in which it occurs, we shall therefore have to start from *verb structures*. This demands a complete change in our way of thinking. The story told in the Old Testament is then not a salvation history in the sense of a series of God's salvation events, but rather a history of God and man whose nucleus is the experience of saving. It does not, however, remain only a story of deliverance. In the middle of the Pentateuch stands the confession of praise of those who experienced this saving, and in the middle of the Deuteronomistic historical section (Joshua to 2 Kings) the confession of sin of those on whom judgment was passed. The Pentateuch is further subdivided into primeval history, patriarchal history, and history of the people. Within this subdivision, the beginning of the history of the people (Exodus through Deuteronomy) receives a forestructure which encompasses God's activity in the world and human life and thus God's blessing.

In the prophetic books, the framework of the presentation does not emerge from what the individual prophets said, but rather from the structure of the judgment oracle common to all judgment prophets (to which corresponds the confession of sin in the middle of the Deuteronomistic historical work) and its correspondence within the salvation oracle. The varying individual prophetic pronouncements are then to be understood from the perspective of these constants.

In the Psalms, this constant factor is given by the structure of the Psalms of lament and praise, the two major types, from which then both the varying individual expressions and any subordinate forms are to be understood.

Wisdom has no place within this basic framework of an Old Testament theology, since it originally and in reality does not have as its object an occurrence between God and man; in its earlier stages wisdom is overwhelmingly secular. A theological wisdom develops at a later stage, and is then to be understood according to its theological statement (e.g., from the perspective of the contrast between the pious and godless). The theological home of wisdom can be found within the context of human creation; the creator gives humanity the ability to understand its world and to become oriented within it.[4]

So far we have only hinted at a few main features. They should show that, from such a starting point of an Old Testament theology, the whole of what the Old Testament says about God continually stays in view. The theology of the Old Testament thus remains determined in every aspect by the outline of a story entrusted to us which includes the occurrence of God speaking and the response of those who experience these events.

With that the structure of Old Testament theology acquires a systematic as well as historical aspect. The systematic aspect emerges from the talk about God which remains constant throughout the entire Old Testament. This constant is found primarily in an interaction between God and man (more precisely; between God and his creation, his people, humanity), and includes speaking and acting on both sides. In addition to this we find a series of other constants throughout the entire Old Testament, e.g., the fact that both saving and blessing belong to God's acts from beginning to end, or that human response finds its center in lament and praise, or that from beginning to end God is *one*.

The historical aspect emerges from the fact that this God of whom the Old Testament speaks has bound himself to the history of his people. Since this is a people like any other, it, too, is subject to historical change and historical contingency. This accounts for the fact that the elements of this interaction between God and humanity change in the course of history. So, for example, the facticity of response in service remains constant, while the worship service itself is subjected to changes during the course of this history. Or it manifests itself in the fact that the saving God is simultaneously always the judging God, although both God's saving and judging occurs in a history in which each, in and for itself, as well as their relationship to each other, changes. This simultaneity of constants and variables inhering in this talk about God also accounts for the fact that the history of God with his people as a whole—in this structure of constants and variables—is characterized by absolute singularity and uniqueness. The elements, however, out of which this whole is put together are able to represent a connection between the religion of Israel and other religions (see below, pp. 58-61).

The History

What kind of story does the Old Testament tell? It differs from history as understood by modern historical science in that what happens happens between God and humanity, between creator and his creation. The nineteenth century of history alone cannot be the standard for an Old Testament theology because it *a priori* excludes an act of God as an integral part of history. In the Old Testament, God's acts and words belong to every event; reality without the working of God does not yet exist for Old Testament people. What moves history takes place between God and humans; this is what Martin Buber calls an event in dialogue.[5] This has its roots in the creation; God created humankind in his image, to correspond with him, so that something may happen between him and this creature.

The discussion begun between G. von Rad and F. Hesse[6] about whether Old Testament theology should be concerned with historically demonstrable events or with the conceptions of Israel's faith about these events started from false presuppositions on both sides, since both presuppose the distinction between reality and the reality of faith. What the Old Testament says about reality, it says about God; what it says about God, it says about reality.

That is the fundamental difference between the story told in the Old Testament and the concept of history used in historical science. The latter is oriented towards political history or the history of peoples, i. e., towards the history of the societally organized human community. The determining factor for this is that the historical events can be documented; historical verification consists in proving something from historical documents. This kind of documentation arose only within the context of civil organization, so that historical writing itself presupposes this organization.[7] Herein lies a limitation of historical science: It is limited to events which are documented. This limitation shows itself above all in the investigation into early human history; other sciences are also engaged in this study, particularly ethnology. It is concerned with primitive peoples and in general is not able to work with historical sources or historical documents. Since it does work with peoples, tribes, and other groups in a prehistorical stage, it must reckon with conditions not corresponding to the criteria of historical science. To mention but two examples: Narrative precedes historical writing. This narrative, however, portrays an event differently than does historical writing. It does tell of something which really happened, but not in a way enabling it to be ascertained as "historical." The figuring of time in genealogies precedes that in historical dates, and the same holds true here.

These two examples can also be applied to the Old Testament, since it encompasses both the prehistoric and historic stages of a certain group. One conclusion from this is that the alternative historical-unhistorical can be applied to one part of the Old Testament texts, but not to all, e.g., not to the patriarchal history. Another conclusion is that no strict separation of the historical from the religious is possible in the Old Testament.

The most important difference, however, is that God's activity is universal, that it encompasses the entirety of what happens from beginning to end. The "historical" cannot simply be extracted from this comprehensive action.

This history occurs in three circles: In its middle stands the history of the people of God, corresponding to the political, historically portrayable history of one people among others. In a larger circle it is the history of the "family of man," of generations of families and their individual members in their personal, completely apolitical sphere of life as portrayed in the patriarchal history. In the largest circle it is the history of humanity as a whole, divided into nations, on the earth as a whole, just as it is the subject of primeval history at the beginning and of apocalyptic at the end. This corresponds to the conception of the Yahwist, which is apparent in his combination of the primeval history (Gen. 1—11) with the patriarchal history (Gen. 12—50) and with the history of the people (from the Exodus to the conquest of Canaan). It is clearly manifested in the introduction to the patriarchal history (Gen. 12:1-3), in which the promise of Abraham is not limited to Israel, the people of God, but, looking back to the nations into which humanity branched out (Gen. 10), the promise of blessing includes the nations of the earth: "by you all the families of the earth shall bless themselves."

The *concept of salvation history,* however, coined in the nineteenth century and dependent on that century's understanding of history, cannot, at least not alone, be fully determinative for a theology of the Old Testament.[8] In contrast to a narrowly conceived concept of salvation history, the Old Testament speaks of an event between God and humanity not limited to a history of God's salvation acts. To be sure, the history of the people of Israel begins with a divine act of salvation, and the confession of God as savior remains decisive right into the New Testament; but in the first place God's saving is contrasted with his judgment, and to this saving is added God's blessing activity, which cannot be simply inserted or subordinated to God's salvation acts. In the structure of the Pentateuch this is demonstrated by the fact that the center (Exodus to Numbers) is determined by God's saving, while the framework (Genesis and Deuteronomy) is predominantly determined by God's blessing. The narrow salvation-historical interpretation of the Old Testament presupposes that God's activity as salvation activity is in general consistently the same, and that it is related to the entity of the people of God. However, the specific character of the history told in the Old Testament consists in the fact that God's activity is not the same from beginning to end and is not always related to the same entity, i.e., the nation, but rather embraces all important forms of community in human history in a universal conception, in the center of which stand the people of God and their history: the family, tribe, nation, and the cultic congregation, and beyond that humanity as a whole. All areas of human life participate in this history: economy, culture, social life, and politics. All these spheres belong somewhere in what happens between God and humanity, but they are and must be different as they appear in a family, a tribe in the process of settlement, a village community with agriculture, and at a royal court. In this process everything has its meaning and its necessity: what the patriarchs experienced on their wanderings and in their families about and with God; the Exodus group from Egypt at the Reed Sea, in the wilderness, and at Sinai; the experience of the immigrating tribes in their struggles for a settlement. To this we add the new experiences of the call of a leader; the encounter with the sanctuaries of the inhabitants of Canaan; the experience of God's blessing in the new, agricultural form of economy with its annual feasts; the adoption of kingship with new promises and new dangers right up to the suffering through the collapse, which had been announced long before by the prophets; and on up to the humiliations of the exile and the new beginning of the temple congregation in the province of an empire. This diverse reality in its multitude of forms, portrayed in a multitude of linguistic forms, is embraced by God's activity, moved by God's word, and out of it there emerges the response.

The Word of God in the Old Testament

God's activity with his people, with man, with the world *includes action and speaking.* Psalm 33:4 summarizes thus:

> For the word of the LORD is upright;
> and all his work is done in faithfulness.

The second part of the canon, the Prophets, has as its actual subject matter the occurrence of the word of God, the words of the individual prophets are presented in the context of the historical process in which they occur. But it is not only this part of the canon that deals with the word of God; on the contrary, the word of God in various forms belongs to everything the Old Testament says about God. The significance of God for his people consists of both his working and his word together (Ps. 33:4). The prophetic word is most closely associated with the story told in the Old Testament, and this accounts for the fact that precisely this word forms a part of the canon.

What does the word of God mean in the Old Testament? It is here not primarily understood on the basis of its content, but as an action which takes place between a speaker and a listener. We find this understanding of the word particularly in the case of prophetic words. If one says "the word of the LORD came to Jeremiah," this sentence introduces a process corresponding to the commissioning of a messenger and continuing further in the prophet's delivery of the word and the reaction of those addressed. The word is a process in time between two or more persons. It is inherent in the nature of the word that it reaches the listener and causes a response.[9] Understood in this manner, the word of God in its many expressions belongs to the history told in the first part of the canon.

The word of God does not exist for modern historical understanding because it cannot be historically documented. The modern historian must place the prophet's subjective consciousness, the consciousness which believes it has heard the word of God, in the place of the word coming to the prophet from God. But with that the historian changes the meaning of "word" in the Old Testament. He is able to adapt the phenomenon of the word of God encountered in the Old Testament to his own historical understanding only by understanding it differently than the text intends.

However, modern theology also understands the "word of God" to a large extent differently than the Old Testament intends, namely, on the basis of its content. According to that understanding, the word of God is what God has said. As such it can be found as given and becomes accessible to objective reflection. This separates the word of God from the process of its occurrence and puts it at one's disposal.

God's speaking, throughout the Old Testament, occurs in multiple forms. Every word of God, no matter what it says or how it occurs, functions within the event between God and man; separated from it, it would no longer be the word of God. One might order the profusion of God's words in the Old Testament such that they are either words occurring within the flow of daily life or in the particularity of the cult. The word of God spoken and heard in the worship service differs from that coming to a person in the middle of daily occurrences primarily in one aspect. Those who have come together at a particular place at a particular time do so expecting to listen for God's word;

this holy time and holy place form a quiet enclave complementing this preparedness for hearing. Particularly characteristic of the word of God occurring within a daily life is the word of the messenger, the *mal'ak jhwh*, who with his message encounters a person in the field, at home, or underway. This type of word of God also includes the prophetic word which comes unexpectedly and often unwanted to people without the security of the holy space.

As regards its content, we can understand the word of God in a manner commensurate with the two main aspects, prophecy and law, as announcement or proclamation and instruction or directive.

The word as announcement has its center in prophecy, but it is not confined to it; it also comprises a significant part of the historical books. It is two-sided to the extent that it announces salvation or doom, either as promise or as the announcement of judgment. Both belong together throughout the Old Testament, although in quite different relationships, from primeval history, the promises to the patriarchs, beyond the Exodus from Egypt and the conquest of Canaan, through the period in the country, the exile, the post-exilic period right up to apocalyptic. The announcement oracle, either as promise or as judgment, demonstrates a profusion of manifestations that can occur in extremely different ways. Summarized, it can only be represented by a history of the promises and a history of the words of judgment throughout the Old Testament. If, however, it is correct to say that the announcement—either of salvation or of doom—can only be summarized in a history, then the word in its function as announcement is necessarily related to the history of the people and is one of the moving elements behind this history. Indeed, in every case an announcement introduces an event curve, from the moment the announcement occurs until the moment what was announced actually arrives. A promise is made to Abraham; the messengers of God tell him: "I will surely return to you in the spring, and Sarah your wife shall have a son." The messengers continue on their way and daily life returns to normal. But there is a tension causing the family to look forward, and it remains until the child is born. The hour of the child's birth, however, is simultaneously an hour of recall: It has happened, what they said! And only in this way is what happened preserved and carried on.

Another example: Jeremiah announces during the period of political ascendancy that Jerusalem will be taken and destroyed by the Babylonian king. This announcement is disputed and resisted, and Jeremiah is silenced. After it indeed happens, however, the announcement is reawakened; thus it is preserved and handed on.

These two pronouncements are undeniably different. The one announces salvation, the other doom. The one occurs in the familiar, the other in the political sphere. The one is accepted, the other rejected. Nonetheless, they have something in common: They create a context. By means of the word event, both cause a given time period to become an organic whole: the temporal distance from the utterance itself up to the occurrence of what was announced. This is how historical consciousness emerged in Israel, where one began to see and experience contextual relationships within what was happening. This seeing and experiencing was one of the roots of tradition. [10]

From here we can see the connection with the introduction to the Gospel of Luke. It begins in the prologue with a family history whose motifs are very similar to those of the patriarchal history. A child is promised—a child is born. The child, however, is the savior, and its birth fulfills the promise of such a savior. The people of God in the Old Testament learned to understand time within a certain context, from the promise of a child to Abraham onward, through the announcement of judgment upon Israel up to the promise of Israel's savior in the exilic and post-exilic periods. The introduction to the Gospel of Luke becomes comprehensible only against the background of this preliminary history. A word issues into daily events, into daily occurrences, creating contextual relationships and connections in its extension up to the point where what was announced indeed comes to pass. In creating these connections it thus establishes history. Behind the messenger's announcement, "To you is born this day a Savior," stands the history of the people of God with its path from the promise to the fulfillment. It is the word of God functioning as announcement. From the smallest event curve within the family sphere to the broader ones of the nation and of humanity, it makes history into a particular context. It was thus also able to connect the history of the old with that of the new people of God.

The key words in the "salvation-historical" interpretation of the Old Testament are promise and fulfillment. [11] It is intended such that the entire Old Testament is understood under the concept promise, the entire New Testament under the concept fulfillment. However, quite different situations are possible as regards this fulfillment of Old Testament words of salvation. By no means were all the words fulfilled in this way. A profusion of possibilities is possible, from the clearly, unambiguously recognizable fulfillment, the subsequent variation of a promise, all the way to the clear absence of any fulfillment.

The majority of Old Testament salvation pronouncements are fulfilled in the time with which they deal, and that means within Israel's history. This is the case, for example, with the promised land, the promise of victory, Jeremiah's salvation oracles during the seige of Jerusalem, and many others. The curve described by this kind of salvation oracle from its utterance up to the occurrence thus remains within the history of Yahweh with Israel, and does not extend beyond.

One group of salvation oracles concerned with all of humanity, or with the entire human world, announces something which to this day is still outstanding—that death will no longer be. A salvation oracle such as Jeremiah 31:31-34, however, announces a new community with God for which the mutual exhortation as well as the tradition in general will simply no longer exist. This has not yet come about. Concerning the broad promise of blessing in Genesis 12:1-3, one can also ask whether it has already been realized. The Old Testament thus contains a group of promises whose realization has not yet come about.

Between these two groups there is a very small group of promises which one can say point to Christ or are fulfilled in Christ. In these, however, the reference to Christ is often not clear and is thus disputed. This looks quite different from the perspective of the New Testament. In the New Testament only those promises are relevant which are fulfilled in Christ; all others are of no interest and thus never arise. Only for that reason can the Old Testament promises in their totality be said to be fulfilled in Christ in the New Testament, 2 Corinthians 1:20: "For all the promises of God find their Yes in him. That is why we utter the Amen through him." That is, all the Old Testament promises find their fulfillment in Christ. This sentence is understandable from Paul's perspective, since for him promises are only those which point to Christ and are fulfilled in him. But how are we to understand a sentence such as 2 Corinthians 1:20, if according to our own understanding of Old Testament salvation oracles the sentence does not apply in this way? The sentence can acquire meaning for us, and even be affirmed, if from our own understanding of Old Testament salvation oracles we see them in all their differentiation and multiplicity as the constitutive parts of a history, and if we recognize a goal-orientation in this history pointing beyond the Old Testament. To be sure, the fact remains that a large number of salvation oracles in the Old Testament do not point to Christ; however, the fact also remains that the history of promises in the Old Testament began with the promise of saving. The history growing out of this promise led to the promise of a saving of the people of Israel on the basis of God's forgiveness (Deutero-Isaiah), and in this context we hear of an individual who representatively dies for the people's sins and is confirmed in his work by God beyond death (Isa. 52/53). In view of this one line we can affirm Paul's sentence. We must simultaneously say, however, that this does not apply to each individual Old Testament salvation oracle in and for itself and in each individual context.

From the perspective of fulfillment in Christ we must then, of course, return to the many other Old Testament salvation oracles their independent meanings. Just as all the promises running through the Old Testament form a history, so also does the fulfillment in Christ introduce a history reaching from Christ's coming to his return. Fulfillment can then only be seen in the whole agitation of historical occurrences. The history of the many and various salvation oracles in the Old Testament then function to give historical perspective to this fulfillment in Christ, and to unfold this fulfillment into the multifariousness of human existence and its changes. The history of salvation oracles leading to Christ is then to be expanded from the center of fulfillment out into the changes in the community and into the new tasks and problems of changed eras. We then need to ask how the three areas in which salvation oracles in the Old Testament have moved are intended from the perspective of the center of fulfillment; how are they intended for the people of God, for the individual person and for humanity itself; and how these areas are affected. The narrative in Luke 4:16-21 shows us this additional meaning of fulfillment in Christ. In the concluding sentence, "Today this scripture has been fulfilled in your ears," the promise in Isaiah 61:1f. is interpreted as fulfilled in Jesus' activity in all its richness, in a fulfillment story beginning with his coming.

The directive word (*torah* understood as instruction) later comes to be described in summary form as Law, but the different designations in Deuteronomy (commandments, statutes, and laws) still show that the overriding concept of Law embraces different forms and processes. Commandment (prohibition) and law are basically different processes. The commandment or prohibition consists of only one sentence in the form of a direct address, while the law is expressed in two parts connecting the deed with its consequence. The law presupposes an institution which has the power to punish and make decisions; the authority of the commandment is that of whoever gives it. Closely related to the commandment is the exhortation (warning, above all in the deuteronomic paraenesis), which sets out a positive or negative consequence in the form of a conditional clause. Commandments and laws originally belonged to a different *Sitz im Leben* and have been transmitted in different ways: in series of commandments and legal corpora. Only afterwards did they come together in the legal collections of the Pentateuch, and only at that point did the "Law" arise comprising commandments and laws. In this combined form they have been assigned to the Sinai theophany and together have become the Law which God has given his people.

But in the Old Testament the word of God as instruction is not confined to the series of commandments and legal collections. It also includes commissions, orders, and commands throughout the entire Old Testament in the flow of daily life, from the prohibition against eating the fruit of the tree in the middle of the garden on up to the commissions to a prophet and God's other commanding and instructing words in all the Old Testament writings. These instructions or directives are given to an individual person in a specific situation and are confined to this situation, as with the command to Abraham: "Go out from your father's house . . ." (Gen. 12:1; cf. Gen. 46:2). The commandment applying to everyone and for all times is totally different, as e.g., "You shall have no other gods before me." This kind of commandment, applying to everyone and for all time, could thus become an integral part of the worship service.

This directive or instructing word is also to be seen in the widest context, not from the perspective of a theoretical and abstract legal concept, but rather in its function in reality. A person stands at a point where he does not know further what to do, since the signposts at hand are inadequate. In this situation only an authoritative directive can help him. Abraham heard the directive to set out in just this kind of situation, and the rich young man heard the directive "Sell what you possess," while another was told, "Take up your pallet and walk." People need this authoritative directive; every person can come into a situation in which only this can really help him further. Whether a person's path leads to his goal depends at certain times on whether he hears a clear, unambiguous directive. Because this kind of directive is vitally necessary, we encounter it in both the Old as well as the New Testament; in no way can it be subordinated to an abstract legal concept. Just as the directive to Abraham introduces the patriarchal history, so also does the directive to a prophet introduce the history of prophecy; and Jesus' directive "Follow me" equally introduces the history of the apostles. God acts in the history of his people as well as in the life of individuals through these directives; they specify a path, command a reversal, a turn towards the suffering and away from a falsified worship service, or command a step into new spheres. The word as directive or instruction is a necessary function of the word of God.

The cultic word has its place in the context of a sacred act. It presupposes the assembly of the congregation for worship and the occurrence of God's word through the cult mediator, the priest. A word typical of the continuing worship service is the blessing, or the priestly word imparting God's blessing. In contrast to the prophetic word (future) and to commandment and law (imperative), it has a perfective-present character. God blesses his people when the priest speaks the blessing and thus extends it to the people. The affirming or forgiving answer (salvation oracle) following the lament in the worship service has the same character; the priest mediates the divine answer in the perfective form: God has heard. A cultic curse can correspond to a cultic blessing, as the series of curses in Deuteronomy show. The proclamation of commandments is based on the fact that the commandments were assigned to the Sinai theophany. We must be aware here that the individual commandment and the commandment series have different functions. The individual commandment, heard in a situation corresponding only to it (e.g., "you shall not kill"), functions as a directive to the extent that it influences or guides a person's decision in a certain direction. The commandment series, on the other hand, to the extent they are an address to the entire liturgical congregation in the worship service, function to keep alive what God has commanded (perfect tense) as a whole and to transmit it further. The perfective character of the commandments, as that which God has commanded, made it possible for the proclamation of God's commandments in the worship service to be expanded later by the reading of the Law.

Corresponding to the cultic word of God are the liturgical answers of the congregation, the Amen, the praise of God, the sacrificial saying, and the confession. The cultic word as directed to the people and the liturgical response of the people come together in the act of worship.

The word of God which occurs in worship is at the same time the word that has been transmitted or handed down, as is especially clear in the commandments (see above pp. 20ff.). In the act of worship, protected and secured by the particular time and place, it is received and handed down from generation to generation. But this word of God which is transmitted in the cult, secured by the institution, and preserved unchanged by this holy act, would become fossilized if it did not also stand in a lively, alternating relationship with the word of God as it occurs and is heard outside worship in the flow of daily life. Only these two together form the word of God, never the one without the other.

These three functions of the word of God can only approximately and inexactly encompass the richness of God's words in the Old Testament. Some cannot be assigned unequivocally to one of these functions, and some combine several of them. There is a profusion of connections between these functions, for example in the patriarchal promises when a directive to set out is combined with a promise (Gen. 12:1-3); when in Deutero-Isaiah the prophetic promise is expressed in liturgical language (salvation oracle); when the commandment becomes a liturgical word. Such combinations, however, do not change the fact that the three functions continue to exist with and next to each other throughout the entire history. The promise cannot take the place of the commandment or law, and the liturgical word cannot stay alive without the word of God occurring outside the worship service. Neither the commandment nor the law can exist without the future-oriented word. The entire Old Testament is permeated by the multifaceted word of God which is connected with history and is a part of its many forms. It has its own history in each of these three functions: (a) the word of announcement at the center in the history of the prophetic word, in the whole Old Testament in the history of promise and judgment; (b) commandment and law in the history of the forms of commandments and legal statements, as well as in the history of commandment series and legal collections; (c) the liturgical word in the history of the worship service.

If in these three basic functions of the word of God only the word as announcement has formed an independent part of the canon, this does not mean that prophecy constitutes the center of the Old Testament. It is the center only for one of the three integral parts, for the word of God. It is prejudicial to characterize Israel's religion as a prophetic religion, and it is prejudicial to give the prophetic word a one-sided priority position in the Old Testament. Only in the center between the directive and liturgical word does the word as announcement acquire significance. There, pointing towards the future, it characterizes God's journey with his people, with humanity, and with creation as history, from the patriarchal promises on up to apocalyptic. This history is determined from beginning to end by the word of God occurring in it. Of the three basic functions of the word of God it is thus also the announcement which unequivocally connects the Old with the New Testament. The announcements of salvation as well as of judgment point beyond the Old Testament.

An essential difference between the Christian and Jewish understanding of the Old Testament is that for Jewish understanding the directive in the form of the Law is most important, not the word as announcement. In this understanding, the Law is God's word without qualification. It can refer here to the fact that it is anchored in the founding event of the Sinai revelation; it is the word revealed at the beginning at Sinai. One can ask, however, how this Sinai pericope is related to the preceding Exodus pericope, which is determined by the promise at its beginning. The fact that the prophets, and not the Law, form an independent part of the canon speaks against the Jewish understanding. Even if the first part of the canon received the designation "Law," this is a later interpretation.

However, decisive for the understanding of the word of God in the Old Testament is the fact that it is inseparably connected in these three functions with the history of God with his people. It cannot be separated out of this history as something God said. The Old Testament knows nothing of an abstracted, objectified word of God, and that is why the word of God in the Old Testament cannot become a doctrine. It is also the reason none of these functions can be absolutized apart from the others. This absolutizing takes place not only when in the Jewish understanding the Law becomes the dominant word of God. It is also the case in Christian theology when the Old Testament as a whole is understood from the perspective of the concept of Law and in contrast to the New Testament.

It is equally the case when in the Christian church the word of God in the prophetic function is understood as promise from the perspective of the New Testament. Every one-sided view of the word of God in the Old Testament can be countered by the fact that only together can the three functions of the word we have ascertained express what the word of God is in the Old Testament. In the following discussion this will be presented in detail within the context of these three functions.

Revelation in the Old Testament—how is the concept related to the words and acts of God? The Old Testament does not have a general concept of revelation. In Christian theology the concept of revelation is overwhelmingly determined from the perspective of the result: Revelation is what God has revealed, the revelation is what is revealed. The Old Testament has no such objectified concept of revelation (neither does Hebrew have a word for it). It only knows it as a process, as something which happens. These revelatory processes, however, can have various forms. The most important distinction is that different processes are assigned to God's speaking and to God's acting; these processes then also have different designations. The God speaking to his people or to an individual reveals himself differently than does the God acting in the life of an individual or the people. An *epiphany* belongs to God's acting, a *theophany* to God's speaking. Epiphany and theophany are different processes; they are portrayed in a different linguistic fashion, and one can follow their different histories through the entire Old Testament.

The saving God is the coming God. He appears in order to help his people, and appearance has here the same meaning as coming. In every case it is a coming into a situation of distress. In earlier times this was represented as an advent of God which shakes the cosmos with tremendous uproar in nature, as in the rescue at the Reed Sea or in the time of the Judges, e.g., at the beginning of the Song of Deborah in Judges 5:4-5:

> "LORD, when thou didst go forth from Seir, when thou didst march from the region of Edom, the earth trembled, and the heavens dropped, yea the clouds dropped water. The mountains quaked before the LORD, before the LORD, the God of Israel."

In the laments of the people this appearance of God is entreated: "Thou who art enthroned upon the cherubim, shine forth before Ephraim and Benjamin and Manasseh!" (Ps. 80:1-2). Or this kind of coming is announced:

> God came from Teman, and the Holy One from Mount Paran. . . . His brightness was like the light, rays flashed from his hand . . . he stood and measured the earth. . . . Thou wentest forth for the salvation of thy people. (Hab. 3:3-15)

Later it is the God punishing and judging his own people who comes to judgment in his epiphany, and finally it is the God who appears at the world judgment. The coming of the saving God also belongs to God's dealings with the individual, and has its place in the supplications of the lament Psalms. This supplication has two parts. The request for God's coming precedes the request for God's saving intervention (see below, pp. 168-169). The saving God is the coming God.

The theophany, on the other hand, always introduces God's speaking. The Sinai theophany shows this particularly well, as portrayed in the Sinai pericope in Exodus 19–34. Its goal is an act of speaking. It is also different from an epiphany in that it establishes a holy place (Gen. 28) or occurs at a holy place (Isa. 6). The theophany establishes the divine presence at the sanctuary. We encounter it in the patriarchal stories (Gen. 28), leading us from these to the Exodus (Exod. 3), to the divine revelation in the burning bush and in the middle of the desert sojourn in the divine revelation at Sinai in Exodus 19; we also encounter it in a changed form in the call visions of the prophets.

As regards the epiphanies and theophanies we can thus speak of revelations, since God "appears" in both, though in different ways.[12] Both should be distinguished from God's speaking to an individual where nothing is said about an appearance of any sort. Just as the Old Testament speaks about God's many different acts which do not stand in the context of a revelation, so also about various acts of speaking not designated or characterized as revelation. In the patriarchal stories we read simply: "God spoke to Abraham." God's word can come through a dream or through a vision, through a sign or through a messenger. God has many ways of speaking to a person. Designating this varied speaking as revelation, however, does not accord with the Old Testament, just as understanding revelation onesidedly as revelation through history (W. Pannenberg) or as revelation through the word (G. Fohrer) does not accord with it.

Excursus: Thus one cannot apply a general, comprehensive concept of revelation to the Old Testament. L. Köhler uses this kind of general concept of revelation as a point of departure in his theology (1936; 4th ed. 1966) when in part 6 he treats "God's revelation" (34 Revelation in the Old Testament, Conceptual considerations; 35 God reveals himself in his works, 36 in visions, 37 through men, 38 in the Law, 39 through the Spirit, 40 through representations). G. Fohrer proceeds similarly in his theology

(1972), albeit with critical restraint, chapter 2 "Old Testament and Revelation." A general and comprehensive concept of revelation is also presupposed by W. Pannenberg, *Revelation as History (Offenbarung als Geschichte,* 1961; 3rd ed. 1965). He designates revelation as God's self-revelation, from which we have the singularity of revelation (7—11). This idea of self-revelation would then have to be biblically justified (11). He differentiates an indirect self-revelation of God through history from the former. This is a typical example of nominalistic thinking which proceeds from general concepts and intends to approach biblical facts through conceptual distinctions. When Pannenberg says (17): "It can thus only be the case . . . that we understand the entirety of the event as God's revelation," I agree with him that the theology is concerned with the "entirety of the event." It does not, however, accord with the Old Testament to subsume this under the overriding concept "revelation."

In the volume mentioned by Pannenberg, R. Rendtorff gives an overview of "The Ideas of Revelation in the Old Testament" (21—41). He ascertains that "the Old Testament has no clearly defined concept for revelation" (22) and concludes: "Yahweh's self-revelation in Israel's history and the world is for Israel the point of departure of all faith and all theology." This concluding sentence echoes Pannenberg's thesis. He concludes from it: "A theology of the Old Testament oriented on Old Testament thought itself will always have to start from the Israelite understanding of history and its historical changes."

Humanity's Response

We are concerned here with a particularly important point for the theology of the Old Testament.[13] If one understands the story told by the Old Testament as an interaction, then the human response becomes one of the three integral parts of the Old Testament and belongs to everything said in the Old Testament about God, from creation to apocalyptic. In all God says and does one needs to ask how people react, since all of God's acts and speaking is directed towards eliciting a response.

This has trans-theological consequences. In the tradition of Western theology there has from the very beginning been a tendency to separate the human response in speaking and action from theology in the real sense, from dogmatics. Thus the basic response is often unconsciously regarded as subordinate in significance. It is treated as different from theology. Human response as action, to the extent it affects behavior in daily life, is treated in "ethics." To the extent it affects behavior in worship, it is considered under the heading of "liturgy." Human response as speaking (prayer) is generally treated in either ethics or liturgy. This separation into distinctive, individual divisions of study necessarily results in a kind of arbitrariness. It misleads us from seeing that human response belongs to the nucleus of theology, that only the Bible in its entirety can say what prayer is, what worship is, and what obedience in daily life is. A change can occur here from the perspective of the Old Testament if the human response is seen as one of the three main parts of the Old Testament.[14]

Human Response in Words

Just as God's work consists of his deeds and words, so also does the human response consist of word and action. That response includes the immediate reaction in the flow of daily life, e.g., a shout of praise, a word of thanksgiving, a vow, as well as that particular word directed to God in the sanctuary in the characteristic form of liturgical prayer as transmitted in the Psalter.[15] The close relationship between the two finds expression in the fact that elements appearing in the historical books as immediate responses from the flow of daily life are fused together into a whole in the Psalms. All the individual components of a lament Psalm—to call to God, the lament, the request, the vow—can also appear as components of a narrative, as in Jacob's vow (Gen. 28:20-22) or in the lament of Samson (Judg. 15:18). In all these cases, the elements of prayer form a necessary part of the story, which would be incomplete without the human response.

In the Psalms the two main groups, Psalms of praise and lament, correspond to God's action in salvation and judgment, and to the respective two-sided announcements. G. von Rad confines Israel's response in his theology to Israel's praise; this is commensurate with a one-sided conception of salvation history. Lament and praise (as in the theology of W. Zimmerli) respond to God's judging and saving actions. The experience of suffering is voiced in the lament directed to God; the experience of joy is voiced in the praise of God. In lament and praise people speak to God, the humans God created for life but whose lives he simultaneously limited by death. Lament and praise are to be understood as a polarity implying the entirety of human existence. Praise of God is the joy of life directed to God, while human suffering which turns to God comes to expression in the lament. The elements of prayer in psalm-form are rooted in what happens between God and his people and are integral parts of this history.

Here we must call attention to a distinction between prayer as we normally understand it and the understanding of prayer in the Old

Testament. According to our understanding, prayer is something a person does on his own. One can decide to pray, can be called to pray, or can himself call to prayer. This understanding of prayer arises where liturgical prayer is determinative and has lost its connection with spontaneous prayer as it arises quite naturally within daily experience. In the Old Testament, on the other hand, the liturgical Psalm-prayer is simply a fusion of the elements of spontaneous call to God arising within daily experience, but in a liturgically determined form. It lives from the elements of that spontaneous call to God from which it has grown. These spontaneous calls to God from daily life come together with the members of the cultic assembly in the liturgical Psalm-prayer, and this prayer then returns with them to daily life.

Every person reacts to external impressions either in action, speech, or reflection. There are numerous possibilities for the reaction in words, including the possibility that our reaction unconsciously and unintentionally elicits an address to something moving or unnerving us: "Thank God you're here!" "Oh, how wonderful!" "Oh my God, he's going to kill us all now!" and so on. We need to remember that our language contains far more address forms than we realize, since the so-called interjections such as Oh! and Ah!, among others, actually introduce addresses and also maintain this function when the address itself is missing. This shows us that within verbal human response there are also reactions requiring an address. This kind of reaction includes the outcry which transcends our reality even if we are not at all thinking about God. Otherwise the language could not preserve expressions such as "Oh my God" in a defunct form. This manner of reaction is part of human existence, and thus prayer, in its center, is also something belonging to human existence. There is no such thing as human existence without any trace of prayer. That is why it is so important to understand prayer again as a reaction, as is the case in the Old Testament, and not as something one undertakes from his own initiative, something like a pious work.

This is also why lament and praise cannot exist simultaneously; each has its time, just as do laughing and weeping (Eccles. 3). Here the call to God participates in the historicity determining everything that happens between God and man. Like laughing and weeping, lament and praise are steps along a path. The structure of the Psalms confirms this: In the lament Psalm the lamenting person looks forward to the praise of God in the vow of praise; in the Psalm of praise the person saved looks back into the abyss from which he called out to God. Depth and height are leveled out in prayer just as little as they can be leveled out in life.

A peculiarity of the Psalms consists in the fact that in them, the speaking to God within a polarity of praise and lament encompasses the entire person in the entirety of the world. This polarity corresponds to human existence in the world between birth and death. The separation into Psalms of the individual and Psalms of the people suggests that the experiences of personal life as well as the events of public life have their place in this speaking to God. The correspondence between brief words of prayer and the liturgically determined Psalms combines daily life and festival, work and celebration in the call to God. In the Psalms we encounter all the locales of daily life: the house and highway, field and workshop, sickbed and bedroom, the ages of life from the child to the aged, and the community forms of man and wife, parents and children, brothers and friends.

Above and beyond that, the history of the people of God forms an important part of the Psalms, from the early period up to the present time of the various Psalms. We hear of the tribes, of the kings and princes, of victory and defeat, captivity and liberation.

And, finally, the language of the Psalms encompasses all creation. When in Psalm 148 all the creatures in heaven and earth are called out to the praise of God, this is the same understanding of what happens as we found in the historical books. What transpires between God and his people, and is reflected in the call to God in praise and lament, stands within the context of a comprehensive occurrence between the creator and his entire creation.

Human Response in Action

Human response in action includes the execution of what is commanded for daily life as well as the specific act directed towards God in the sanctuary, particularly the sacrifice.

The historical books speak of human response as everyday actions; one of the dominant event structures in them is that God commands something and this is then carried out. Within the historical books, it is the entire complex of commandments and laws summarizing what God has commanded and stipulated. The Old Testament presupposes that a person who has been commanded by God to do something is able to do it, and under normal circumstances would do it. When God commands Abraham "Go out . . ." and it is then reported that "Abraham went . . .," Abraham has thus complied with God's will. Even a pagan seer, Balaam, can do the will of God when God commands him not to curse but to bless Israel. God's commandments are such that they comply with human capabilities: "For this commandment which I command you this day is not too hard for you, neither is it far off" (Deut. 30:11). Only in this way is it possible to distinguish through all of history between obedient and disobedient actions, between periods of obedience and periods of disobedience. The prophets' accusation and message of judgment only occur when disobedience has risen to such a level as to necessitate them. The relationship to God in the Old Testament presupposes that a person can say "Yes" to God and act according to this "Yes."

The act directed specifically towards God in the context of worship, the *sacrifice,* has a fluctuating history in the Old Testament. We hear reports of it from primordial history onward up to the post-exilic period, and a large part of the laws are concerned with the nature of sacrifice and the corresponding cultic institutions. The primeval history presents sacrifice as necessary for human existence, in Genesis 4 as an immediate response to God's blessing, in Genesis 8:20-22 as a response to his saving. Here as elsewhere in the Old Testament the assumption is that sacrifice is a phenomenon of religion as a whole, and not something peculiar to Israel's relationship to God. It has remained a decisive factor for the understanding of sacrifice in Israel that humans were created not, as in the Babylonian creation myths, to serve the gods, but rather to cultivate and preserve the earth. Consequently, sacrifice could never in the Old Testament take the place of the observance of God's will in everyday life. The Old Testament emphasizes obedience as opposed to sacrifice: "Obedience is better than sacrifice" (1 Sam. 15:22), but never the reverse. This enables the history between God and his people to continue even when the destruction of the temple makes sacrifice impossible. With the destruction of the second temple, sacrifice in the form of animal sacrifice then also ceased to exist for the Jewish religion right up to the present. Responsive speaking, however, remained significant for liturgical prayer. This explains why it forms a part of the canon in the Psalms.

The Oneness of God as That Which Makes Context Possible

With that we have expressed in a few broad lines what the Old Testament says about God. What the Old Testament says about God is a history developing between God and his creation, between God and humanity, between God and his people from creation to the end of the world. As in all stories of the world, there is on both sides action and reaction, word and response. The actions of God, the words of God, and the words and actions of people in response are the elements forming the constant basic structure of this history.

But what makes this incomprehensibly rich profusion of events between beginning and end into a context, a connected history? It is the oneness of God which Israel confesses: "The LORD our God is one LORD" (Deut. 6:4), "I am the LORD your God, you shall have no other gods before me" (Exod. 20:3). Because the creator is the same as the savior, because the God who blesses his creation in a universal horizon is the same who saves and judges his people, because the God whom the individual person trusts is the same who "gives to the young ravens their food" (Ps. 147:9), and because there is only one to praise and only one to whom to lament—therefore there is coherency and connection in everything that happens between God and man, between God and his creation. Therefore it is a real story from beginning to end.

The fact that God is one is decisive for talk about God in the Old Testament from beginning to end; God's oneness determines the unity and hence the continuity of the history between God and his people. However, the fact that God is one has not always been understood and expressed in the same way during the course of the history of the people of God. God's oneness is not a timeless doctrinal statement in the Old Testament. We can, with extreme simplification, differentiate three stages of talk about God's oneness. The first stage is expressed most clearly in the first commandment (Exod. 20 and Deut. 5): "I am the LORD your God, who brought you out of the land of Egypt, out of the house of bondage. You shall have no other gods before me." There is no reflection here on the existence or non-existence of other gods. The verses proceed from the fact that other people worship other gods. The commandment is concerned only that Israel has only one God as Lord, whom it can trust and serve.

The second stage found expression in the confession of Deuteronomy 6:4: "The LORD our God, the LORD is one." This word brings Yahweh's oneness to consciousness and expresses it conceptually. This confession to the one God grew out of the long and difficult struggle for the independence of the Yahweh-faith in polytheistic surroundings. The centralization of the cult in Jerusalem is commensurate with this: *one* worship for the *one* God.

The third stage, which we encounter in the prophecy of Deutero-Isaiah, stands against the background of the collapse and exile in which the Israelites held fast to Yahweh, the God of Israel, in the sphere of alien worship services. In this time of helplessness, God's oneness found its strongest expression in the confession of his singularity (Isa. 43:10):

> Before me no god was formed,
>> nor shall there be any after me.
> I, I am the LORD,
>> and besides me there is no savior.

Before Deutero-Isaiah no one ever spoke a sentence this unequivocal and this fundamental concerning God's singularity. This confession to Yahweh as the one God has the consequence that divinity is denied for any other gods. Deutero-Isaiah sees Yahweh's singularity in the dimension of time, and that means in its relation to history (Isa. 44:6):

> "I am the first and I am the last;
>> besides me there is no god."

"Monotheism" is not important for the Old Testament in the theoretical sense as a sublime, spiritual conception of God. It is vitally important for Israel, however, that its God as the One is not turned toward other gods with his divinity, but rather alone toward his people and his creation. Because there is no history of the gods for Yahweh, he is the God of history. Because God is One, there could be no myths for Israel in the sense of theogony. Thus his whole being as God unfolds in the history with his people, with humanity, with creation. The fact that God is One, and that he is the God of history, are two sides of the same understanding of God.

The confession to Yahweh as the only God in total exclusivity ("besides me there is no god") has yet another implication: If there is only one God, then he is the one involved in everything. Hence it is only logical when the prophet Deutero-Isaiah advocates a universalism the likes of which cannot be found earlier with such clarity and such consequence. In his proclamation, the savior of Israel is the creator, and he awakens new trust in the downtrodden precisely by pointing toward the creator and Lord of history in spite of the seeming failure of the God of Israel; this is the Lord of whom Israel's Psalms sing (Isa. 40:28-31):

> Have you not known? Have you not heard?
>> The LORD is the everlasting God,
> the Creator of the ends of the earth.

> He does not faint or grow weary,
>   his understanding is unsearchable.
> He gives power to the faint,
>   and to him who has no might he increases strength.

When the prophet speaks here in one breath about the creator of the world as the savior of Israel, about the savior of Israel as the creator of the word, these two lines of tradition—separated until now—come together in the *one* God who is the Lord of *all*. The savior of Israel is the Lord of world history and the creator of the cosmos. The fact that God is one means that everything is in his hands.

PART II

The Saving God and History

Introduction

Both the Old and New Testaments speak about the saving God. One example is the healing of the man blind from birth, in John 9: "As he passed by, he saw a man blind from his birth" (vs. 1). On his way Jesus sees a suffering person. Jesus' look is the look of compassion with human suffering. The narrative begins here with this look of compassion in the face of human suffering, just as at the beginning of the book of Exodus: "I have seen the affliction of my people who are in Egypt, and have heard their cry because of their taskmasters; I know their sufferings" (Exod. 3:7).

An interlude follows the beginning of John 9; the disciples also see the blind man, and have a question: "Rabbi, who sinned, this man or his parents, that he was born blind?" (vs. 2). The disciples thus bring up the orthodox doctrine of recompense: Suffering must have its cause in sin; the only question is whether the blind man or the parents are to blame. They look at the blind man with a question similar to that with which Job's friends look at the suffering Job. It is not the look of compassion, but rather the interest in theological doctrine. Jesus answers: "It was not that this man sinned, or his parents, but that the works of God might be made manifest in him" (vs. 3). Along with the disciples' question Jesus also rejects Job's friends' doctrine of recompense as well as the abstract teaching of a universal human sinfulness: "It was not that this man sinned, or his parents." He places the view of a suffering person into a different context, the context of God's saving action which springs from his compassion with the suffering creature. The history of Israel began with the saving action of God which was motivated by compassion. There exists a compassion on the side of God which does not ask who is guilty. Thus Jesus has pity on the blind man and heals him. The healing has a subsequent history. A dispute arises concerning the healing. A group of strict pharisees demands the healed man turn away from the person who healed him: "Give God the praise; we know that this man is a sinner" (vs. 24). And the healed man answers: "Whether he is a sinner, I do not know; one thing I know, that though I was blind, now I see" (vs. 25). The healed blind man's answer shows how saving is understood in the Bible. It can only be experienced; it is not enough that it is only spoken to him. However, it can only be experienced as a change in the time of need; the change brought about by the saving must be experienced as such. It is experienced as an encounter, an encounter with the savior. Through this experience of saving, the saved person belongs together with the savior, the healed person with the person who healed him. The assertion of the pious that he is a sinner cannot change a thing. At the end of the chapter there is thus a turn to him who has helped: "He said, 'Lord, I believe'; and he worshiped him" (vs. 38).

The Meaning of God's Saving Action in the Old Testament

"The story of the saving from Egypt forms the crystalization point of the entire Pentateuch narrative" (M. Noth, 1948, p. 54). The "little historic creed" (G. von Rad, 1938) also shows this; it summarizes the reports of the book of Exodus in a few sentences, and therefore in its structure corresponds in broad outline to the structure of the whole book. The importance of this short summary is shown by the fact that it is spoken in a fixed form in the introduction to the Decalogue (Exod. 20), at the presentation of sacrifice (Deut. 26), and in parents' recitation to their children of the acts of God (Deut. 6), and says what God has done for Israel. Indeed, in all those passages where the history of Israel with God is summarized in short reviews, the starting point is always this encounter with the saving God. Encounter is a personal category; it dominates the whole of God's history with Israel, and opens up a dialogue between God and his people.

This encounter occurred as an experience of saving. This is witnessed throughout the entire Old Testament in such depth and density that its significance is evident. In the Old Testament nothing of commensurate significance can be placed side by side with it.

The rescue from Egypt begins the history of the nation in the book of

Exodus. It is already announced in Genesis 50:24, where Joseph says: "I am about to die; but God will visit you, and bring you up out of this land to the land which he swore to Abraham, to Isaac, and to Jacob." This fuses the patriarchal history with the history of the people. The confederation of tribes in the worship of Yahweh is based on this during the transition to the settlement (Josh. 24). Deutero—Isaiah refers to it at the end of the history of the state with his promise of deliverance from the Babylonian exile.

The rescue from Egypt is related to Israel's worship in many ways: at the presentation of the first fruits (Deut. 26); in the historicizing of the festivals, which is anchored by the transferal into the accounts of Exodus of the establishment of the Passover feast (Exod. 12); and finally in the liturgical Psalms as well as in the praise of God (e.g., Ps. 136) and in the lament (e.g., Ps. 80; Isa. 63/64). God's saving act at the beginning of the history of Israel is regarded as the nucleus of the tradition, of the transmission to future generations (Deut. 6; Judg. 6:13). The commandments and laws are based on this event at the beginning, especially in the prologue of the Decalogue (Exod. 20; Deut. 5) and the Deuteronomic paraenesis. The prophets refer to this event in particular as a contrast-motif in their historical reviews (e.g., Amos 2; Jer. 2; Ezek. 16, 20, 23).

Only the most important passages are mentioned here.[1] All parts of the Old Testament (with the exception of the Wisdom literature) contain evidence for the lasting memory of the encounter with the saving God at the beginning: it has apparently permeated many areas of Israel's life. But it is not just a memory of the past; it has a very clear function for the present, as is particularly evident from the passages in the prophets and the Psalms (Josh. 2:10, 24:5-7; Judg. 6:13; 1 Kings 12:28). The significance of this event is preserved on into the later period: Judith 5:9-11; Wisdom 10:17-20; in the new Testament Acts 7.

The experience of the deliverance at the beginning means for Israel that Yahweh will *remain* Israel's savior. As he was the savior at the beginning, so his rescue continues to be expected, prayed for, and experienced. Yahweh is the saving God. This applies to the existence and history of the people as well as the existence and history of the individual. That could be further developed in a history of verbs and rescue in the Old Testament.[2] U. Bergmann (THAT II, 96-99) says the following concerning *nṣl*: "The background for the use of *nṣl* with a divine subject is the experience and expectation of Israel that Yahweh will liberate the people and the individual in various ways from distress, will rescue them when they are threatened. This is reported (Exod. 18:4 f.; Ps. 18:18, 34:5, 56:14), recalled (Judg. 6:9; 1 Sam. 10:18; 2 Sam. 12:7), and announced (Exod. 3:8, 6:6; 1 Sam. 7:3; Jer. 39:17); one entreats Yahweh for it (Gen. 32:12; Ps. 7:2, 31:16, and so on), and one counts on it (2 Kings 18 f.)."

The historical books report further acts of saving and liberation. The rescue from Egypt is followed by many experiences of saving and preserving on the way through the wilderness, during the settlement, in the time of the Judges and (less frequently) of the kings, especially at the beginning of the latter: A king is granted to Israel for the purpose of rescue from the Philistine threat. We must remember here that God's saving deeds in the various chapters of Israel's history change with the varying situations, and that the experience of saving is thus always new. It is not enough simply to say that God is the savior of Israel; only the reports and narratives dealing with this can say what this meant in reality.

The rescue at the Reed Sea is thus followed by the series of preservation miracles during the desert period. The first threat to Israel on this path was not enemies, but rather hunger, thirst, and fatigue. It was a matter of simple survival. These experiences of continually new preservation ingrained themselves in Israel's memory, as is shown by that particular group of murmuring-stories. In their core these stories very likely go back to the actual experiences during that wilderness period, since the verb used here for "murmur," *lun,* occurs only in these narratives; it never occurs again subsequently (Köhler–Baumgartner Lexikon). Their uniqueness lies in the fact that, in the majority of cases during the march through the wilderness when the people murmur against God or the mediator Moses, God does not punish them, but rather answers with a deed saving them from distress.

In these narratives Israel preserved the experience that God not only proved to be the saving God during a threat by enemies, but also in the time of elementary distress. Since then Israel learned to differentiate between the "bread of blessing" growing during the yearly cycles, bread in which man's own work participated, and the "saving bread" received as the preserving gift of the saving God during the distress of hunger (e.g., 2 Kings 6—7).

After entering the promised land, that saving took place in an entirely different manner. Here it was again a matter of being rescued from enemies, but things stood differently than during the rescue at the Reed Sea. Now Israel itself had to fight for possession of the land. The liberation deeds of the charismatic leaders are characteristic for these struggles during the period before the state (see below pp. 75ff.). Israel was able to experience God's saving action in these struggles only if and as long as the struggles were clearly a liberation from extreme distress (as e. g., in Judg. 6—7). The thoroughgoing change in the relationship to God during the time of kingship manifested itself especially in the fact that wars of conquest were now added to the defensive wars (Saul and David's wars with the Philistines belonged to the latter). The wars of conquest could no longer be experienced as God's saving deeds.

In addition, however, the period of kingship knew enough situations in which the acts of the saving God could be experienced. The transmission of this experience of God's saving is most explicit in the communal laments, where the worshipers call to God for rescue from a present need by an express reference to his previous acts of salvation (as in Ps. 80 and Isa. 63—64).[3] During the exile, Deutero-Isaiah promises liberation from the Babylonian captivity as a new exodus.

Indeed, this speaking of God as the savior in present and future extends throughout the historical books, the prophets, and the Psalms.

The reference to God as the savior is also applied to private life in the personal sphere. The majority of the Psalms of the individual tell of the saving acts of God: the cry out of need in the individual laments; the telling of experienced rescue from death in the individual praise-narrative; the praise of the saving God "who looks into the depth" (Ps. 113, author's translation) in a group of descriptive Psalms of praise (hymns). But this experience of the saving God in the life of the individual is not related to the saving acts of God in the history of Israel (almost the only exception is Ps. 22). The experiences of one's private life belong to a different sphere. The patriarchal stories would more likely offer a corresponding example here, stories which speak of God's saving actions in private life: in the saving of the child dying of thirst (Gen. 21); of the jeopardy of the ancestress in a foreign land (Gen. 12:10-20); in the saving of a brother from his brother (Gen. 32); and of the youngest son in Genesis 37 and 44.

There is a further expansion. In the old Testament the saving acts of God are not confined to his people and its individuals. In the primeval history and in apocalyptic, it is extended to all of humanity and to the animals. In the flood story (Gen. 6—9), the God who destroys his creation is at the same time the saving God who in a remnant preserves humanity and the animals from destruction in the flood. Apocalyptic speaks similarly of destruction and rescue (Isa. 24—27). This is to say that no boundaries exist for God's saving action; they occur among the people of God, in the life of the individual, in humanity.

By speaking of God's saving in the spheres of national history, the life of the individual and of humanity within the whole of creation, the Old Testament indicates that *God's saving has comprehensive significance.* The experience of saving belongs to human existence. It is something that everybody knows and which has occurred always and everywhere throughout the history of humanity up to the present day (hence a secular word).

It is based on the fact that human beings are creatures. Man is created for life (as *naephaes ḥājāh*), but this life for which he is created is limited. It follows from the limitations of human life, as portrayed in Genesis 2—3, that as long as humans live they are in danger, assailable, and vulnerable. To the extent they survive the danger, they know the experience of being saved. This applies to the individual, to every human community, and to humanity as a whole. There is no human existence void of all danger. Being saved is a part of human existence.

Because the dangers and threats to human beings can be as varied and can take on as many forms as human existence itself, the acts *and experience of saving* can be very different indeed. This dissimilarity does not, however, alter the fact that God was, is, and shall be the savior. The Old and New Testaments thus also agree in the statement that God is the savior. The fact that God is the savior is an aspect of his divinity in the Old as well as in the New Testament. In the middle of the New Testament stands God's saving act in Christ; Christ is proclaimed as *soter,* and *soteria* is a central term in the New Testament. It may seem that what is called *saving* in the book of Exodus and what is called *saving* in the New Testament have hardly anything in common. It is a fact, however, that God is the savior both in the Old and in the New Testament. This conclusion needs no special exegesis; it stands quite independent of how one otherwise understands the relationship of the Old Testament to the New. This is a fact which cannot be disputed: in the Old as well as in the New Testament, the saving God is of central significance.[4]

For a long time the concept of election played an important role in the theology of the Old Testament. It designated the entirety of God's actions concerning Israel. Thus one spoke in a comprehensive fashion about "Israel's traditions of election" (e.g., K. Galling) and used it to refer to the patriarchal stories, the Exodus account, and other texts as well. (See THAT I, 1971, 275-300; more sources listed there.)

We need to point out, however, that in the texts called by this name the verb *bhr* (to elect) does not occur. The Old Testament never uses this word when it reports what has happened. In the Old Testament the word has rather a subsequent, interpretive function. It is a late interpretation, looking back from a distance, of what happened. It was not God's election which made Israel into his people, but rather his saving deed at the beginning. This act of God was explained by subsequent reflection such that God elected Israel. The use of the word in the Old Testament shows this clearly (I refer to the article by H. Wildberger in THAT I, 275-300: "There is almost a consensus in Old Testament scholarship that there is no explicit talk of Israel's election before Deuteronomy," p. 284). There is a full consensus that the concept of election acquired its final and valid definition in Deuteronomy. The "locus classicus" is Deuteronomy 7:6-8:

> The LORD your God has chosen you to be a people for his own possession, out of all the peoples that are on the face of the earth. It was not because you were more in number than any other people . . . but it is because the LORD loves you, and is keeping the oath which he swore to your fathers, that the LORD has brought you out with a mighty hand, and redeemed you from the house of bondage. . . .

This passage clearly shows that the concept of election is an interpretation. Yahweh delivered Israel from Egypt because he elected Israel "out of all the peoples that are on the face of the earth," so that he might perform this saving deed on them. This interpretation stands in Deuteronomy 7 within the context of the commandment which decisively separates Israel from the Canaanites and their worship; and indeed, Deuteronomy 7:6-8 is the foundation of the commandment of separation in 7:1-5, which is then taken up again in the paraenesis verses 9-11. The concept of election is to be understood within this paraenetic context, the vitally important emphasis (as far as Deuteronomy is concerned) on the first commandment in the face of the danger of syncretism. The concept was determined by this context. However, this also means that one misunderstands the concept of election if any claims are made concerning it. Deuteronomy 7:6-8 already expresses this implicitly, and Amos 3:2 does so even more sharply. Precisely this paraenetic context, in which the first commandment is put forth to Israel because of the danger of apostasy, seems to advise us not to generalize the concept of election in order to speak then in an abstract sense about the election tradition, the condition of election, or about an elect people. Only in the previously mentioned context does that concept acquire significance. In this kind of abstract generalization the danger is too great that some sort of claim is derived from the concept of election.

This kind of generalized use of the concept of election is also controverted by the fact that, in the formation of the tradition of God's initial saving deed, the verb "to elect" never occurs, not even in the long chain of traditional words which recall that initial saving deed (see above). It is then no accident that the pre-exilic prophets virtually avoid the concept of God's election.[5] One cannot then say that the concept election is of decisive significance for the entire Old Testament; any use of this concept requires full clarity concerning its limited significance.

It is a characteristic of previous theologies of the New Testament that they attributed a higher significance to the noun concepts than to the verbs. This is particularly true for the concept of "covenant." In a so-called "covenant theology" one has tried to attribute to this concept a significance determinative for the entire Old Testament.[6] A bias comes to expression here which does not do justice to the reality of the Old Testament. Talk about God in the Old Testament is primarily verbal, not nominal. What is said about God is without exception an occurrence between God and human beings. It is never primarily a condition. To the extent that a "covenant" is understood as an existing, permanent relationship between God and man, such a concept cannot function determinatively for the Old Testament; it can only be a subsequent designation for an event which has happened between God and his people. Aside from this, three objections can be raised against the determinative significance of any concept of covenant for Old Testament theology.

First, the fundamental significance of the covenant for Old Testament theology is generally supported by Exodus 19 f., in which God makes a covenant with Israel at Sinai. This assertion is problematic. As is now generally recognized, the Sinai pericope Exodus 19—24 and 32—34 (without P) cannot be taken as a closed, continuous textual unity. The actual account of the theophany at Sinai only encompasses chapter 19. The P-parallel to it is Exodus 24:15b-18. This account says nothing of the making of a covenant; 19:3b-8, where in verse 5 we encounter the sentence, "and keep my covenant," is a later addition in Deuteronomistic language. A text independent of this account in Exodus 19 is Exodus 24:3-8, which speaks expressly about the making of a covenant. It is continued in chapter 34. But in this text, too, Sinai does not come up. It is a later text which was subsequently inserted into the account of the Sinai theophany (according to L. Perlitt, 190-203, among others). This text typically expresses a later understanding of a covenantal relationship between Yahweh and Israel, but cannot be taken to support a covenant making at Sinai.

The second objection emerges from the meaning of the word *berit* (covenant) in the Old Testament and its history.[7] In the expanded discussion concerning the understanding of this Hebraic word, there is full agreement that it originally did not mean a condition, but rather an act. Translating the word as "covenant" through its entire spectrum is thus shown to be a mistake from a lexicographic standpoint. In its entire earlier employment, *berit* means the act of someone giving a ceremonious, binding guarantee. Such a guarantee can resemble a vow (or oath) (N. Lohfink, SBS 28), or even a promise, if the subject is God. This meaning becomes clear through the ritual of a ceremonious guarantee or self-obligation, *karat berit* (usually translated: to make a covenant), in the sense of a self-curse: the stepping through the pieces of dead animals as in Genesis 15 and Jeremiah 34.[8] The phrase *karat berit* does not then mean "to make a covenant," but rather "to give an obligation pledge." The connection with the meaning "covenant" can easily be explained, since in making a contract or covenant one or both parties gives obligating explanations or pledges. The concept first acquired theological significance in the Deuteronomic period (according to L. Perlitt, op. cit.), and it is extremely uncertain whether earlier there was any talk at all in Israel about a *berit* (in the sense of covenant) between God and his people. In any case, *berit* originally meant the act of obligating guarantee. It is thus not possible, on the basis of the text recounting the Sinai event, to say that Yahweh made a covenant with Israel at Sinai. This is rather an interpretation of the Sinai event from a much later time, the late Deuteronomic period (Deut. 5:2): "The LORD our God made a covenant with us in Horeb." What follows this introduction is not the act of making a covenant, but rather the Decalogue. *Berit* is understood here in the sense of law, just as it directly becomes a designation for the Law in Deuteronomic language. From this later stratum we can distinguish an earlier one in which *berit* is used in the sense of promise (Deut. 7:9): "Know therefore that the LORD your God is God, the faithful God who keeps covenant and steadfast love." This is referring to the *berit* Yahweh vowed to the patriarchs: "The theological uniqueness of Deuteronomy 7 consists in letting the 'covenant' live not from the Law, but rather from the promises" (L. Perlitt, op. cit. 63).

The comparison of these two passages shows that the word *berit* serves to interpret the events at the beginning of Israel's history for a later time. The change in usage is clearly reflected in two chapters in Genesis, both of which speak of God's *berit* with Abraham. In Genesis 15:7-21 the word does not have the meaning "covenant," but means rather a ceremonious pledge, corresponding to an oath or vow. As regards content, it is a promise. It stands quite close to the meaning of *berit* in Deuteronomy 7:9, and probably even belongs to the same period. In Genesis 17, on the other hand, which belongs to the priestly tradition, *berit* has the meaning of covenant. It is here a two-sided agreement obligating both parties which establishes the continuing status of the covenant. Just as in Genesis 17 *berit* refers to the circumcision commandment, so also in Deuteronomy 5:2 to the Decalogue; in both passages *berit* now includes both commandment and law. These two passages, however, only belong to the period of the exile.

The concept of covenant between God and his people thus arose relatively late in Israel and was first used at an equally late time to refer to the mutual relationship between Yahweh and Israel; it is a subsequent interpretation intending to transform the relationship to God into a static concept.

The so-called "covenant formulation"[9] is to be distinguished from this. It is a false designation because it originally had nothing to do with the word *berit* or the idea of a covenant. An example is Jeremiah 11:14 (cf. 7:13): "Listen to my voice, and do all that I command you. So shall you be my people, and I will be your God." This formulation is particularly emphasized and expanded in Deuteronomy 26:16-19 and the end of the section comprising chapters 12—26 with the commandments and laws, and before the conclusion in chapters 28—29 containing the curse and blessing. In the middle stand the words:

> "You have declared this day concerning the LORD that he is your God . . . and the LORD has declared this day concerning you that you are a people for his own possession."

This emphasized concluding section summarizes the two main constituents of Deuteronomy: that which Moses said of God's work concerning Israel in the past up to this day, and of his work in the future in the promises. There Yahweh spoke through the mouth of Moses: "that he is your God." The other constituents are the "commandments, statutes and laws" in which Israel—to the extent it accepts them—declares that it intends to be "a people for his own possession."

This so-called "covenant formulation" nowhere has anything to do with a covenant ritual or any other kind of liturgical act. We encounter it overwhelmingly in speeches of God, where it formulates the reciprocity of what occurs between God and his people. Its intention is "to stabilize the relationship to God" (L. Perlitt, op. cit. 114). The formulation stabilizes it such that it is not confined to any concept (including that of covenant) or any ritual, but rather leaves this reciprocating relationship open in the fullness of its possibilities. The "event in dialogue" (M. Buber, 1954) between God and his people finds its clearest and most succinct expression in this formulation.

The Act of Saving and History

The uniqueness of this talk about God as the savior and about God's saving is that this saving is understood as an event which is narrated or reported, an event with a pre- and post-history. "Salvation history" as a summarizing term for God's saving deeds presents difficulties, since the word "salvation" (*das Heil*) is a concept of condition or state, corresponding to Latin *salus* and Hebraic *šalom*. The Old Testament does not mean a state of salvation when it speaks of God's saving deeds, but rather a process, which therefore in our languages, too, is best rendered verbally. God's saving is portrayed in the Old Testament as a "tearing out" (the verb *nṣl*) from mortal danger; the result of this tearing away from the power of death is not a condition of salvation, but rather normal life, restored by the saving. The only thing new about this life is that it now includes the experience of saving and the bond with the savior.

This process of saving occurs in a particular sequence of events. Saving can take place in many different ways and can be presented in very different forms. One can, however, always recognize the basic structure, which remains the same: need—call out of need—hearing—saving—response of the saved persons. Two of these five elements are common to all discussions of saving, including secular talk: the need and the turning away of need (saving). The other three elements add the word to mere events: on the human side the call out of need and the response of the saved persons; on God's side the word of the savior, which, as the hearing of that call out of need, precedes the saving intervention. These three elements turn the saving into an event in dialogue. By them the experience of saving from need becomes an encounter with the saving God, with which Israel's history began.

This sequence or structure of events is shown by the "historic creed" in Deuteronomy 26:5-11 (author's translation):

The previous history	vs. 5: "An Aramean ready to perish was my father . . . "
Need	vs. 6: "But the Egyptians oppressed us . . . "
Call from need	vs. 7a: "Then we cried to Yahweh . . . "
Hearing	vs. 7b: "And Yahweh heard us and saw our affliction . . . "
Saving	vs. 8: "And Yahweh brought us out of Egypt . . . "
	vs. 9: "and he brought us to this place and gave us this land . . . "
Response of the saved persons	vs. 10: "And now I bring the first fruit . . ."
	vs. 11: " . . . you shall bow down and rejoice."

This creed does not describe individual historic acts (as von Rad maintains[10]), but a continuous process whose individual elements form part of a whole. The text of Deuteronomy 26:5-11[11] is not a collection of themes, but rather a description of a process in its individual elements. The strength of the tradition of this creed is not based on an addition of individual events, but rather on the fact that so many and such diverse events from Egypt to Canaan have been melted into a single, self-contained event arc leading from need to saving.

The composition of the book of Exodus is based on the same structure, even if considerably extended. It is necessary to sketch it in its broader lines (continued up to Numbers):

Chapters 1—11: The Need
                1: Oppression in Egypt
            2—6: The Promise and the Mediator
          7—11: Moses and Pharaoh, the Plagues

     12—14: The Saving
          12—13: Passover and Departure
          13—14: Journey Through the Desert;
                 Pursued and Preserved

        15: The Praise of Those Rescued (Historical Psalm)

     16—18: Preservation During the Journey Through the Desert (continued in Num. 10—36)

     19—34: The Sinai Pericope
          19: Theophany (par. 24:15-18 P)
          20: Decalogue 21—23: Book of the Covenant
          24: The Covenant
          32—34: Break and Judgment

     25—31; 35—40; Lev. 1—27; Num. 1—10: The Priestly Code (P)
          25—31: Instructions for Building the Sanctuary
          35—40: Execution of the Instructions in 25—31

This structure of the book of Exodus (up to Numbers) forms the basis for the section portraying God's saving action. The elements of this structure, however, are not confined to the book of Exodus, but rather extend through the entire Old Testament wherever there is talk about God's saving action.

G. von Rad (ThB 8, 10f.) sees in the Hexateuch "an end stage, something final. . . . This baroque structure of the fundamental idea . . . is not a first attempt, it is . . . something final which must have had its earlier stages. . . . The historical creed as such is stable . . . but the treatment is variable." Von Rad's thesis can be carried further. The correspondence between creed and Hexateuch is confined to parts of the Hexateuch, namely to Exodus through Numbers, without P, while Genesis and Deuteronomy for the most part have no parallel in the creed. One first needs to ask about clear correspondences or parallels, then about expansions corresponding to the creed, and then, about those which do not.

First the clear parallels. The previous history alluded to in Deuteronomy 26:5 corresponds to Exodus 1:1: "those who came to Egypt" (author's translation; cf. Gen. 50:24). The oppression in Egypt (Deut. 26:6) is described in detail in Exodus 1:6-22. The call from distress (26:7a) is presupposed in Exodus 3:7, 9. The hearing (Deut. 26:7b) is contained in the promise of deliverance (Exod. 3:7-8). The deliverance itself (26:8, 9) encompasses the account of Exodus 11 to the end of the book of Numbers. The response of those saved (26:10, 11) is the psalm of praise in Exodus 15.

Concerning the expansions: We need to differentiate those emerging from the structure of the saving event from those not belonging to it in any way.

The creed itself already contains an expansion. The saving is divided into two acts, the leading out and leading in (26:8, 9). This expansion is developed in Exodus. The saving takes place in such a way that those rescued only reach the place of freedom, which was announced during the rescue, after a long journey. This expansion extends beyond the book of Exodus and forms a considerable part of the Pentateuch: the account of deliverance into the promised land by means of the journey through the wilderness in Exodus 16—18 and Numbers 10—32.

The second expansion is grounded in this long journey. The hearing of the cry from distress, expressed in the two-part promise, promises guidance along this long journey. However, this promise and journey require a mediator; he announces the promise and leads during the journey.

A third expansion is the narrative about the mediator (Moses), who mediates the promise and leads the people in the wilderness (Exod. 2—6). In this story we need to notice the similarity with the stories of the prophets; it begins with a call and has further correspondences as well.

A fourth expansion is that the Exodus is described in two acts: in the liberation from the long distress of oppression (the miracles and plagues in Egypt in Exod. 7—11, and the departure in connection with the final plague in Exod. 12), and the rescue from mortal danger, the miracle of the Reed Sea (Exod. 14). The two possibilities of saving which run through the entire Old and New Testament are combined here: saving (or liberation) from a continuing situation of distress, and saving from acute danger. (Concerning this distinction, see U. Bergmann, Diss. 1968, and also THAT, article on *nṣl.*)

A fifth expansion is the insertion of Passover before the departure in Exodus 12—13.[12] This expansion connects the deliverance from Egypt with Israel's act of worship and anchors it there. In the older sources (J, E) this happens as a narrative: In Exodus 12:21-39 the departure from Egypt is associated with the final plague. The first-born of the Egyptians are smitten, while the Israelites are spared (the blood ritual, Exod. 21—28); this sparing establishes the Passover feast (Exod. 25—27). The festival of unleavened bread (Exod. 13:3-10), established in the context of departure, is added subsequently, as well as the requirement of the first-born for Yahweh (Exod. 13:11-16), based on the sparing of the Israelites when the first-born of the Egyptians were killed. In P the cultic establishment of the Passover replaces the narrative 12:1-20 with the subsequent addition 12:43-51 and the requirement of the first-born 13:1-2. However, the priestly (P) Passover law itself also includes an allusion to the history from which it emerged:

> In this manner you shall eat it: your loins girded, your sandals on your feet, and your staff in your hand; and you shall eat it in haste. It is the LORD's passover. (Exod. 12:11)

This expansion in 12—13 has a three-fold significance for the theology of the Old Testament. First, it shows that God's saving deed at the beginning is determinative for Israel's relationship to God in general and remains so for all time. The celebration of the Passover will recall this event yearly: "You shall eat it as those who are going away . . ." and the bringing of the first-born, as primatial sacrifice, once the most important sacrifice, will each time recall God's saving deed. Sacrifice and feast, the two main elements of an ongoing cult, are based on God's saving deed at the beginning.

In the second place, this expansion shows the close connection between worship and history which is so characteristic of the Old Testament. The worship service of a sedentary people has a cyclical character corresponding to God's blessing activity. This close connection between worship and history opened the act of worship in Israel to history and thus also to the future.

Thirdly, it is significant for the relationship of Exodus 12—13 and Exodus 19—34. The regulations for feasts and sacrifices in P actually have their place only in the Sinai pericope, and are attributed to the theophany at Sinai. If we already encounter some of them here in the context of the departure, and indeed in J, E as well as P, this shows that important parts of Israel's worship have their foundation in history, more specifically in God's fundamental saving deed concerning Israel at the beginning, and not first in the theophany at Sinai. This establishes the sedentary cult which presupposes the sanctuary at a fixed place. Israel's worship, however, is unthinkable without reference to that time in history which preceded the settlement, namely the period of the wandering group.

The expansion Exodus 32—34 does not belong to the expansions developing the history of saving; it leads us beyond that. Exodus 32—34, the story of the golden calf, deals with the breach and the renewal of the covenant made in chapter 24. This expansion is based on the fact that those who have been saved deny their response in word (Exod. 15) and deed (Exod. 12—13). This section recounts the first falling away of the people from God, to whom it owes its life. This section in Exodus 32—34 is conceived from a later stratum. Many exegetes see in it a reflection of the events surrounding the apostasy of the northern kingdom and the steer cult in Bethel and Dan (1 Kings 12—14). Those transmitting the Pentateuch wanted to show with this expansion that Israel's history with its God offered the possibility of disobedience and apostasy from the very beginning, and that the new element of guilt and punishment thus entered into the relationship with God. The breach, characterized by apostasy, enters the history of belonging together, characterized by the saving. Viewed in this way, Exodus 32—34 forms the connector between the Pentateuch and two other Old Testament complexes which deal with guilt and punishment, the Deuteronomic history and the judgment prophecy. In the introduction we said that the Pentateuch is based on a confession of praise, and the Deuteronomic history on a confession of sin. Exodus 32—34 shows why a transition had to occur from the one to the other; it is a connector between the two. This conscious connector is seen from the other side in the Deuteronomic introduction to the Book of Judges, in which God's saving action encounters the people's repeated apostasy. Here we see the change the creed undergoes because of the motif of guilt and punishment:

> And the people of Israel did what was evil in the sight of the Lord, forgetting the Lord their God, and serving the Baals and the Asheroth. Therefore the anger of the Lord was kindled against Israel, and he sold them into the hand of. . . . But when the people of Israel cried to the Lord, the Lord raised up a deliverer for the people of Israel, who delivered them. . . . So the land had rest forty years. (Judg. 3:7-11)

The judgment prophecy can also already be heard clearly in Exodus 32—34. The mediator who brought his people the promise of saving becomes the proclaimer of judgment; the figure of the judgment prophet as well as the prophetic announcement of judgment are already prefigured here. Also prefigured, however, is the possibility that the prophet can become an intercessor for his people. God the savior becomes God the judge.

The Sinai pericope Exodus 19—34 falls completely away from the previously described structure of events. While Exodus 32—34 stands in a direct relationship to God's saving action (the savior becomes the judge), the events at Sinai have nothing whatever to do with it. It is thus absent from the creed, and G. von Rad justifiably concludes from this that we are dealing here with a separate, originally independent tradition. In the theophany at Sinai, Israel receives the basic elements of worship as the holy act (see below pp. 187ff.). To be sure, this theophany is an occurrence during the journey, but the form of worship established here is that of a sedentary service, as P (the priestly tradition) clearly shows in Exodus 24:25-40. The commandments and laws were ascribed to this theophany; these laws also belong to a sedentary form of existence.

The Sinai pericope also includes the texts of a covenant between Yahweh and Israel in chapter 24. The making of the covenant then does not belong to the saving at the beginning, which establishes the nation's history, but rather to that period of transition from saving history to sedentary life.

The Sinai pericope in Exodus 19—34 thus represents a bracket between the saving at the beginning and the act of worship in the promised land. The Sinai pericope does not belong to the elements of the saving event and its expansions.

The elements forming the history of the Exodus from Egypt up to the entry into the land of Canaan not only make up this period at the beginning of Israel's history, but also extend beyond that and determine a large portion of the Old Testament texts. God's saving acts continue, and God remains for Israel the saving God. In them Israel experienced God's miracles, and the concept of miracle has its real place in them. Miracles of saving occur in the life of the people as well as of the individual. If the saving is announced beforehand, then an arc of tension is formed from promise to fulfillment which runs through the entire Old Testament and is taken up in the New Testament. The announcement of judgment appears whenever the savior is denied the response. Prophetic announcements of judgment and salvation are thus already prefigured in the Exodus history, and the history of the mediator already appears with the announcement through Moses.

Since, however, the events in the book of Exodus occur between God and man, they also include human reactions. The encounter begins with the call from distress; and the praise of those saved answers the savior. Praise and lament are the two main forms in the Psalms, and they also accompany God's history with his people outside the Psalter. The three main sections of the Old Testament are thus determined by the elements one already finds in the story in Exodus. The history of these elements can be followed throughout the entire Old Testament. First, however, we need to ask what has been found concerning the Old Testament understanding of history.

Findings for the Old Testament understanding of history. If the entire Old Testament were determined by God's saving action such that one of God's saving deeds followed upon another from the departure from Egypt onward, then one might speak of a history of saving or of salvation in the strict sense of the word. However, the structure of the book of Exodus has shown that God's history with Israel does not just remain a history of saving. The process of saving forms the framework, but then expansions are added to this framework.

The continuation of the history occurring between God and his people, following the book of Exodus, corresponds to these expansions.

The expansion of the promise of saving is most closely connected with the structure of the saving process itself: "I will lead you out . . . " with the promise of blessing: "I will lead you into a land flowing with milk and honey." The promise of land, and with it of settled life, is associated with the promise of saving. One can view the book of Deuteronomy as a development of this promise of blessing. Neither is it merely an accident that the central theological concept in Deuteronomy is that of blessing. A new period in Israel's history begins with the crossing of the Jordan, a period no longer only or primarily characterized by God's saving deeds. The distress is now alleviated for a time, even though new and other dangers will come. The activity of the blessing God is added to that of the saving God; that is a main theme in Deuteronomy.

God's saving deeds do not cease with that, but a change does take place in them. With the transition into the promised land God's saving deeds no longer occur directly, as at the Reed Sea or in the wilderness, but rather with and through Israel's weapons. Joshua and Judges show this in different ways. The first part of the book of Joshua (chapters 1—11) portrays battles dealing with the land promised during the departure. In the saving deeds of God portrayed here it is no longer a matter of the necessities of life, of sheer survival, but rather also of the new domicile. This new element finds literary expression in the kind of narratives which speak of these acts of God: They are etiological stories[13] belonging in their etiological character to this land and in the various examples saying something about the land.

The book of Judges expresses this new element in a different way. The fact that the God of Israel now remains the savior of Israel in the promised land in threatening situations is carried out in the calling and commissioning of "saviors." These saviors are mediators of God's saving acts which occur in battles of defense. Both complexes, however, the stories of God's saving acts in Joshua and Judges, have in common the fact that one now speaks about God's saving acts differently than in the book of Exodus, in a manner corresponding to the nation's new form of life.

To God's saving acts is now added his perpetual activity, corresponding to the promise of blessing. If we say that Deuteronomy develops this promise of blessing, continuing activity must find clear, even decisive expression in the epoch of historical portrayal following the struggle for the land. This is indeed the case. The historical books following Joshua and Judges are determined by the two great institutions dominating Israel's settled life in the land: kingship and cult.[14]

The figure and kingship of Saul very clearly establishes the transition from the "saviors" of Judges to the static nature of kingship, finding its theological foundation in the Nathan-promise of 2 Samuel 7. The other static quantity determining the entire period of kings appears with the kingship of Solomon: the temple in Jerusalem (1 Kings 6—8). The temple cult institutionalizes what was established in the second expansion of the Sinai pericope. Just as Saul's kingship constitutes the transition from judges to kings, so also does the story of the ark David brings to Jerusalem constitute the transition in the history of worship. The wandering sanctuary of the early period, the sanctuary from the wilderness period, finds its place in the sanctuary of the royal city.[15]

This second expansion of the Sinai pericope not only establishes the settled cult, to it is also attributed the Law, the regulations of sedentary life (according to the Covenant Code, Exod. 21—23). The covenant between the people and God is also anchored in it (Exod. 24). This transformed the saving event into a condition, i.e., the continuing covenantal relationship, and we can compare it with the conclusion of the book of Joshua, the making of the covenant at Sichem in Joshua 24. However, the static quality of the Sinai pericope finds its strongest expression in the great Priestly Code which regulates the fixed worship at the sanctuary; the tabernacle is the model for the temple.

The third expansion, Exodus 32—34, which prefigures the possibility of apostasy and of judgment, corresponds to the later version, acquired by the portrayal of the history of the royal period in the Deuteronomic historical word as a history of apostasy. The historical period of Israel's settled life in the promised land has not come down to us as the history of the blessing through the two great static institutions of kingship and cult. What is emphasized is the threat to Israel, from the beginning of settled life onwards, by the disobedience of the kings and people causing the announcement of judgment. Israel is also threatened while living in a secure land and secure cities, secured as well by the continuous harvest from the land. Now, however, this threat comes from within, the turning away from Yahweh. The prophets' announcement of judgment commences in the face of this threat. This is the context expressed by the designation of the historical books as "former prophets." Only here does the function of the expansion Exodus 32—34 in the story portrayed in Exodus as saving become clear as a connector between this and the history of apostasy in the period of kingship. The announcement of Yahweh's judgment over his own people is intended to be seen—even if this sounds paradoxical—within the further context of the history of his saving deeds. In it Yahweh wants to turn away the mortal threat to his people. The prophetic announcement of judgment, which begins with the period of the state, continues the history which had begun as God's saving action concerning his people. It continues this history, however, against the background of the security provided by the sedentary lifestyle and the power of the state.

In conclusion, one can say that the broad lines of the history which unfolded between Yahweh and his people are prefigured in the book of Exodus. In its nucleus it proves to be the history which arose from the experience of saving. The elements of this saving event can, in their various strands, be followed through the entire Old Testament (see the following section). Israel encountered Yahweh as its savior, and Yahweh remains the savior of Israel.

Other theological motifs appear already in the expansions in the book of Exodus, motifs which determine the further history beginning after the Exodus and the wilderness period. On the one hand, this is the line of God's continuing activity in blessing, developed in Deuteronomy and receiving its determinative structure in the two static institutions dominating the period of kingship. The other line is that of apostasy and judgment, determining the later portrayal, in the Deuteronomic historical work, of the history of the settlement period as well as—in a different fashion—the history of prophecy.

We can thus recognize a threefold context in that which the Old Testament historical books say about the history between God and his people Israel, a context in which each of the historical books had its part, but whose nucleus is the history of saving at the beginning in the book of Exodus. The three expansions show that a historical section characterized by blessing follows that characterized by the saving. This new period is identical with the period of the settlement. A new threat to Israel arises here because of apostasy which turns away from Yahweh, a situation characterizing that arc of tension from the announcement of judgment up to the judgment itself. There appears with that the two great speech complexes by God (presented in Parts III and IV), the one dealing with God's continuous activity, the other with God's judgment and God's mercy. The biblical books in their canonical sequence were the basis for this working out of those broad lines. We will deal later with their combination into historical works and its theological significance.

Elements in the Saving Process

Saving as Miracle

One cannot verify a miracle. Israel experienced both saving at the beginning as well as God's saving acts permeating the history, as miracles. What the Old and New Testaments understand under miracles becomes most clear from the perspective of this context. Psalm 77:11-15 can show this:

> I will call to mind the deeds of the LORD;
>> yea, I will remember thy wonders of old.
> I will meditate on all thy work,
>> and muse on thy mighty deeds.
> Thy way, O God, is holy.
>> What god is great like our God?
> Thou art the God who workest wonders,
>> who has manifested thy might among the peoples.
> Thou didst with thy arm redeem thy people,
>> the sons of Jacob and Joseph.

These verses introduce the miracle at the Reed Sea, portrayed in the fashion of an epiphany. It is a late Psalm, but even in the later period this event is seen straightaway as a miracle. It shows the God who works miracles. In verse 12, miracle and works stand in synonymous parallelism; to speak about God's works is to speak about God's miracles. The following sentence in verse 14 is an expression of astonishment, of the astonished silence in the face of the holy, majestic God's activity. God's greatness and majesty are by no means static concepts here; one encounters them rather in the experience of the miracle: "Thy way, O God, is holy." God shows himself in his works as the Holy One, the Majestic One. The Psalm shows that astonishment is one of the essential characteristics of the experience of miracles. Astonishment necessarily contains a moment of incomprehensibility within itself. A miracle which is explained is no longer a miracle. Astonishment is thus much more frequent and natural in children than in adults. This childlike element within astonishment is inseparable from the experience of a miracle. However, precisely this element demonstrates that a miracle is never comprehensible according to the phenomena accompanying it which one can verify. One cannot verify miracles. The German "miracle or wonder" (*Wunder*), too, does not really mean astonishment or wonder (*Verwunderung*, as in the expression *"es nimmt mich wunder"*: "I wonder at it"). To the extent that it tries to comprehend miracles from the perspective of what is verifiable, i.e., as a deviation from natural law, all of Western theology has traversed a path in its talk about miracles which itself deviates from the Bible.

The miracle itself is expressed in Psalm 77:14-15 in the simple sentence: "Thou didst with thy arm redeem thy people." This sentence comes from the historical creed, in which one does not find the word "miracle" or "wonder." If the word "wonder" is used, as in Psalm 77, that does not order something like the event at the Reed Sea into the category "miracle," but rather emphasizes a particular aspect of the event, namely that it comes from God. The word "wonder" is described in precisely this way in Psalm 118:23: "This is the LORD's doing; it is marvelous/wonderful in our eyes." The sentence here is also an expression of astonishment in the context of the praise of God as in Psalm 77. We will later show how astonishment is an essential element in the praise of God.

If we now take the prosaic, narrative portrayal of the same event in Exodus 14, we see a difference in the talk about God's wonders which is grounded in the history of tradition. The multi-layered portrayal in Exodus 14 shows no miraculous features in its oldest form; these come only in the later portrayals. The same holds true for Jesus' deeds in the New Testament. It makes a difference whether those immediately affected speak about a miracle they experienced, or whether those coming later do so, to whom the event has been handed down. In the immediate account the miracle consisted in the fact that in the moment of highest need God brought about a turn on which those affected could not count. Without their astonishment, what they experienced was not a miracle. The miracle is an occurrence between God and his people, and has its reality alone in this vis-à-vis. Therefore there can be no externally acquired criteria for it, no standard according to existing norms. Something seen objectively, from a distance, is no longer a real miracle.

Psalm 77 shows yet another feature of talk about miracles. An actual miracle is God's helping in greatest need. However, God's approach, portrayed as an epiphany, proceeds under miraculous accompanying circumstances: the shaking of the cosmos, of the sea, of the earth as well as powerful storms. They show the majesty of the one approaching, and precisely that makes them miraculous and wonderful. We find that the miracles occurring on and in creation are subordinated to the actual miracle. The juxtaposition of "nature miracles" and "healing miracles" (i.e., miracles of saving intervention) in the Synoptic Gospels becomes comprehensible against this background. They are not two kinds of miracles next to one another. One must rather clearly subordinate the miracles which are a show of power to the miracles of helping.

A later expansion of the concept of wonder occurs in those passages which understand the creator's work as a miraculous deed, as does Psalm 139:13-14:

> "For thou didst form my inward parts,
>   thou didst knit me together in my mother's womb.
> I praise thee, for thou art fearful and wonderful.
>   Wonderful are thy works!"
> (Text uncertain; cf. also Isa. 28:29)

This expansion of meaning lies quite in line with the original understanding of miracle. Here, too, one speaks about God's wonders in the context of the praise of God. If this broadening to include God's work in

creation were possible, that confirms that in the Old Testament a miracle is
not to be understood as the violation of natural laws. It can be understood
alone from the perspective of that vis-à-vis between the acting God and man,
who is overwhelmed by those acts. Whenever we believe we experience a
miracle in an encounter with something overwhelmingly beautiful, this
corresponds with this broadening of the concept of wonder.

We need to differentiate between miracles and those signs which are
supposed to distinguish a word as having come from God (e.g., Isa. 7). They
have different functions and belong in a different context. "Signs and
wonders" could only secondarily be equated.[16]

The Coming of God in the Old Testament

The saving God is the coming God. The Exodus account already says
this: "And I have come down to deliver them" (*wa'ered lehaṣilo* 3:8), and from
here a line of talk about God's coming runs through the entire Old and New
Testaments up to Revelation: "Behold, I am coming soon," "behold, he is
coming!" The song of praise in Exodus 15:21 corresponds retrospectively to
the announcement:

> "Sing to the LORD, for he has triumphed gloriously;
> the horse and his rider he has thrown into the sea."

As short as this song is, God's action is still recounted in two acts: God's
saving intervention includes a movement which precedes it. We find
something similar in the ark sayings in Numbers 10:35f. This call "arise,
Yahweh!" or "Come hither" then flows in a broad stream into the call to God
from distress in the laments of the people and of the individual. This
movement of arising and coming belongs to God's saving intervention from
the oldest documents onward up into the later period.

Whereas in Exodus 15:21 and most of the other passages God's coming is
expressed only in a simple verb, a special linguistic term emerged during a
certain period, the period of the land conquest. This form was the epiphany,
i.e., a portrayal of the coming (= appearance) of God under powerful natural
occurrences.[17] The passages: Judges 5:4-5; Psalm 18:8-16; Habbakuk
3:3-15; Psalm 68:8f., 34; 77:17-20; 97:2-5; 114; 29; Micah 1:3-4; Nahum
1:3b-6. An example is Judges 5:4-5:

> LORD, when thou didst go forth from Seir,
>   when thou didst march from the region of Edom,

> the earth trembled, and the heavens dropped,
>> yea the clouds dropped water.
> The mountains quaked before the Lord,
>> yon Sinai before the Lord, the God of Israel.
> (God's intervention in the battle follows.)

The epiphany is divided into three parts: God's coming—cosmic tremblings accompanying it—God's intervention for or against. It is likely that parallels from outside Israel had an influence here (see bibliographical footnote 17). Epiphanies in the Old Testament, however, show no sign of mythical thinking. The drama of this coming is not that of a theogony, but is rather that of an occurrence between God and his people in the hour of serious threat. We find this especially wherever, in a lament Psalm, the epiphany is an expansion of the petition for God's coming, as in Psalm 80:2 and Isaiah 64:1:

> O that thou wouldst rend the heavens and come down,
>> that the mountains might quake at thy presence—
> as when fire kindles brushwood
>> and the fire causes water to boil— . . .
> When thou didst terrible things which we looked not for.

The epiphany as an integral part of supplication reaches on up into the song of advent: "O Savior, rend the heavens open. . . ." This motif of epiphany lies at the basis of the early Christian epiphany festival in which the appearance of the Son of God is celebrated. Here, too, it is the appearance of the savior, and here, too, the saving God is the coming God.

The primary element in all epiphany portrayals is the coming of God, the secondary element, the "how" of this coming. Ideas about the "how" of this coming have changed radically. Concerning Judges 5:4f. (similarly Deut. 33:2), compare Psalm 18:9f. (from heaven); Psalm 77:19f. (through the sea); 50:2f. (from Zion). Reference to God's coming in an epiphany must have gone through a long, varied history, of which only pieces have been preserved. God's coming as such, however, a coming to one's aid, remains constant. The accompanying appearance of the shaking of the cosmos also remains relatively constant. It is the earliest context in the Old Testament in which God's work in history is associated with an occurrence in creation (or nature). We encounter the power or majesty of God first with the coming God, and only later with the existing (reigning) God. The praise of the creator is prefiguring itself in such statements.

There is a great deal of reference, in various contexts from the exile onward, to the anticipated advent of God in the future. This is especially the case in Deutero-Isaiah, where it is a primary motif from the prologue (40:9) through his entire announcement. It is equally the case in post-exilic prophets such as Zechariah 9:9: "Lo, your king comes to you; triumphant and victorious is he!" and in Psalms of Yahweh's kingship, Psalm 96:11f.: "Let the field exult . . . for he comes, for he comes to judge the earth."

Between these two groups of passages in the early period (God comes, epiphany) and in the later period (God's advent is anticipated) stands the large group of passages of prophet judgment announcement in which God's coming is a coming to judge Israel (e.g., Isa. 2:12, 19). Just as the saving God, so also is the judging God the God who comes.

God's coming and "eschatology": The saving God is the coming God, i.e., wherever the Old Testament speaks about God's saving work, it portrays it as an event which comes to man from without. The advent thus necessarily belongs to saving, since the preceding distress is experienced as God's distance ("why are you so far?"). The change in the distress is experienced in God's approach, in his advent into the situation of need; that is God's future. The future in the Bible is not primarily *what* is coming to me, but rather *who* comes to me; the future is identical with the coming God. That is why the use of the term "eschatology" in reference to God's coming is problematic in the Bible, since eschatology means *that* which is future, the "doctrine of the last things." To the extent that eschatology means *that* which is future, which is ascertainable as teaching, God's future becomes accessible in it. This does not correspond to biblical talk of God's coming.

In the Old Testament the future is contained in God's coming. There is, to be sure, a profusion of statements concerning that which is coming, but God's coming is more than all utterable futurity; God cannot be pinned down in that. God precedes all utterable futurity in his coming; he remains the coming one. The entire future is contained in God's coming, the future of the individual person, of the people of God, the future of humanity and of the world. The only absolutely certain thing we can say about the future is that we are going towards God and God is coming towards us, just as the final sentence in the New Testament says: "Behold, I am coming soon."

The Oracle of Salvation and Its History in the Old Testament

In the departure story, deliverance is announced to the Israelites, who are languishing under the burden of forced labor. Deliverance can come unexpectedly, but it can also come during a long journey. The history of saving then begins with the announcement coming to the distress situation. That is why the oracle of salvation is an integral part of the saving event, both in the Old as well as New Testament, the latter of which begins in the Gospels with the message of deliverance. Accordingly, the oracle of salvation is of decisive significance for the entire Bible and has a varied history.[18]

Characteristic of the talk of God in the entire Old Testament is that he speaks a word turning the distress situation around, an oracle of salvation, into that distress, into fear, dread and despair, into pain, debasement, and hopelessness. However, the words of salvation in the various periods and various spheres of life are so different that a summary term such as "oracle of salvation" or "promise" can only serve as an overview. Beyond that it cannot say a great deal.

We can initially differentiate three main forms of the oracle of salvation in the Old Testament: the salvation confirmation, salvation announcement, and salvation portrayal.[19] The salvation confirmation, or statement of hearing, is perfective; it says that something has happened, that the distress has been turned (as in Exod. 3:7f.; Isa. 40:1f.). The salvation announcement is future-oriented; it announces that something will happen (in Exod. 3:7f. it is combined with the salvation confirmation). The salvation portrayal is future-present oriented; it portrays a condition of salvation in the future, and portrays how things will be one day (e.g., Isa. 11:1-10). These three main forms of the oracle of salvation point to three entirely different processes. The salvation or hearing confirmation is a response to the lament; it always occurs through a mediator, in the laments of the people usually through a prophet (Exod. 3; Isa. 40), in the lament of the individual in the worship service through the priest (the "priestly oracle"). The salvation announcement is the typical prophetic form of the oracle of salvation (an example is Jer. 32:14f.), particularly for the prophets of salvation (1 Kings 22:11; Jer. 28:2-4). It corresponds formally to the prophetic announcement of judgment, except that it needs no supporting explanation. This form of salvation announcement is not, however, confined to prophecy; we encounter it otherwise as well, e.g., in the patriarchal promises. The salvation portrayal goes back to the office of the seer to his vision of the future (e.g., Num. 24:5-7a) and to statements of blessing (as in Gen. 49:11-12) which perhaps stand in some connection with the statements of the seer. The salvation portrayal has become associated with prophecy (e.g., Isa. 2:1-4; 11:1-10), but receives its richest development in apocalyptic: The apocalyptic is a seer.

To the differentiation according to primary forms is added that according to whom is addressed. Just as in the case of God's saving action, the word of salvation can come to Israel or to individuals, but can also be meant for the world and humanity. In view of these two aspects we can then inquire into the history of words of salvation through the Old Testament.

Promise to the people. The history of saving at the beginning began with a word of salvation which set this history in motion. It spans the entire course of events from the departure up to the settlement, in which it came to fulfillment. But it does not lose its significance at this point. The land in which the Israelites now live remains the promised land,[20] and the Israelites have a different relationship to it than other peoples have to the land bequeathed them. This is shown by the continuation of the land promise after the settlement, particularly in Deuteronomy. In the context of the new threats associated with remaining in the land, the old promise to the patriarchs is reawakened. This combines the promise associated with the deliverance from Egypt with the land promise already given to the ancestors Abraham, Isaac, and Jacob. Its fulfillment is seen in the Israelite's settlement of the land, as Genesis 50:24 shows:

> And Joseph said to his brothers, "I am about to die; but God will visit you, and bring you up out of this land to the land which he swore to Abraham, to Isaac, and to Jacob."

The patriarchal history is closely associated with the history of the people by means of the land promise. The insertion of the patriarchal history in Genesis 12—50 in front of the history of the people beginning with Exodus was made possible by this connecting link. The promise of blessing (e.g., Gen. 12:1-3) and the promise of descendants (e.g., Gen. 13:14-16) also have their goal not in the patriarchal history itself, but rather in the history of the people of Israel. The abundance mentioned in the promise of descendants ("like the sand of the sea," "like the stars of heaven") can only refer to the numbers of the people of Israel.

These promises, however, first coming to fulfillment in the people

Israel, combine with much older promises and carry those forward which can be traced back to the patriarchal period itself, since they find their fulfillment in this period: It is the promise of a son (Gen. 15, 16, 18), the promise accompaniment during the journey (Gen. 26:3; 26:24; 28:15) and the promise of new living space or new pastures (contained in Gen. 12:1-3). They are understandable from the perspective of the patriarch's life style and are firmly anchored in the old narratives. Here the promise encompasses only a very small span, commensurate with the narratives from the patriarchal period.[21]

The patriarchal promises, however, contain one more in addition to those already discussed, a promise in which the arc between promise and fulfillment spans a much larger area. The fulfillment reaches here into the distant world of the nations in general (Gen. 12:3):

> I will bless those who bless you, and him who curses you I will curse; and by you all the families of the earth shall bless themselves.

This sentence, standing in the Yahwist's prologue to the patriarchal history, can only be understood in its place within the transition from primeval to patriarchal history.[22] Just as the insertion of the patriarchal history in front of the history of the nation receives its theological articulation in the promise of land and descendants given the patriarchs, so also does the insertion of primeval history in front of them both find its articulation in the promise of Genesis 12:1-3, which expands to include the multiplicity of peoples as previously presented in the table of nations in Genesis 10. This promise places the history of God with his people Israel from the very beginning into the wider horizon of the history of God with all of humankind. It will resound repeatedly in the history of the people of God until at the end of the nation's history it again acquires determinative significance in the songs of the suffering servant, which then extend into apocalyptic.

Thus from the promises at the beginning (promise of departure and patriarchal promises), the three areas have already become visible to which the promises throughout the Old Testament refer: the people Israel in the sphere of its history, the individual in the personal sphere of the family, and humanity, created by God and proceeding towards its goal in a world created by him.

The promise at the end of the history of the nation corresponds to the promise at the beginning. The promise to Israel of deliverance from the Babylonian captivity stands in a clear, oft-mentioned correspondence to the promise of deliverance from Egyptian bondage. It comes into a similar situation: formerly to the forced laborers in Egypt, now to the deported people in Babylon. Here as there it is a promise of saving and homecoming, it can be accepted or rejected, and it comes through a mediator. The prophet Deutero-Isaiah sees the liberation he announces as a parallel to the liberation from Egypt (Isa. 43:14-21). He juxtaposes the new liberation and homecoming to the old one, so that the old one pales before the new (43:18-19). But this is not the essential difference. The new one is the connecting link between the promise of saving with the confirmation of forgiveness (40:1-3; 43:22-28). The deliverance from Egypt was based on nothing more than God's compassion with the suffering people ("I have seen your distress"). However, between this rescue at the beginning and the deliverance from the Babylonian exile lies the mountain of guilt which had accumulated in the history of the people of God (43:22-28). The promise of deliverance now presupposes the pledge of forgiveness with which Deutero-Isaiah's message begins: "Cry to her that her iniquity is pardoned" (40:2).

This difference is of great significance for talk about God in the Old Testament. Deliverance from compassion with the sufferer and deliverance associated with the forgiveness of the person who has become guilty *both* are meaningful and necessary in the history of God with his people. Aside from this essential difference, the correspondence is quite extensive. Only in these two passages do we encounter the unconditional, perfective pledge of deliverance (cf. Exod. 3:7-8 with Isa. 43:1-3), associated with the future-oriented announcement which is in both cases an announcement of return. And both times an element of salvation portrayal is added, in Exodus 3 the land flowing with milk and honey, in Deutero-Isaiah the portrayal of the new blossoming in 54—55.

The history of words of salvation between these two fixed points at the beginning and end, which is extremely varied, needs only to be sketched in. The promise of saving at the beginning is directly continued during the time of the settlement in the pledge of victory in the defensive struggles of the immigrant groups in "Yahweh's wars."[23] An inquiry is made to Yahweh during a threatening situation, and the answer given to the leader chosen by Yahweh is the formula of deliverance: "See, I have given into your hand the king of Ai" (Josh. 8:1; passages in G. von Rad, 1951, 7f.). The promise of victory is confined to the early, pre-state period.

Just as God's continuing work for Israel acquires significance with the beginning of the settlement, so also is the promise of blessing added to that of deliverance. In it blessing becomes linked with history. The promise of blessing is developed within the context of God's blessing action.

From the beginning of kingship onward, the announcement of judgment replaces the announcement of salvation for Israel in increasing measure. However, the promise of salvation never completely ceased during this period characterized by the announcement of judgment; during the exile it again became dominant. (Concerning the history of salvation prophecy, see below pp. 141ff.)

The promise to the mediator. The promise to the mediator stands in the middle between that to the people and that to the individual person. To be sure, it comes to an individual person, but it refers to the office this person occupies within the people as a whole. Two very different strands can be differentiated here.

In the one case the promise comes to a helpless person for whom the burden of the office becomes too heavy. It is thus normally the answer to the mediator's lament. We find it with Moses (an echo with Joshua), with Elijah, Jeremiah, and with the suffering servant. The people's burden becomes too heavy for Moses; in desperation Elijah wishes for death; and the lament of the mediator is most fully developed in Jeremiah and the suffering servant. The promise being issued is usually extremely subdued; only endurance, not victory or success, is pledged to the mediator. Only in the final suffering servant song does the servant receive God's "Yes" for his work beyond death (Isa. 53:10-12).

In the other case the promise is issued to a powerful person, the king. The so-called promise of Nathan in 2 Samuel 7, however, is so different from the previous group as far as its form and content is concerned, that the common term "promise" is almost no longer applicable. Nathan's statement, which pledges to David the continuation of his house and dynasty, is a confirmation of the status quo. It serves to stabilize and legitimize David's kingship and is characterized by a royal theology totally alien to Israel's early period. It marks a turning point in the history of the promises. For the first time the promissory word of God bound itself to a political institution and promised it duration and longevity. There has never, neither before nor afterwards, been a similar divine confirmation of a human institution. And precisely this promise—at any rate according to the historical reality—was broken. It was one of the most serious crises in Israel's faith when the Davidic dynasty was toppled with the Babylonian exile. Psalm 89, in which the promise of Nathan is taken up almost verbatim, shows the deep shock precipitated by the apparent breach of this promise.

The so-called "messianic prophecies" can be explained from the perspective of this collapse. They presuppose the collapse of the kingship and at the same time the question concerning the breach of the promise of Nathan.

The promises to the mediator throughout the Old Testament end in two points: the promise to the king, changed into the promise of a king during the salvation period, and the promise to the helpless mediator of the word, reaching its goal in the promise to the suffering servant of God beyond his death. In the New Testament Gospels Jesus is seen in the corridor between the two promises to the mediator. He is called the Messiah in the sense of the king of a coming kingdom of peace; but the other line of promise to the helpless mediator corresponds even more to the Gospel accounts, the mediator whose suffering brings about forgiveness.

Oracles of Salvation to Individuals

Excursus: The relationship between God and the individual in the Old Testament. In the history of the oracle of salvation, we come upon the fact that it is addressed with about equal frequency to the people and the individual. This shows that God's activity in the Old Testament is by no means concentrated only on the people of God, on Israel, but rather that it is directed with equal intensity to the individual person. Indeed, it is not just directed to individuals to the extent that they are members of the people of God, but simply to individuals as people. We see this in the creation of man, in the book of Job, and in wisdom. It is particularly the case in the Psalms, in which the suffering and joy not only of the people of God, but also of the individual person in his personal life comes to expression. The relationship between God and the individual person occupies an important position next to that between God and Israel. The two are not identical, and it would be an impermissible abbreviation of what the Old Testament says about God if one fails to keep it in mind. A brief look might illuminate this.

Primeval history (Gen. 1—11) deals with humanity *before* its separation into nations and religions. Here man in all his possibilities and limitations as God's creation stands across from his creator. In the patriarchal history (Gen. 12—50), the individual man in the community form of family takes on a significance which is decisive for everything which follows, including the history of the people of God. In the history of the people we repeatedly see that the personal relationship between God and the individual within the familiar sphere of life remains a necessary element in the history of the people of God. One need only think of David's family history, or of Jeremiah's lamentations. The relationship between God and the individual in his personal sphere of life participates just as much in Israel's worship as does the people of God with its history; this is shown particularly by the considerable importance of the individual in the Psalter. During the exile the family and individual again took on a significance which was decisive for Israel's religion, a significance it always kept in the Diaspora. The book of Job witnesses to the fact that the fate of an individual person, of a person suffering before his God, has something decisive to say to the people of God even if this suffering person is not an Israelite. Finally, one can think of the strong humane line of thought running through the entire Old Testament: in the humane commandments of Deuteronomy, in wisdom, and in the universalistic coloring of many folk proverbs. It is essential for what the Old Testament says about God that the individual person and his personal, familiar life sphere is appreciated along with the history of God with his people. Such an appreciation would understand him as God's counterpart in his simple existence as a human.[24]

Just as the lament of the individual in Israel has its place next to the lament of the people, so also the oracle of salvation to the individual never fell silent next to the word to the people. Even during the period characterized by the great prophets' announcements of judgment, men and women in Israel received encouragement and consolation in their questions and needs in which the link with the preserving, saving God was maintained.

A unique significance regarding the insertion of the patriarchal history in front of the history of the people lies in the fact that it is here an individual human being in his personal sphere of life, in his family and his house, to whom all of God's promises are issued, indeed in extemely personal distress: childlessness, danger to life and limb, the threat of powerful people, the breach of peace in a family. This remained determinative for the entire later history. God's activity includes the personal life of the individual, his promises reach into the houses, the places of work, and into the days and nights of every individual.

Here lies one of God's essential functions in Israel. Whereas the promises to the people almost always occur in the course of history through leaders or prophets, the mediation of oracles of salvation to the individual occurs overwhelmingly in the institutions of worship. Commensurate with the two main kinds of divine activity, saving and blessing, the promise of saving as well as of blessing to the individual could occur in the words of worship. When he came to the sanctuary in a particular situation of need or danger and "poured out his heart" there, a successful hearing could be granted his lament. This "priestly oracle" (J. Begrich, ZAW 52) has not been handed down to us, but one can presuppose it behind many Psalms of lament in which the lament passes over into the certainty of a successful hearing or even into a praise of the saving God (Pss. 6; 22; 28). It is even mentioned once in a Psalm (Lam. 3:57):

> "Thou didst come near when I called on thee;
> thou didst say, 'Do not fear!'"

The proclamation of Deutero-Isaiah, who often uses it for his salvation message, repeatedly confirms that the cry "Do not fear!" was constitutive for the salvation oracle to the individual. It is particularly characteristic for the relationship between God and the individual person in Israel. He expected his God to hear this cry in the hour of distress or despair. If one considers that the lament of the individual is the most common genre in the Psalter and that the Psalms of trust and praise of the individual also belong to this experiential sphere, one can no longer say that in the Old Testament everything is centered on the relationship of God to his people. The word of salvation directed to the individual occupies an extremely important position in the Old Testament, and thus also the personal relationship between God and the individual person.

Whereas in the answer to a lament in the salvation oracle it is always a matter of some word of distress situation, the Old Testament also knows of a promise of blessing directed to the individual; its situation is continuing, day-to-day life. In the patriarchal stories it is the promise of blessing and of accompaniment: "Behold, I am with you and will keep you wherever you go" (Gen. 28:15).[25] In Psalms 91 and 121 a liturgical celebration is suggested in which a pledge of blessing is given an individual who speaks a confession of confidence beforehand. In Job 5:18-26, the first speech of Eliphaz reflects this pledge of blessing; it is also found in a variation in Proverbs 3:23-26. Although this is only sparse documentation, the texts permit us to conclude that in Israel's worship, in addition to the blessing conferred on the congregation (Num. 6:24-26), there was also the bestowal of blessing on individuals during special occasions.

A change occurred here in Israel's later period. The pledge of blessing to the individual was previously conferred without any conditions, just as was the pledge of a positive hearing. Just as in Deuteronomy the conditional promise to the people now takes the place of the unconditional one, so also does this occur in the post-exilic period with the promise to the individual. It acquires a prerequisite condition: The promise is only valid for the pious person. This is schematically stated in the first Psalm, the introduction to the book of Psalms in the post-exilic period. Blessing is promised to the pious person, whereas the wicked "are but chaff which the wind drives away." The relationship to God is now only possible in this polarity: All blessing and all that is good is promised to the man who fears the Lord (Ps. 112:1-9), "the wicked man sees it and . . . gnashes his teeth" (vs. 10). Psalm 73 and the book of Job show that this alternative was too simple.

Promise for humanity and creation. One cannot call Genesis 8:20-22 a promise in the strict sense; it is, however, a pledge of enduring existence for the human world. This pledge after the flood gives to mankind as a whole the guarantee that no catastrophe will ever again destroy the human world "while the earth remains": "While the earth remains, seedtime and harvest, cold and heat, summer and winter, day and night, shall not cease." This pledge at the end of primeval history needs no continuation and no repetition. It is valid once and for all and presupposes that the God of which the Bible speaks holds our earth and space in his hands. The earth will not exist forever, but no one can put an end to it except its creator.[26]

In the transition from primeval to patriarchal history the Yahwist alluded in Genesis 12:1-3 to a promise of blessing extending far beyond Israel to "all the families of the earth." How is that intended? We must first consider that in all the promises going beyond Israel the addressee is not directly addressed. That can only mean those addressed are first the Israelites, and that these promises going beyond Israel are first to mean something for the Israelites. That is clear in Genesis 12:1-3, where the Yahwist is speaking to Israel in these words, the Israel of his time. He is saying to them that Abraham's descendants will mean something for all the other peoples at some time in the future. It can remain quite open here just what this blessing is to be or how it will come about. That special thing God sends to his people is one day to have an influence on others. The same thing

J intends to say in Genesis 12:1-3 is also suggested by P in the scene at the end of the patriarchal history in which Joseph introduces his father to the pharaoh and Jacob blesses the pharaoh (Gen. 47:7-10). The scene radiates a peculiar solemnity by means of the contrast between the mighty, powerful pharaoh in the splendor of his court and state, and the old man, a poor nomadic shepherd, who is nothing and has nothing, and who nonetheless is the giving one in this scene. It is he who blesses pharaoh. This scene is of portentous significance for P at the end of the patriarchal history, before the beginning of the history of the people.

To these two passages we now add a totally different one from the later period, an oracle of salvation for the people, Isaiah 19:18-25, in which a highway from Egypt to Assyria is announced for the salvation period. Israel is to be "the third in alliance" and beyond that "a blessing in the midst of the earth." Israel is promised here that it will one day be a gift to the other nations, with whom it will then no longer live at war, and that from it a stream of blessing will go out to the others. In neither of the three passages is this blessing issuing from Israel tied to any conditions. It is God's free, unconditional blessing which flows out to the others from that which God does for his own people.

The final promise in apocalyptic is to be distinguished from this. In it, the promise directs itself to the entire world. This can occur in extremely varied fashion, but the typical is an apocalyptic drama in which both God's judging as well as his blessing activity come to a final conclusion. All anti-divine powers are destroyed in a world judgment, and after this there will come a state of salvation which is no longer threatened, no longer changed, which is final. A new heaven and earth are created, suffering and death will no longer exist. This apocalyptic promise, too, is a promise of blessing; that which grows out of the apocalyptic drama is described as an enduring condition in the language of blessing. It can no longer be changed. History has ceased.

In conclusion, a retrospective overview of the history of words of salvation in the Old Testament is needed.

We first encountered the promise as an integral part of the saving process: God's word, promising deliverance, comes to the situation of distress. This word creates a tension, a tensed inclination towards the occurrence of the promise; this creates a context. This context, however, does not just remain one-tracked, i.e., it does not go on such that when the first promise is fulfilled, the second is issued, and so on. Rather, the first promise introduces a history which itself participates in the multifariousness of all history. The historical changes determine a change in the words of salvation, as the three fundamental forms of the words of salvation have shown. The most important change as regards content is that the promise of blessing is added to that of saving. Then, however, on the basis of the denial of response, the word of judgment is added to and in part replaces the word of salvation. This word of judgment then has its own history.

In its variety and diversity the history of the word of salvation is a distinguishing characteristic of the theology of the Old Testament. Through it a strong movement, a strong inclined motion, the drama of real history comes into the history going on between God and his people. Just as the ancestors were on their way without knowing their goal, but led and directed forward by the promissory word, so also did the people of God remain on their way, without knowing the future, but trusting in this word.

How do the people in the Old Testament react to an oracle of salvation?[27] The oracle of salvation opens up a future; the person to whom it is directed can orient himself toward it or not. The normal reaction is that one takes a step into that future opened up by the word of salvation:

> Gen. 12:4: . . . so Abram went . . .
> Exod. 3: The departure from Egypt into freedom.
> Judg. 6—8: The departure into battle for liberation.

This first step implies that the word of salvation is believed; in most cases, however, this is not stated in the text. Only in reflective retrospect, from a distance, is it said that the Israelites believed the word of salvation which came to them:

> Exod. 4:31: . . . And the people believed . . .
> Ps. 106:12: Then they believed his words;
>   they sang his praise.

This same is true for the word of salvation to Abraham:

> Gen. 15:6: And he believed the Lord, and he reckoned it to him as righteousness.

Only in reflective retrospect does faith lose its matter-of-factness. Now one notices that the person to whom the word of salvation came believed it. Regarding the promise issued to Abraham, for example, the later transmitter knows that Sarah laughed at the promise of a son to the old couple, that she thus did not believe. In the face of this other possibility it is emphasized that Abraham believed.

This is much more strongly the case in the prophet Isaiah. It is said that Isaiah came to King Ahaz with a word of salvation and the king did *not* believe it (Isa. 7). This king's disbelief has decisive significance: The anointed of Yahweh does not believe Yahweh's word! That is why "to believe" acquires such a special significance in Isaiah's proclamation. From here it becomes understandable that the verb *'āman* hi. in the early strata of the Old Testament is encountered overwhelmingly in its negated form. Faith becomes noticeable and is mentioned wherever one does not believe. Faith comes to expression where it loses its matter-of-factness. Most of the time it is normal and natural, and thus does not need to be mentioned. In all these cases it is implied in the answer of speech or action. That is why the term "to believe" (there is no noun "belief") is relatively infrequent in the Old Testament and is encountered only where it is something special.

"To believe" is used in the Old Testament only in those situations in which it designates a clear alternative, i.e., where there is the possibility of no believing (as with Ahaz). This possibility is always present in the case of a word of salvation ("I heard the message well, I simply do not believe"). The term "to believe" is not used wherever this alternative is not possible. This is the case, for example, in God's creative activity. For ancient Israel there is no alternative to the fact that God created the world or humankind. There is not yet any other explanation of their origin. Thus the Old Testament never speaks about faith in the creator or faith in being created. There is no creation faith. The relationship of man to the creator is characterized differently. The consequence is that "to believe" is not a general, comprehensive designation of the relationship to God or one's connection with God in the Old Testament as it is in the New. One does not in the Old Testament find the general designation "to believe in God" or "faith in God" or anything similar. Only in very few passages—as, for example, in Isaiah—is the word "to believe" used absolutely; otherwise it only occurs in certain relationships in reference to certain situations: Someone in a certain situation believes someone else or does not believe him. In the Old Testament it cannot designate one's relationship to God as such or, on the whole, with the exception of a few passages; otherwise it is always one of many possibilities of the relationship to God. It remains bound to a certain situation and does not become a static term designating state or condition. If it has become customary in Old Testament scholarship to speak generally and comprehensively about "Israel's faith," about the "faith of the prophets," or about "creation faith," then one must keep clearly in mind that the New Testament concept of faith is being transferred to the Old Testament here. (K. Koch, *Šaddaj. Zum Verhältnis zwischen israelitischer Monolatrie und nord-westsemitischem Polytheismus:* VT 26, 1976, 299-332, 301: "The term *hä'ämin,* normally translated in the Old Testament as 'faith,' never refers to the difference between the Israelite and other religions, and never becomes a means to set the one God apart from the others, but rather always refers to promises and to prophetic words about the future [Gen. XV 6; Isa. VII 9"].)

But wherever a situation arises in which the word of salvation (and thus also the reaction to that word) acquires decisive significance, faith, too, becomes comprehensively significant. This is the case in the message of Deutero-Isaiah. In the prologue (40:1-11) and epilogue (55), this situation is framed by an emphasis on God's word: "But the word of our God will stand for ever" (40:8), and the metaphor of rain and snow signifying that the word of God brings forth fruit (55:10-11):

> So shall my word be that goes forth from my mouth; it shall not return to me empty, but it shall accomplish that which I purpose, and prosper in the thing for which I sent it.

The word intended here is the prophet Deutero-Isaiah's message of salvation. Even if "to believe" does not occur here in an emphatic manner, the announced future nonetheless depends on the message being believed. We encounter the term "to believe" emphasized in the final suffering servant song at the beginning of Isaiah 53: "Who has believed what we have heard?" In the use and meaning of "to believe" in Deutero-Isaiah and in suffering servant songs, one can discern the path leading from the Old to the New Testament.

The History of the Mediator

The message of saving comes to the oppressed through a human mouth, from the mouth of one of them. It is a mediated word. However, the guidance through the wilderness is also carried by a person, i.e., in a mediated fashion. The mediator belongs both to the announcement as well as to the process of deliverance.

God's words as well as God's actions can be mediated to his people through a human. The mediator is not a timeless figure; the working of the mediator can only be presented in a history. The history of the mediator is an essential part of the history of Yahweh with his people Israel.

The patriarchal history does not yet know of the mediator; what is said and done between God and the patriarchs happens directly. The history of the mediator begins with the history of the people, and begins such that Moses, the mediator at the beginning, is a mediator of God's words and actions. In the middle period, the time of the settlement, the mediator of the word and mediator of action emerge separately. At the end, but only in a suggestive fashion, the two strands merge again in the figure of the suffering servant.

Moses belongs to the epoch of the wandering group as the leader of this group and thus as mediator of God's action ("I will deliver you . . . ") and as the mediator of God's word at the departure and along the way. There was never again in the history of Israel an office such as that of Moses.[28] Moses' historicity is grounded in this office. The Exodus event in general is unthinkable without God's spokesman, who is simultaneously the leader of the group.[29] Moses is the mediator necessary for the liberation from Egypt, the path through the wilderness, and the guidance into the promised land; his historicity is grounded in this. Moses was not, as earlier maintained, an originator or founder of a religion. Only in the later stages of religious history do we find something like the establishment or founding of a religion.[30] Religions are not established or founded in the early period. Neither is there a beginning for a religion in the strict sense. Every beginning is a transition—because there are no communities without religion—and indeed a transition associated with a social or political change.

The texts at the beginning of the book of Exodus show with astonishing clarity that, at the departure from Egypt, it was a matter of only a relative beginning which was actually a transition. The connection with the religion of the fathers is shown in chapters 3 and 6 with the transition to various names of God, explained differently in the different strata. Precisely this threefold different explanation points to a real transition. The old God receives the name Yahweh, thus it must be explained here (Exod. 3:14: "I AM WHO I AM"). The new name grows out of the new experience, out of the event of encounter with the saving God. The new name gives continuity to the event beginning with it.[31]

It is part of the uniqueness of Moses' task as mediator of the Exodus event that he never becomes the leader in battle, is never a warrior, that he is powerless. However, he is also powerless as the leader of the group; he has no disciplinary or executive power whatever. Thus he must suffer in his office. With the mediator at the beginning we thus also encounter the lament of the mediator, which then recurs profusely at the end of the history of the office of mediator.

After the settlement, the office of mediator is diversified. The mediators of the word and those of the action of God emerge separately. The charismatic leaders are the mediators of God's saving action in the period before Israel became a state. God frees his people by mediators of action, as the book of Judges portrays it. Here God's saving comes about differently than before: The mediator is called by God and brings about liberation through the force of arms. This is how the variation in the old creed at the beginning of the book of Judges portrays it (see above p. 53). G. von Rad has drawn attention to the unique form of these struggles in the work, *Der Heilige Krieg im alten Israel* (see also R. Smend, FRLANT 84). These are not wars in the strict sense, but rather always only individual skirmishes, locally and temporally confined; it is never a continuing waging of war. Their uniqueness lies in the fact that the Israelite tribes, in their struggle for survival, called on God for rescue in a situation of acute danger. When the liberation came about, they experienced it as God's saving deed. That is why the military events were so closely associated with Yahweh. When in distress a young man was willing to take up the struggle, he was considered commissioned by God, and he understood himself to be acting in the service of his God, who was saving his people. One thus made inquiries of God in critical situations, and the word of salvation was received as a response in the form of the formula of deliverance: "Behold, I have given the enemy over into your hand." In the songs of victory God is thus praised as the liberator (as in Judg. 5). The understanding and portrayal of these struggles as God's saving deeds was only possible, however, because their goal was only the liberation from a situation of acute distress, and never the acquisition of power. Precisely this was true of the leader as well in these struggles; he attains no power for himself in these struggles, but is rather the same thing after the struggles as he was before. That is why these so-called wars of Yahweh were confined to Israel's brief period before statehood in which the tribes carried on battles which were exclusively defensive.

Excursus: Ruaḥ—The term *ruaḥ jhwh*[32] is rooted in these liberation struggles of Israel's early period. The "spirit of Yahweh" seizes the savior chosen by God and enables him to carry out the deed of liberation: Judges 3:10; 6:33f.; 11:29; 14:19; 15:14; 1 Samuel 11:6. The verbal term "to breathe out heavily through the nose" underlies this; *ruaḥ* can mean breath or wind, but this implies heavily exhaled breath. The common element is the power encountered in heavily agitated air. John 3:8 shows that the basic concept is the same in the Old and New Testaments. One speaks about the spirit of God in the sense of the basic meaning in the context of charismatic leadership, but also in the early ecstatic prophecy: The *ruaḥ jhwh* seizes a person such that he falls into prophetic ecstasy (1 Sam. 10). The term "spirit of God" is almost completely lacking in the prophetic writings. This is negative in the rejection of ecstatic prophecy, positive in the concentration on the prophetic word. The prophets are messengers of the word of God. The second center of use lies in the promise of the spirit of God for the period of salvation. In one case the expected savior of Israel is understood as the bearer of the spirit of God (Isa. 42:1; 61:11 and Isa. 11:2), in another case the future people of God become the bearer of the spirit (Isa. 44:3b; 32:15; Ezek. 37; 36:26f.; Joel 2:28; 3:1; Isa. 59:21; 63:11). The deepest break in the history of its meaning lies in the fact that the *ruaḥ jhwh* becomes a static concept (Isa. 11:1; Joel 3:1). This broadens the concept such that in the later period all of God's activity becomes an activity through the spirit, including that of the prophets (Neh. 9:30; Zech. 7:12; 2 Chron. 15:1; 24:20). It is this static concept of spirit which then becomes dominant in the New Testament, although within the important context of the Pentecost narrative in Acts 2, the "spirit of God" is used in its original sense as an element enabling one to perform a special, unique deed.

The kings as mediators of God's action in Israel (the theological aspect of kingship). As followers of the charismatic leaders (the transition takes place in the figure of Saul), the king in Israel could only be of significance for the relationship of Israel to its God as the mediator of saving, and this is precisely how his emergence is portrayed. Israel was threatened in its existence by the Philistines; the charismatic leaders were no longer up to this threat, so the people turned to Samuel for a king. The king was thus to be the mediator of saving. Kingship, however, which as an institution was international and inter-religious,[33] contained within it its own religious structure which had to come into conflict with the Israelite understanding of the king. The saving function of the king necessarily receded when the enemies threatening the people's existence were defeated. After the consolidation of the king's power, the kingship had to become a static institution just as it did everywhere else (in contrast to the charismatic leaders), and the king became the mediator of God's perpetual action; the king became a mediator of blessing. This static character of kingship is expressly grounded theologically in the prophecy of Nathan in 2 Samuel 7, in which the king and his house are promised continuance (2 Sam. 7:16): "And your house and your kingdom shall be made sure for ever before me; your throne shall be established for ever."

The danger thus arose that the king would no longer remain just a mediator, but would himself become divine, i.e., the danger of divine kingship. Israelite kingship did not fall prey to this danger of divine kingship, though the king—just as everywhere—did indeed acquire sacral functions in Israel as well. The greater danger was that the king as mediator of blessing abandoned the old, strict traditions of the Exodus creed and let himself be influenced by the understanding of kingship in the surrounding area, so that through the king's activity and the royal ritual, alien elements made their way into the Yahweh faith. This danger accounts for the fact that the history of kingship from beginning to end is accompanied by an element of criticism.

If one views the books of Kings as a whole, then one notices that the entire weight lies on the kingship of David. One might say that the books of Kings speak about kingship as an aborted possibility for Israel under Saul, and then about the only really successful possibility under David which then remains in suspension under Solomon, only to become a history of failure after the division of the kingdom. This is commensurate with the fact that, in the Deuteronomic historical work, the portrayal of the history of kingship to a large extent proceeds quite critically. David receives a positive evaluation first because he really was a mediator of saving, but also because he brought the ark to Jerusalem and thus combined the traditions of ancient Israel with the new state. After Solomon, the majority of kings receives a negative evaluation. The criterion is the first commandment, and the kings' sin is "the sin of Jeroboam," idolatry. It is commensurate with the largely critical evaluation of kingship that in the presentation of the Deuteronomic historical work, the history of kingship from the beginning onward is accompanied by the critical authority of prophecy. Before the prophetic writings the most important addressee of the prophetic word is the king. From Amos onward the announcement of judgment to the king is directed to the entire people. The theological evaluation of kingship in Israel's history requires that one consider its portrayal in the prophets as well as in the

Deuteronomic historical work. Here the kings belong in the context of the history of apostasy and defection from Yahweh to other gods. This is confirmed through the entire history of kingship—not, to be sure, always uniformly, but consistently at various points. This only becomes comprehensible if one presupposes that in sacral kingship the king represents the people, is responsible for the welfare of his people, and thus can also cause a disaster for the entire people. Here the Deuteronomic historical work judges that Israel's kings did not conform to the demand for obedience set forth in Deuteronomy as the condition for blessing, but rather denied the response of obedience.

Because of this thoroughly critical view of kingship in the prophets and the Deuteronomic historical work, we can assume that under other auspices kingship and its history could be viewed more positively than here. In contrast to the Deuteronomic evaluation, we also find an at least partially positive view in the Old Testament in other contexts. In the royal Psalms (Pss. 2; 18; 20; 21; 45; 72; 89; 101; 110; 132) the kingship is fully affirmed; the intercession for the king shows particularly that the king was of essential significance for Israel's worship. This positive significance emerges with particular impressiveness in the lament on the end of the dynasty in Psalm 89 and Lamentations 4. This deep shock was possible only if the king had considerable significance as the mediator between the people and God. This positive meaning of kingship in the role of mediator is shown most clearly by the fact that the collapse of the prophecy of Nathan for the house of David was not accepted, but was rather changed into an expectation directed toward the future in the promises of a king in the time of salvation.

We need to consider that in these three contexts the king is meant primarily as a mediator of blessing, as shown in particular by Psalm 72. Kingship in Israel had a totally positive significance as the mediator of God's blessing activity.

The priest as mediator of God's word. Priests are mediators of God's action only to the extent that they administrate and confer blessing; God blesses his people in the priestly blessing (Num. 6:24-26). They are mediators of God's word in the context of the worship service; it is the institutionally bound word of God, associated with the liturgical ceremonies, whose mediator is the priest. These two limitations taken into consideration, it must still be said that the priest, as a mediator between God and man in Israel, was of much greater significance than the Old Testament suggests at first glance.

The office of the priest is a perpetual office associated with the sedentary form of life and is a part of the sanctuary and its rhythm of festivals throughout the year. From the beginning of kingship onward, the priesthood is firmly associated with that kingship; the priests are royal officials and subordinated to the king in their duties. The office's perpetual nature also manifests itself in the fact that the priesthood is inherited just as dynastic kingship; the son followed the father in priestly service. This perpetual character of the priestly office also accounts for the fact that the priests, unlike the prophets, rarely played a role in Israel's history, and for the most part did not appear at all in the historical movements. For this reason their actual significance cannot be ascertained from the historical books alone. In addition, in prophetic accusations the priests are often portrayed as being partly to blame for Israel's defection from its God. This should not, however, be allowed to mislead us into false generalizations. Along with the regular worship service, the perpetual service of the priests throughout Israel's entire history is an irreplaceable part of what happened between God and his people in Israel. As those commissioned to confirm blessing on the people, they constituted an integral part of worship, which itself stood in the middle of the community's life. As the mediators of the liturgical word, they were the most important carriers of tradition; they preserved the word of God through the centuries and presented it anew to each generation. (Concerning the priests' specific functions, see below p. 198.)

The prophets as mediators of the word. The prophets are mediators of the word alone. They are neither leaders in any sense (like Moses and Joshua), nor possessors or administrators of some power (like the kings), nor mediators of God's blessing within an institution (like the priests). However, since Moses was also a mediator of the word, the activity of the prophets is related to that of Moses. Like him, they are mediators of the word of salvation as well as of judgment, and like Moses they initially performed a positive and guiding task concerning the people of Israel. In the early period a prophetess named Deborah worked together with the charismatic leaders. At the beginning of kingship the prophets performed a task at the court which supported the king and kingship (Nathan, Gad), even if when necessary, they announced judgment to the king. There were salvation prophets up to the exile and then afterwards as well, and in certain situations the prophets of judgment also spoke oracles of salvation. The prophets of the exilic period, just as Moses at the beginning, announced deliverance to the people.

The fact that judgment prophecy then became decisively significant has its roots in Israel's history. It corresponds to the threat to the relationship with God accompanying the kingship, and set itself against that threat. Thus judgment prophecy stands within the wider context of God's saving action: Israel is threatened in its existence by apostasy. This is already implicit in the conditional announcements of salvation and disaster in Deuteronomy. Viewed in this way, judgment prophecy is the task of retarding the divine judgment hanging over Israel by raising a voice of accusation against Israel and in that way making the people conscious of the coming judgment. In contrast to the divine judgment of the flood, which breaks in on men unannounced like a merciless fate, Israel's fall is announced long in advance so that the people move towards the collapse consciously and with the warning in their ears. Viewed in this way, the history of judgment prophecy as a whole acquires positive significance for the history of Israel with its God. Israel's God, who himself announces the judgment upon his people, remained *beyond* this judgment. One could not say after the coming of the catastrophe that the God of this people fell with it, that the God failed along with his anointed one, or that the worship of this God ended with the destruction of his cultic locale. By announcing judgment through the prophets and declaring through them that he would destroy his own people, Yahweh remained the one acting through this catastrophe and beyond it. This is shown by the history of prophecy which continues during the exile. Precisely this is a decisive argument in the proclamation of Deutero-Isaiah, who is related here to judgment prophecy: God has here proven to be dependable, since the judgment he announced did occur; the newly issued word is then also dependable, the promise of return. The positive significance of judgment prophecy is shown in another way by the Deuteronomic historical work, in which the history of Israelite kingship acquires comprehensive meaning: The collapse of Israelite and Judaean kingship can be shown to be meaningful and necessary by pointing to the prophetic announcement of judgment.

The epochs of prophecy. It is essential for the understanding of prophecy that it occupies a clearly defined period in Israel. Prophecy is not something which always must be. The historical period of prophecy is essentially the same as that of kingship. This has already been explained from the perspective of kingship: The prophets are the critical authority accompanying kingship. From the perspective of prophecy this means that they became necessary for a certain historical constellation and that their function ended when it did. We can conclude from this that it is then not possible to call Israel's faith a prophetic faith, or Israel's religion a prophetic religion.[34] The significance of judgment prophecy lies in the fact that it followed a historical period characterized by deliverance and indirectly carried it further.

For the New Testament and the Christian church we can then conclude that the question whether there must be or cannot be prophecy in the Christian church is falsely put. Prophecy would be misunderstood if one made a perpetual institution out of it. The question is rather whether and how certain elements of Old Testament prophecy can acquire significance in certain situations and in limited temporal periods.

The prehistory. Strands from various religious-historically known and disseminated phenomena come together in prophecy: ecstatics, seers, and the figure of the man of God. Elements from all three have gone into prophecy. Elements of ecstatics can be found in the early period in Elijah and Elisha and in the later period in Ezekiel. Otherwise, they are virtually absent from prophecy, and the early attempt to explain prophecy from the ecstatics (H. Gunkel, 1917; G. Hölscher), have for all practical purposes been abandoned. The visions have gone over into prophecy as an essential element from the seers, as well as the developmental presentation in announcements of judgments as well as of salvation. The visionary element breaks through fully again in apocalyptic. The apocalyptic is a seer; he no longer announces events, but rather sees the future. The man of God and prophet can almost merge in the early period, as with Elisha. One characteristic of the man of God, the fact that he has the power-word at his disposal, continues to exist below the surface throughout the history of prophecy.[35]

The main phase of prophecy has two divisions. In the first, the prophets' activity and words are transmitted in the historical books; in the second, the prophetic tradition is made independent, and collections of prophetic words and books arise. In the first period, the accusation and announcement of judgment is only raised against individuals, usually the king, and the span from the issuance of the announcement up to its occurrence is small. In the second period, the announcement of judgment is broadened to include the entire people, and the span from the announcement to its occurrence encompasses several generations. It is characteristic of this main phase of prophecy that not one of the prophets is successful with his message, and yet one prophet follows the other until the announcement of fall, common to them all, occurs.

The post-history. The prophecy of the exile constitutes the conclusion of the main phase of prophecy inasmuch as it remains related to the end of the state, of kingship, and of the cult of pre-exilic Israel. This includes Ezekiel, Deutero-Isaiah, and many nameless prophets of the period of exile. All subsequent prophecy belongs to the post-history, which is actually only an echo of the pre-exilic and exilic prophecy. It presupposes the preceding prophecy, which has become tradition, and builds on it. Salvation prophecy, in all its mixed forms, is dominant. The end of prophecy is seen in two transitions: that into apocalyptic in the prophet Zechariah, and that into doctrinal disputation in the prophet Malachi.

The mediator at the end: the suffering servant. The texts:

Isa. 42:1-4:	The king who is a servant (designation).
49:1-6:	The calling of the servant.
	The servant's seemingly futile activity concerning Israel.
	In contrast to that: designated as a light to the nations.
50:4-9:	He who receives and carries on the word becomes the suffering one. His confession of trust.
52–53:	The dying and elevated servant and his congregation.[36]

The texts must first be seen in the context of Deutero-Isaiah's proclamation. Deutero-Isaiah announces his people's deliverance from exile on the basis of forgiveness. But with that the deliverance becomes something different. Deutero-Isaiah cannot proclaim that Israel will again become what it previously was. To be sure, Israel can return to its country, but the returning Israel is powerless, and no longer holds political power over that land. Deutero-Isaiah can also promise future blessing (Isa. 54—55), but not political greatness and power. The servant songs issue into the question of the future, which thus remains open. They, too, must also be seen within the broader context of pre-exilic judgment prophecy. The third text, Isaiah 50:4-9, says that the servant is a mediator of the word, and 49:1-6 says that the activity of the prophet of judgment was apparently futile. This suggests that the suffering servant is understood as the one who carries on or consummates the activity of the pre-exilic prophets of judgment. In this, however, the task is broadened to include the nations. What is new in the suffering servant in contrast to the prophets of judgment is his representative suffering, which is already prefigured in the last of the pre-exilic prophets, in the Lamentations of Jeremiah.

Finally, these texts must be placed into the even broader context of the history of God with Israel. This broader context is suggested by Deutero-Isaiah's proclamation when he describes the liberation from the Babylonian captivity as the new Exodus. With this, the correspondence of the mediator at the end with the one at the beginning emerges quite of itself. Moses and the suffering servant are the two cornerstones in the history of the mediator. The difference, of course, is that the suffering servant is not a historical figure in the same way as Moses at the beginning. He stands in no recognizable historical context, remains anonymous, and his activity is portrayed in veiled language. Both have in common that they are commissioned by God for a task to Israel and that in this task they can both be called *'ebed,* servants of God. Both are mediators next to which there are no others, and with both the office of the mediator embraces more than words: As leader, Moses is simultaneously the mediator of God's action, while suffering takes the place of action for the suffering servant. Both are mediators without power and must suffer in their office. The suffering servant is different in that his suffering is representative for the sins of the entire people and does not end in death. His work is to extend beyond Israel: God will give him as a light to the nations (Isa. 49:6).

The obvious correspondence between the mediator at the beginning and the mediator at the end acquires its significance in this broad context of Israel's history. The mediating office of Moses introduced the history of a people which was like other peoples. The guidance into the promised land led to settlement, to the state, and to kingship. Moses himself, however, remained outside (Deut. 32:48-52); he was a leader without power. This history reaches its goal again in a servant without power, a mediator with whom the history of Israel as one power among others is at an end. The goal does not lie in the strand of the state and kingship; it lies in the strand of the judgment prophets and their powerlessness. The end of the mediators of action is contained in the mediating figure of the servant. Instead, suffering acquires the positive significance of suffering for others. Simultaneously, however, the task of the mediator is expanded beyond Israel to other nations. In these two features: The fact that suffering now acquires the positive possibility of a representative function, and that the mediator between God and Israel now becomes the "light to the nations," the mediating figure of the suffering servant reaches beyond the Old Testament, and the fundamental correspondence with the Gospel accounts of Jesus' representative suffering, death, and resurrection is unmistakable.

The structure of the fourth servant song (Isa. 52/53) has the same basic structure as the accounts of the suffering, death, and resurrection of Jesus in the New Testament gospels. The events portrayed in it take place between three characters just as in the three-part structure of the lament and just as in the structure of the book of Job: between God, the person who suffers, and the others. The word of God frames the account (Isa. 52:12; 53:11b, 12). The suffering person becomes a mediator (intercessor), and his fate is changed. This process changes the enemies, who have erred, into friends, and the new congregation emerges from those who despise and condemn the servant. All this occurs before the forum of humanity (Isa. 52:14, 15; 53:11b, 12): "he bore the sin of many."

The History of the Lament and the Praise of God

The elements of the process of saving include, on the side of humanity, the lament and the praise of God. These two form the framework in the portrayal in the book of Exodus. The sequence of events is precipitated by the Israelites in Egypt crying out to God, and it issues into the praise, in the Song of Miriam, Exodus 15, of those rescued. Both lament and praise belong to what happens here. Lament and praise will be treated thoroughly later. Here we need only to point out that both accompany the history of the people of God and the life of the individual from beginning to end, and indeed do so on a recognizable path. The early stage is characterized by short cries to God; the second stage is that of the Psalms; the third is that of the long prose prayers. In the changing forms the elements of praise and lament remain constant.

PART III

The Blessing God
and Creation

The Creator and the Creation[1]

To speak of God means to speak of the whole. Wherever people call to God, they mean the one who holds the whole in his hands. Wherever people praise God, they praise the one beyond the limitations of human existence and human thought who oversees the whole and knows the meaning of the whole. Thus the Bible speaks of God the creator of the world and of humanity.

Whenever we speak about the creator or about creations, we are consciously or unconsciously coming from the first article of the Apostles' Creed: "I believe in God . . . Creator of heaven and earth." The second and third article of faith begins with the same "I believe. . . ." This presupposes that the relationship of man to God the creator is the same as that to God the savior. The unavoidable consequence is that faith in the creator, similar to faith in Christ as the savior, is understood alternatively: Do we believe that the world and humanity were created by God at the beginning, or are we persuaded with the scientifically thinking people of our time that the world originated within the context of astronomical processes, and that human life originated in the context of the gradual emergence of organic life?

Now, the Old Testament itself does *not* speak about faith in the creator or about creation faith (see above p. 72). This kind of alternative is originally alien to any reference to the creator and creation. There is no such alternative or anything similar for any of the references to creation in primeval history, in the Psalms, in Deutero-Isaiah, or in the book of Job. A contradiction between an explanation of the world from a faith in God and a scientific explanation of the world has no foundation in the Bible itself. The fact that

God created the world, and that God created human life, does not contradict the scientific explanation of the origin of the world and man. This contradiction as such is a fateful misunderstanding of biblical talk about the creator. This talk, in its essence, cannot come into competition with the scientific explanation of the origin of the world and of humankind.

Reference to the creator and to creation in the Old Testament itself stands in two great contexts. When we open the initial pages of the Bible, we ask first: What kind of meaning do they have within the whole of the Bible? The preceding section has shown us that Israel encountered its God as a savior. This was an experience which could be verified and carried on. We saw what significance it acquired for the entire tradition of Israel. The experience then went further: God *remained* Israel's savior. And with that the experience expanded; God became the savior in all spheres of life. However, only he who is active in everything could be the savior. Since God is One, the savior must also be the creator. It follows that in the Old Testament the history established by God's saving deed was expanded to include the beginning of everything that happens. The savior of Israel is the creator; the creator is the savior of Israel. What began in creation issues into Israel's history.

This connection is shown by the fact that in Israel, praise of God combines the activity of the saving God and the activity of the creator. The really specific way of speaking about the creator is the praise of God, as shown by many Psalms in which the creator is praised. We can include here the taking up of the praise of the creator in the book of Job (e.g., Job 9:38-41) and in the proclamation of Deutero-Isaiah (e.g., Isa. 40:12-31).

The other great context emerges from the fact that, for millennia before Israel, in the wide spectrum of the peoples of the world, there was and is talk about creation and the creator. Not one of the motifs in the Old Testament story of creation is absolutely new; they all have close or distant parallels.[2] The question of how the world came about cannot be comprehensively answered, and it cannot be answered in one sentence. But one thing can be said for sure: The question of the origin of human life and the world was not originally a question of the intellect (this came later). It was rather the question of the endangered, threatened, astonished human. As such, it is a question of meaning. When in a group of people one tells how a god made man, this brings to expression the fact that behind man there stands some purpose and thus some meaning. It thus becomes immediately clear that the creation of the world and the creation of human life are independent. The question of the meaning of human life is different from the question of the meaning of the world or the meaning of what exists. It also becomes understandable that the traditions of human creation, viewed within the whole of creation stories, are older than the traditions of the creation of the world, since the endangered, threatened person asks first about the meaning of his own human existence.[3]

The concepts of the whole, of the whole of humanity, and of the whole of the world first emerged in this talk about creation. In all the world's languages the word designating the genus "man" just as the word "world" are late arrivals. In many languages, the designation "man" is still identical with the name of the people, and in others it is derived from "man." In all the world's languages the word "world" is the gradual expansion or extension of a smaller sphere. Neither "the man" nor "the world" belong to the experiential sphere of primitive history. They could not be conceived other than from their origin, and this origin could not be understood other than as creation by a creator.

This second great context suggests that talk of creation in the Bible, in its roots, reaches far into the history of humanity. With it, the church has been entrusted with something extending far beyond the Old and New Testaments and belonging to the oldest religious material and simultaneously to the oldest cultural material of mankind. Long neglected and misunderstood by the church itself, it is today again suspected as something necessary for the future of humanity.

Primeval History, Genesis 1–11

The first sentence of the Bible implies that the Bible wishes to speak of the whole of being. When it speaks of the creator, it speaks of the universe. The creation narrative at the beginning of the Bible points to the horizon in which what it wants to say about God takes place. It is the whole world (Gen. 1) and the whole of humanity (Gen. 2) with which the God of the Bible deals. If both the Yahwist and the author of the Priestly Code begin their respective works—which aim at the history of Israel (J) and at worship in Israel (P)—with creation and primeval history, then they wish to express that the God of the people of Israel is not limited in his working by the boundaries of that people, but that he is the Lord of universal history and the Lord of the cosmos. Everything that happens between Israel and its God, everything that happens between an individual and God stands in this broad context.

Primeval history as a whole. The first eleven chapters of the Bible speak of this broad context. They constitute a context which can only be understood as such. Each individual text in Genesis 1—11 has its own context within this whole.[4] Now, this has never been expressly disputed. But in the tradition of the Christian church, when the first three chapters—which according to church doctrine deal with the creation and fall—were given a much greater significance and the following chapters 4—11 only a very small one or none at all, the context of Genesis 1—11 as such lost its significance. That, however, considerably changed what the Bible says about creation.

We need to ask about the changes from the perspective of the structure of Genesis 1—11. These chapters contain narrative and enumerative texts. The narratives are first those of the creation and of the flood (Gen. 1—2 and 6—9), J and P together. To this is added a series of narratives about guilt and punishment which only J has (Gen. 3; 4:2-16; 6:1-4; 9:20-27; 11:1-9). The enumerative texts are the genealogies in Genesis 4, 5, 10, and 11. If these enumerative texts, the genealogies, are not taken into consideration, one cannot see that the blessing of humanity in Genesis 1:28: "Be fruitful and multiply," is portrayed in the genealogies. The blessing works itself out in the sequence of generations; with P in chapter 5 it extends into the depth of time, and in chapter 10 into the breadth of space. Thus a large portion of the texts in Genesis 1—11 deal with the effect of the blessing.

Creation and flood belong together and correspond to one another. The flood narrative implies that the creation is threatened by catastrophes, and that a catastrophe can also be based on God's will. The first conclusion of the flood story says what the creation of humanity in the world means for the present. The creature threatened and endangered in his own world is told that God holds his creation in his hands up to the present, indeed "while the earth remains." God pledges its enduring existence through all catastrophes. The way of preserving the world, however, is blessing; God preserves his world in the ryhthms of blessing, summer and winter, sowing and reaping, frost and heat, day and night. The activity of the creator extends as blessing into the present.

The author's intention has been fundamentally misunderstood because of the line of division between the third and fourth chapters. Because chapter 3 was understood as the fall, i.e., as the fall into the existence of the sinner, and chapter 4 only as a heightening of sin, one failed to recognize that the author consciously conceived the two chapters parallel and in exact correspondence. Within this parallel he juxtaposed the transgression against God and that against one's brother. Only both together show man as he is, with his capacity to transgress both against God and against his brother. The creator is just as affected through fratricide as through direct disobedience. Thus God's reactions here as well as there correspond to each other point for point.

The fourth change occurs when the creation in Genesis 2 is confined to verse 7, thus concealing that fact that the entire second chapter deals with the creation of human life; God's creature is man, in and with everything of which chapter 2 speaks.

Creation in the history of religions and in the Bible. Even if what the Bible says about creation is different in some essential points from what was said about creation in religions surrounding Israel, the fact Israel's God was worshiped as the creator of the world and of human life is something which relates the religion of Israel with a great many other religions. The conviction that the world is created and that man is a creature can be found in all of humanity, throughout the millennia. In this talk about a creator and about creation processes, we find an astonishing amount of agreement and an astonishing amount of similarity throughout the world. In the entire, inexhaustible richness of ideas about creation there are only four clearly defined types of creation[5]:

I. Creation by means of making or some sort of activity.
II. Creation by means of (conception and) birth.
III. Creation by means of a battle.
IV. Creation by means of a word.

Creation by means of making belongs to the primitive realm of understanding and is found in primitive creation narratives all over the world. It has been taken up in the Bible in the portrayal of the creation of humankind in Genesis 2, particularly verse 7. The second and third ideas belong to mythical thinking. They are found in the mythical-polytheistic sphere, since both presuppose a plurality of gods or divine beings as well as the two typically mythical motifs of divine battle and love. These two kinds of creation portrayal are dominant in Israel's surroundings. Creation by means of a battle is classically portrayed in the Babylonian epic *Enuma Elish*. Creation by means of divine conception or divine birth is classically portrayed particularly in Egypt. We encounter both in the Old Testament as well. The creation by means of battle echoes in some Psalms, e.g., Isaiah 51:9-10: "Was it not thou that didst cut Rahab in pieces, that didst pierce the dragon?" The creation of the world by means of a series of births echoes distantly in Genesis 1 in the designation of the creation as *toledot* = conceptions and in the linguistic character of Genesis 1, which sounds stylistically like the genealogies. The fourth type, the specifically theological, has a strong abstracting tendency and already serves as a transition to the scientific explanation of the origin of the world. The uniqueness of the Bible's talk about creation is that the latest, abstract conception of creation by means of the word does not extinguish the older, more concrete ideas; rather, the latter maintain their right and significance. In Genesis 1 this is shown by the fact that the chapter has grown out of a combination of an older and a younger stratum, the so-called word-account and act-account. The author of the Priestly Code takes up the older ideas, as, e.g., creation through division, and inserts them into his idea about creation by means of the word. With this he shows that there is no absolutely correct idea about creation at all. These ideas about creation have to change, but this does not mean that the older one is false, and the younger correct. Here the scientific explanation of the origin of the world, in a scientific age, is recognized as justified from the very beginning to the extent that it does not absolutize itself. These ideas about creation are essentially variable, and cannot be absolutized.

The Creation of the World, the World as God's Creation

In talking about the creation of the world, humanity learned to understand the world as a whole. The world as a whole was not accessible to the senses; an individual person could always only perceive a tiny section. The whole of the world could only be comprehended from the perspective of its origin. *All* later philosophy, when it spoke about the whole, e.g., in the concept of being or of what exists, comes from the concept of creation and remains unconsciously dependent upon it, as is clearly shown in the pre-Socratics. All natural sciences, when they proceed from the concept of nature or of material, are coming from the concept of creation and remain dependent upon it. The first generation of natural scientists who paved the way, such as Galileo and Newton, still knew this. Something like the world-view of materialism only became possible because the concept of the creation of the world was coined and defined by hundreds of generations before the materialists. Without it the concept of material would never have been coined, and the same would have been true for the concept of nature.

The intention of the first chapter of the Bible is also to understand *the world as a whole in view of the creator.*[6] The structure of this chapter discloses itself only if one proceeds from the whole. It is divided into the creation of the basic categories of time (Gen. 1:3-5), space (Gen. 1:6-10), the creation of vegetation (Gen. 1:1-13) and of the stars (Gen. 1:14-19), of the animals (1:20-25), of human life (1:26-31) and in the purpose of this whole in Genesis 2:1-4. There is a myriad of parallels for each of the motifs in Genesis 1. The uniqueness resides in the fact that it is ordered into a structure of seven days, through which the creation of the world acquires a progression from the first to the seventh day. In placing the creation of light first, the author gave the temporal category priority over the spatial, so that the creation of the world became an event extending in time and a prelude to world history. Through the schema of sequential creation days he suggests the emergence of our world in sequential epochs, and in the stillness of the seventh he suggested the progession of world history towards a goal transcending the works of creation.

God creates through the word; he creates by speaking. This creation by means of the word is not understood in its real sense if one understands it as a spiritualization of older, more massive ideas about creation. It is correct that it is a later, more strongly reflected idea of creation than perhaps one through a making or some action. However, the word of the creator is not meant as a spiritual process; something happens with the utterance of the word. Thus the word of the creator is not only a word in the usual sense, but rather a specific word, a command. Each of the creation works is divided into the constituents of an order. The order is introduced: "God spoke," and there then follows the order "let it be" and its execution "it was so." In addition, this includes the evaluation of what has been done: "God saw that it was good," and the temporal structuring "and there was evening . . . one day." The consistent sequence of these sentences, which form a whole, gives the chapter its unique character which in its monotony is so similar to the genealogies (Gen. 5 and 10). There is a reason for this: The author expresses in this way that the creation through the word takes the place of creation through a series of births.[7] Through the entire Priestly Code we find the view that everything that happens originates through God's commanding word. At the beginning of the liberation God orders Moses to confront the pharaoh;

in the revelation at Sinai God orders the building of the tabernacle; at the end of the sojourn in the wilderness God orders the crossing of the Jordan and the entry into the promised land. Through this portrayal of creation in a series of creation commands, the author of the Priestly Code intends a conscious association of creation and history.

The creation commands are different from those in history in that they have no personal addresses. Nonetheless, they elicit obedience: In a way incomprehensible to humans, the creator orders that which does not exist to exist. And the recognizing answer is concealed in God's judgment that it is good. Then, however, what is created will answer the creator with praise (Ps. 148).

When the author portrays *the creation of plants and animals as an emergence of the species,* he is not relying on older creation traditions, but rather on priestly lore which grew from priestly circles and traditions. This lore viewed the plants as well as the animals as wholes which were ordered into species. This kind of understanding lies along the path towards a scientific explanation of the origin of plants and animals in species. We can see with particular clarity here that for the author of this chapter the affirmation of the creator on the one hand, and scientific explanations of the origins of the world elements on the other, did not exclude one another. The same thing can be seen, in a different way, in his portrayal of the creation of the stars. The stars are for him simply creations; they totally lose the divinity attributed to them by Israel's neighbors. Because of this extraction of divinity, the sun, moon, and stars become constitutive parts of the world, not accessible to human research.

The creation of the world includes the judgment of the creator, which runs like a refrain though the creation story: "God saw that it was good," and at the end: "And behold, it was very good." In God's eyes it is good in a way not immediately apparent from the works themselves. In human eyes there is much in these works which is not good; much of it is incomprehensible, much is dreadful. But his sentence—that creation was good in God's eyes—relieves the individual of the judgment of the whole. A creature cannot oversee the entirety of the whole and thus cannot evaluate it. But precisely this frees an individual for the joy of creation. One is free to be glad in his or her heart at the sight of a ripe field of corn, even though one knows that hail has destroyed another part of the harvest. One can and should rejoice with those who are joyous. The goodness of creation, which includes its beauty, wants to awaken the echo of joy and thus of praise. This echo of the praise of God is already suggested in the sentence accompanying the works of creation, an echo which then resounds exuberantly in the Psalms in which the creatures are called to praise:

> Praise the LORD from the heavens,
>> praise him in the heights! . . .
> Praise him, sun and moon,
>> praise him, all you shining stars! (Ps. 148)

All creatures participate in the whole of creation, and they are all significant within the whole. These Psalms express that in the orientation of the creatures to their creator, to the praise of that creator. This orientation toward the creator is something the creatures and creations, people, animals, and all the others have in common. Praise is the joy of existence turned towards God, and this joy of existence inheres in the creation as a whole.

The goodness of what is created includes its beauty. The Hebraic adjective *ṭob* can mean good and beautiful. In the concluding sentence the listener thus also heard the echo: "Behold, it was very beautiful." The beauty of creation has its foundation in the will of the creator;[8] beauty belongs to God's works. Whoever speaks about the work of the creator also speaks about what is beautiful. Whoever speaks of what is beautiful, as is done in the Bible, also speaks about the beauty belonging to God's creation. The uniqueness of biblical talk about what is beautiful resides in the fact that this beauty is not something primarily existing, but rather something which happens. In this the biblical understanding of beauty is fundamentally different from that of the Greeks. Beauty is something one encounters in flux, just as in the Yahwist's creation narrative in the encounter between man and woman. This difference accounts for the fact that the echo of beauty in the work of art is typically the plastic arts for the Greeks, while in the Old Testament it is the joy elicited by beauty coming to expression in the word of praise. The joy of beauty in the Old Testament is always close to the joy turned towards God. This need not always be expressed, and not every verbal expression of the joy elicited by beauty has to be praise of God. But both are so close to one another that for the person of the Old Testament the creation never became nature, nature in the sense of something merely there, separated from the creator and his activity. Psalm 104:

> O LORD my God, thou art very great!
> Thou art clothed with honor and majesty,
>   who coverest thyself with light as with a garment . . .

Since beauty belongs to creation, it remains subordinated to the blessing activity of God. It plays no part in the context of God's saving action, and for that reason beauty does not arise in a theology which only intends to be soteriology. The difference can be seen in the figure of the mediator. Beauty belongs to the king, who is a mediator of blessing (Ps. 45); and of the servant, the mediator of deliverance at the end, we read: "he had no form or comeliness."

The goal of creation is suggested by the conclusion in Genesis 2:1-4a. The division of creation into six days' work places the works of creation into a temporal framework in which the work days progress towards the day of rest, the time during the creation week in which the uniqueness of that seventh day was prepared from the beginning. With that the author of the Priestly Code takes up an old motif found in early creation narratives: the motif of the *otiositas* (resting, ceasing work) of the creator god after his work. This accounts for the fact that the creator can no longer intercede in the finished work, so that he cannot disturb it. However, this motif is fundamentally changed here: The days of creation activity have their goal in a day which is different, which is special. The work of creation which began with the separation of light and darkness, ends with another separation. The history of humanity, which begins with the conclusion of creation, is differentiated by means of the sanctification of the seventh day from the rhythm of the perpetually same days and the perpetually same years which constitute the rhythm for all creation. Just as do the days of the week, so also does the history of mankind progress toward a goal. The creative insertion of the uniqueness of that sanctified day into creation suggests the goal for that creature which God made in his own image. At the same time, the author of the Priestly Code uses this conclusion of creation to suggest the goal of Israel's early history, which he sees in the establishment of the worship service in Jerusalem. The number seven recurs in the Sinai theophany (P) (Exod. 24:16: "six days—on the seventh day"), in which it is a matter of the establishment of worship in the promised land.

The Creation of Human Life—Man as Creature

Human existence as a whole. The biblical understanding of humanity acquires its foundation in the story of the creation (Gen. 2). First it is said that a person is God's creature; one is that in no other way than in one's origin from God. This initially has nothing yet to do with his faith or convictions; human existence as such is characterized as creaturely existence. However, this foundation includes something else: The creature existence of human life means human life in all its relationships in existence; the person which is merely made (Gen. 2:7) is not yet the creature intended by God. The creation of humanity includes the living space (the garden), the means of life (the fruits of the garden), the occupation or work (cultivate and preserve), and the community (man and woman) and, as a medium of community, language. This complex understanding of the creation of human life has largely been overlooked in theology, particularly in theological anthropology. There only the fact that human life was made by God seemed relevant for that created existence, i.e., only man in his bare existence. The relationship to God was seen only in view of individuals abstracted from their vital relationships. This has significant consequences for theology as a whole. Under the presupposition of an abstract anthropology, the relationship to God also remains abstract; under the presupposition of this complex understanding of the creation of humankind, it is a matter—in the relationship to God as well—of people in all their relationships in existence: living space, nourishment, work, and the social realm all belong to it.

People in their limitations. Here, too, we need to point out a difference between the traditional church doctrine and the biblical text. The doctrine of the fall and of original sin cannot be based on the narrative in Genesis 3. It comes from the Jewish tradition and can be found in the fourth book of Ezra (7:118), where we read:

> Ah, Adam, what have you done! When you sinned, your fall did not just come upon you, but also upon us, your descendants!

This Jewish teaching of the fall and of original sin was then further developed by Augustine. A citation: "Thus the fall of man is also understood as a sliding down to a lower level of being, so that sin must not be understood as a lack, but as a degradation in existence."[9] This sentence lies along the line of the Jewish interpretation of Genesis 3; it is not commensurate with the text of Genesis 3, as maintained today by Catholic and Protestant exegetes. The text says nothing about a falling or sliding down to a lower level of being. Just as little does the text say that death is punishment for human sins; the punishment for disobedience is rather the expulsion from the garden and thus from proximity to God.

The narrative in chapter 3, which was originally independent, has been combined into one narrative with that of chapter 2, which was also independent. The Yahwist's intention in fusing these two narratives into one was to bring to expression the fact that created existence is intimately associated with human limitations. When one speaks about man as God's creature, one must not just speak about the gifts of the creator to this creature; one must also speak about the limitation set for persons as creatures. In blessing, one receives from one's creator the capacity for propagation; this includes, however, that people are bound to a short span of existence. One exists as a person only in the span which leads from birth to death. The capacity for propagation—the blessing—presupposes death. People must die so that people can live.

This limitation has important consequences for the Old Testament understanding of humanity. Human life, according to the Old Testament, is not a straight line; it is an arc, an arc rising from birth and descending toward death. Any generalizing talk about human life which acts as if life is the same in everything from birth until death is questionable. Every philosophical and every theological anthropology which figures with human life as a straight line is in error. Rather, every human lives in a field of tension determined by two poles. Death projects itself into his existence as a power from the other end of life. The power of death is a power extending into life, as portrayed in Genesis 3:14-19. The power of death projects itself into life not only in aging, but also in sickness, in pain, in fear, in despair, in loneliness, and in resignation. The human is limited.

The other limitation of human existence is the possibility of error. A person can err, transgress, commit a crime, can lose himself—as, for example, in drug intoxication—can be led astray. The Bible takes this limitation quite seriously. That is why the story of the disobedience of the creature against its creator is combined with the story of the creation. Even though humans know that they live by the gifts of their creator, they are disobedient to this, their creator, to whom they owe everything. This fallibility cannot be separated from human creatureliness. The Yahwist does not take this existence as sinner seriously by referring to some abstract concept of sin, but rather by showing it in the multiplicity and richness of its possibilities in the stories of guilt and punishment. Above all, the writer shows in the parallel juxtaposition of Genesis 3 and 4 that the transgression against God and that against humanity belong together. As long as there are people, there will be those capable of error. No religion, no world-view, no political programs, and no social reforms can change that. Infallibility would be inhumanity. It is this limited nature of people in their finiteness and in their fallibility which leads to God's saving deed in the transition from the Old to the New Testament, a deed not bringing an end to these two limitations of human existence, but rather giving persons freedom from them.

People created in God's image. "So God created man in his own image, in the image of God he created him." This is not primarily a statement about human life, but rather about the creation of human life by God. The creature God is now planning is to stand in relationship to him; humans are to correspond to God so that something can happen between them and God, so that God can speak to them and they can answer. Humanity is created so that something may happen between God and humans.

Concerning the discussion permeating the entire history of Christendom about the question of the significance of this similarity with God, the summary of this discussion in the Genesis commentary BK I/1, 203-214 can be consulted. After people long assumed that this must mean something special in them, their spiritual-intellectual capacity or spiritual powers, the freedom of will, personality, the immortal soul, or their upright stature, it was only later recognized that this similarity with God does not refer to something in or on people, but rather means the human as such and as a whole: "It does not consist in anything that man is or does. It consists as man himself consists as the creature of God. He would not be man if he were not the image of God. He is the image of God in the fact that he is man" (K. Barth, CD III, 1, pp. 184, 186).

The statement that God created people in his own image is then to be understood as an explicative one; that similarity to God is not something added to creatureliness. It states rather what it means to say that the human is God's creature. This makes it more clear that something is said of people here which is valid for all beyond any other differences which might exist between them. The people of all nations, all races, all religions, and all world-views are created in God's image. Human dignity is based on having been created in God's image, a dignity inherent in every person as God's creature. This dignity given humans is also what establishes human rights. We can easily see in history that this dignity of creation in God's image, granted to all as God's creatures, receded or was not taken into consideration at all in the epochs of Christendom in which the election of Christians (or of a Christian people) over non-Christians was emphasized.[10]

Work and culture, wisdom. It is part of this complex understanding of humanity that God gives his creature the commission for work; he gives him the task of cultivating and maintaining the garden. One exegete (K. Budde) maintains that this sentence must be deleted, and defends it thus: "Nowhere does the second hand give itself away so clearly as here. Man is in paradise for blessed enjoyment, not for working and maintaining." This understanding is totally alien to the Old Testament. It is the Greek conception of the Isles of the Blessed, which itself has the background of an economic order in which the heavy physical work is done by subordinates or slaves, while the really human activity is purely intellectual. This judgmental differentiation between intellectual-spiritual and physical work is alien to the Old Testament. Physical work has the dignity of God's commission. A person who lives from the work of others is leading an existence not worthy of humanity according to the understanding of the creation story. Work, whether physical or intellectual, is a necessary element in human existence.

With the two verbs "cultivate and maintain" the narrator first means the work of the Palestinian farmers, but one can also view all human work under these two aspects. The prerequisite of this commission is that a human is entrusted with the garden and then with the earth, so that he may gain harvest from it and at the same time protect and preserve this earth, the land, the field as the donor of these yields.[11] Wherever a yield is gained from the earth without simultaneously protecting and preserving the earth as the donor of that yield, it is a case of exhaustive cultivation, which can in no way call itself God's commission. Nothing more is meant by the formulation of the Priestly Code in which humankind is given dominion over the other creatures and thus over the earth as well: ". . . and subdue it." "Dominion" is not meant here in the sense of arbitrary employment of power. That would be a fateful misunderstanding of this commission for dominion. It is meant rather in the sense of the other classic form of dominion, that of kingship. It means the full responsibility of the ruler for the welfare of the people and country entrusted to him. Whenever the king is not capable of bringing about and guaranteeing the welfare of those entrusted to him, then he has forfeited his dominion. There is thus no textual basis when, in the contemporary discussion about *"dominium terrae,"* an unscrupulous exploitation of our earth's resources refers itself to the granting of dominion in the creation story. Every form of exploitation of the earth is contempt for God's commission.[12]

The commission to cultivate and maintain the garden is carried further in chapter 4 from verse 17 on. Work grows and branches out with mankind. This growing and branching out of human work includes the division of labor which becomes necessary with it. God's blessing, active in success, accompanies this branching out, and all human work can participate in it, not just agriculture and livestock farming. Human technical activity in all its ramifications, natural sciences as well as the humanities in all ramifications can be understood under this commissioning by God. Criticism and warning concerning outgrowths and danger can only become significant where this possibility of working in God's commission in all branches of human work has first been clearly stated.

In this cultivating and maintaining, physical and intellectual work belong necessarily together from the beginning. Beyond that, intellectual activity, reflection, and contemplation belong to all spheres of human creatureliness, to the living space, to life's nourishment, to work, and to community. In the Old Testament this is called wisdom. Wisdom belongs to the cultivation of a field, but also to the maintenance of a marriage and to the rearing of a child. Wisdom belongs to the breaking up of a tree stump and to the directing of a conversation. It belongs to the way one comes to terms with life in the broad sense, in all spheres of life. Wisdom was originally given to human existence as a whole, in all its possibilities, and only in a late stage was it separated into an intellectual realm. Only in this separation at a later stage did wisdom become something which is there for its own sake, and which as such becomes the object of human activity—as the Greek word *philosophia* shows. A large portion of the newer works concerning wisdom proceed from wisdom as a separate realm and are thus already questionable in their point of departure.

When Adam and Eve are commanded during creation to cultivate and maintain the garden, wisdom as a coming to terms with life is implied in this commission. G. von Rad thus defines it as "an elementary form of mastering life." We find the phenomenon of human failure in all spheres of human life and human activity. This failure forces one to reflect, and this reflection can lead to insights which then bring about success. The acquisition of wisdom from experiences of failure or foundering is a part of human existence. It is normal and natural that someone transmits insights acquired in this way which can serve in the mastering of life, instead of keeping them just for oneself. For this, they must receive a form in which they can be transmitted further. The form suitable for this, and the most simple form imaginable is the proverb. It serves to preserve and transmit experiences. We thus find this form of proverb or word of wisdom all over the world; it belongs to the language of mankind. The wisdom expressing itself in the proverb is thus international and inter-religious (the opinion of G. von Rad and many others), as is also shown by the wisdom literature of the Old Testament.[13]

> *Excursus:* The theological position of *wisdom* is thus to be determined from the perspective of creation and primeval history.[14] In this commissioning to cultivate and maintain the garden, people are thus not only entrusted with the earth, but with work and maintenance as well. The success of this commission, however, implies wisdom. This wisdom, which acquires form in the proverb—i.e., in the statement collecting experiences and advancing and making possible human self-understanding in the world—stands in direct correspondence to the cultural acquisitions and progress sketched out in the Cain genealogy in Genesis 4. They directly carry on the creation of human life, which includes work and blessing, but also the success of work.
>
> The significance of wisdom as an integral part of the Bible resides then above all in the fact that it makes it clear that the creator gave man the capacity of becoming properly oriented in his world, of understanding himself in his world, and of mastering the daily tasks given him. This requires neither revelation nor theological reflection. Wisdom is secular or profane. It is assumed that a person will progressively experience his world himself, will preserve and assimilate these experiences such that he learns from mistakes and becomes more mature through false steps. The creator has given the creature over to himself in this acquisition and preservation of experience, in insight and knowledge; he wants him to be independent. This is also true for the expansion of wisdom into the sciences. It is the will of the creator that man is independent in this respect; the freedom of the sciences is based on the will of the creator.
>
> Wisdom in the Old Testament finds its continuation in the New Testament. The Synoptic Gospels not only contain a great many wisdom proverbs, the parables of Jesus also stand in close association with wisdom. In them Jesus challenges one to judge independently just as do the old proverbs. One can also say that these parables are expanded comparisons like those we encounter so frequently in Proverbs (particularly Prov. 25f.). With the preservation of biblical wisdom, the church has been entrusted with a precious treasure. Wisdom has priority over all the sciences. No science is

comprehensive; wisdom, in its original form as experiential proverbs, embraces the whole of human life. The preservation of wisdom as a part of the Bible can help counter the centrifugal form of all the sciences—which incline toward ever greater differentiation—with the centripetal force of wisdom, which is concerned with the whole of human existence. It can also help counter the absolutizing tendency of the sciences—which take themselves seriously in that tendency—with the functional tendency of wisdom, which is there only for the sake of man, indeed for the sake of the whole man.

In conclusion concerning creation: creation and universalism. The Old Testament does not just deal with the creator and creation only in the initial pages of the Bible. Apart from a great many individual passages, the creator and creation come to thorough expression in three complexes: the Psalms, Deutero-Isaiah, and the book of Job. Each of these contexts has its own, profound word to say here, and all three would need to be considered in an overall portrayal of what the Bible says about creation. Here we must dispense with it for the sake of brevity.

Only one thing needs to be said. In all three contexts the actual way of speaking about the creator and creation is the praise of God. The praise of the creator stands in the position later occupied by the faith in the creator. It is the joy in the face of creation, directed to God, and the astonishment at the wonders of his creation; it is the joy of the creature which knows itself to be in the knowing thoughts and protective hands of its creator; that is what comes to expression in the praise of the creator:

> Bless the LORD, O my soul!
>> O LORD my God, thou art very great!
> Thou art clothed with honor and majesty,
>> who coverest thyself with light as with a garment. . . .
> O LORD, how manifold are thy works!
>> In wisdom hast thou made them all;
>> the earth is full of thy creatures. (Ps. 104:1-2, 24)

> O LORD, thou hast searched me and known me!
>> Thou knowest when I sit down and when I rise up;
> thou discernest my thoughts from afar. . . .
> Such knowledge is too wonderful for me;
>> it is high, I cannot attain it. (Ps. 139:1, 6)

Wherever the Old Testament speaks about the creator, it speaks about the whole; and wherever it speaks about the whole, it speaks about the creator. In the Old Testament, however, the entirety of the universe is understood primarily as something which happens, and only in a secondary sense as something which exists. If God is the creator of the world and of humanity, then world events and human history are in his hands from beginning to end. What began with the creation of heaven and earth must reach its destination with all that belongs to it: the history of the cosmos and the history of nature, the history of humanity and the history of God with his people. Therefore the Old Testament's speaking of the creator necessarily involves a universalism that attributes to the God—whom Israel meets as her savior—everything that happens from the beginning to the end of time. This universalism seldom appears in the Old Testament, but it echoes through again and again, beginning with the universalism characterizing the entire primeval history. When the beginning of the patriarchal history speaks of God's blessing for all generations of the earth, or when in the Psalms nations and kings, and in Psalm 148 all creatures are called to the praise of God, when in judgment prophecy God effects his judgment on Israel by means of other nations, when in Deutero-Isaiah Cyrus becomes the savior of Israel appointed by God. The final events, corresponding to the first events, are then also totally universalistic. Apocalyptic speaks of a new heaven and earth. This correspondence between primeval events and end events is already prefigured in Genesis 1—11 in the association of creation and flood. The flood has apocalyptic features, and the promise at the end of the flood points to its limit: "while the earth remains." This is the universalism which in many later folk proverbs promises peace and the cessation of wars among the nations, e.g., in Isaiah 19, which in Deutero-Isaiah is expressed in the words: "I am the first and I am the last." And it is the universalism which is taken up in the apocalypse: "I am the alpha and the omega, the beginning and the end."

The Blessing

God's Action as Continuous and as Occurring, Blessing and Saving

In the creation account of the Priestly Code, the creator blesses all manner of life: "Be fruitful and multiply . . .!" The creator works through this blessing, thus the blessing is universal and is valid for all forms of life. As distinct from this, God's saving action is a special turning towards a particular group, and from this experience of saving there thus emerges a particular history, the history of saving or salvation history. God's blessing, on the other hand, also continues outside this particular history; Job, the man from the land of Uz, is also a man blessed by God. But those who have been saved remain human like everyone else and they are therefore in need of the blessing which embraces all people. They share in the gifts of the blessing, in their physical existence, in food and clothing, in social and economic maintenance of the society in which they live, and in the continuation of life from one generation to the next. In the Old Testament all this is understood as the working of God by blessing, which encompasses all people and in which those who have been destined for a particular history with God also share.

Blessing is a working of God which is different from saving insofar as it is not experienced as the latter in individual events or in a sequence of events. It is a quiet, continuous, flowing, and unnoticed working of God which cannot be captured in moments or dates. Blessing is realized in a gradual process, as in the process of growing, maturing, and fading. The Old Testament does not just report a series of events which consists of the great acts of God. The intervals are also part of it. In them God gives growth and prosperity unnoticed in a quiet working, in which he lets children be born and grow up, in which he gives success in work. The saving God is also the blessing God. God's blessing makes it possible for a person to relate his whole life, in its course from day to day and year to year, to God. One receives from God's hand one's whole life, especially in its daily unobtrusiveness in which nothing particular happens. The blessing is a matter not of the extraordinary times when, e.g., one experiences deliverance, but rather of the daily flow of daily life. Evening and morning songs speak about the activity of the blessing God. Something as unobtrusive and seemingly insignificant as a greeting is closely related to blessing. Blessing and peace are simultaneously words of greeting.[15]

The entire Old Testament thus speaks of *God's continuous action in addition to the acts which occur once* in his saving and judging deeds. One should proceed from the fact that in the Pentateuch, the story of that saving at the beginning of Exodus up to Numbers is framed by two textual contexts in which God's blessing is dominant: the blessing of the creator in Genesis 1—11, including the blessing of the creatures (Gen. 1:26-27), the one after the flood (Gen. 8:20-22), as well as the language form of the genealogies; then the blessing of God in the life sphere of the family in the patriarchal story (Gen. 12—50), including the blessing in Deuteronomy directed toward the people in the promised land. The traditionists consciously combined God's blessing activity with his saving deeds in their structuring of the Pentateuch.

In the historical books God's activity in events, in saving and judging deeds, steps into the foreground. Next to that, however, the two institutions characterized by continuity also acquire determinative significance: kingship and temple cult. The promise for kingship is that of duration (2 Sam. 7); blessing is conferred in the temple worship service (Num. 6).

The books of the prophets are characterized by the announcement of judgment. God's blessing action has no place here, though in many passages of prophecy a condition of salvation is promised after the judgment. The language of blessing is spoken in this portrayal of salvation.

In the Psalms, too, we encounter God's continuous action in addition to his momentary events. In the lament Psalms God's saving intervention is requested, and in the narrative Psalms of praise the saving God is praised. But in the descriptive Psalms of praise God's saving and blessing action is summarized in the praise of God (e.g., Ps. 33), the creator is praised (Pss. 8; 104; 139), as well as the blessing God (Ps. 67). The Psalms of confidence (Ps. 23) summarize both together, and in the liturgical Psalms it is a matter of liturgical blessing (Pss. 24; 67). That blessing activity is turned toward the pious in contrast to the godless (Ps. 1). The book of Job is totally determined by God's continuous blessing activity; this is already a factor because the drama of Job takes place outside Israel. The same is true of the wisdom books of Proverbs and Ecclesiasticus. If there is talk here of God's action, then it is that of the creator. The history of God's great deeds concerning his people does not appear.

This brief overview shows that the continuous and occurring, the saving and blessing action is distributed in a proportionate and balanced manner in the Old Testament. Let it be added that, within the context of God's action in the form of events, the course of time is determined according to events within the context of God's continuous action according to the sequence of generations (genealogies).

The History of Blessing in the Old Testament

Blessing in the patriarchal stories. In the patriarchal stories we encounter an extremely early stratum in which blessing is still totally rooted in the community form of the family; the father is here the blessing one. The narrative in Genesis 27, in which Isaac blesses his sons, is based on a pre-cultic ritual which forms the structure of the narrative in all its parts. The action of blessing includes here (1) the summoning of the father (or the request of the son), (2) the identification (or naming) of the one to be blessed, (3) the strengthening of the person conferring the blessing by means of food and drink, (4) the son's approach and touch, (5) blessing. In the three parts of the patriarchal story the various spheres of blessing activity are each particularly emphasized. In the Abraham circle (Gen. 12—25) it is a matter particularly of the continuation of the generations, of the blessing of fertility in the verticle line of sequence from the parents to the children. In the Jacob-Esau circle (Gen. 25—36) it is a matter of the horizontal line of brothers living together, and in particular of the fertility of livestock. In the Joseph story, which belongs to a later stage, it is a matter of the peace (*šalom*) accompanying the blessing, which brings about the soundness of a community.

The blessing of the land as such does not yet play a part in the patriarchal story because of the nomadic form of life; it does indeed, however, play a part in the promise of land, which already looks toward the people Israel just as does the promise of propagation, which itself speaks the exuberant language of blessing. The patriarchal stories also speak about God's saving, but it remains within the context of family events and is still pre-historical.

The association of blessing with history. Blessing acquired new significance through its association with history. The Yahwist schematically carries out this association in Genesis 12:1-3 by structuring the blessing—which is essentially unhistorical—into a promise of blessing for the people Israel.[16] The future people Israel is to be blessed in Abraham, and by echoing the promise of deliverance during the departure from Egypt the Yahwist combines the promise with the commandment to set forth:

> "Go from your country and your kindred and your father's house to the land that I will show you. And I will make of you a great nation, and I will bless you, and make your name great, so that you will be a blessing." (Gen. 12:1-3)

The same thing occurs in a different fashion in the Balaam-pericope (Num. 22—24), in which the power of blessing is subordinated and attached to Yahweh's historical activity. The narrative of Balaam explains how Yahweh, the God of Israel, became the Lord of the power of blessing. It presupposes that other peoples and religions also have gifted ones who have the power of blessing and curse. Balak, the king of Moab, wants to employ this power by commissioning Balaam to curse Israel. Balaam, however, is commanded by Yahweh, the God of Israel, not to curse Israel, but rather to bless it (Num. 22:12). Balaam can now do nothing other than pledge happiness and splendor to Israel in his seer-oracles:

"How fair are your tents, O Jacob,
  your encampments, O Israel!
Like valleys that stretch afar,
  like gardens beside a river,
like aloes that the LORD has planted,
  like cedar trees beside the waters.
Water shall flow from his buckets,
  and his seed shall be in many waters." (Num. 24:5-7)

The proximity of seer-oracle and blessing-oracle is also shown by the sayings in the patriarchal story which are associated with blessing activity (e.g., Gen. 48:15f.) and by the tribal sayings derived from them (e.g., Gen. 49:11). In all these promises the dominant element is the portrayal of a condition, just as the blessing itself is a circumstantial concept. The promise of blessing runs from these beginnings through the entire Old Testament, appearing particularly in the later period of prophecy and in apocalyptic.

Blessing in Deuteronomy. The concept of blessing is dominant in Deuteronomy.[17] God's saving deeds belong to the past. Before the entry into the land, the blessing in the promised land is announced, echoing the promise of blessing from the patriarchal period (Deut. 7:13-16, similarly 28:3-6):

"He will love you, bless you, and multiply you; he will also bless the fruit of your body and the fruit of your ground, you grain and your wine and your oil, the increase of your cattle and the young of your flock, in the land which he swore to your fathers to give you."

With the transition to settlement, the blessing of the land becomes vitally important for the people in the promised land. This is stated in a short note in the book of Joshua (Josh. 5:12): "And the manna ceased on the morrow . . . and the people of Israel had manna no more, but ate the fruit of the land of Canaan that year."

The bread of blessing now takes the place of the bread of saving. This transition involved one of the most difficult internal arguments in the history of Israel, in which the belief in the one Yahweh prevailed, who also has to be acknowledged and venerated as the giver of blessing. The radical struggle against the Baal religion in Deuteronomy and in the prophets, especially Hosea, is directed against the Baal religion as a fertility religion. This had largely led to the false conclusion that Yahweh the God of Israel is only the God of history, and that "nature religion" and the "fertility cult" would be radically rejected in Yahweh religion. Generalized in this way, this is false. For Hosea, who led the most intense struggle against the Baal religion, the God of Israel is also the God who blesses. In chapter 2 he confronts the Baalim not with the God of history but with the God who blesses and gives fertility and prosperity, exactly as in Deuteronomy: "And she did not know that it was I who gave her the grain, the wine, and the oil . . ." (Hos. 2:8). Hosea wishes to say by this that Yahweh, the God of Israel, whom Israel meets as savior in its history, is the *same* God who gives Israel in the *Kulturland* the gifts of the land, growth, and prospering. This does not make the religion of Israel a fertility religion, but the God of Israel as the blessing God gives his people the same gifts that in other religions are expected from the fertility gods. The first commandment has to be understood against the background of this struggle.

In Deuteronomy an eloquent testimony to the unity of the saving and the blessing God is found in Deuteronomy 26. This is the bringing of the first-born as the gifts of the blessing God with the confession of God's saving deed in history, the Creed. What is new in Deuteronomy is the fact that the blessing is now bound to the obedience of the people. The earlier promises of blessing were unconditional; now they are bound to a condition. The conditional sentences, which bind the blessing in the land to the condition of obedience, permeate all of Deuteronomy (28:1f.): "And if you obey the voice of the LORD your God . . . all these blessings shall come upon you. . . ." The conditional announcement of curse corresponds to this (28:15): "But if you will not obey the voice of the LORD your God . . . then all these curses shall come upon you. . . ." The conclusion in chapter 28 once again monumentally juxtaposes curse and blessing under this condition. This combines blessing with the Law, and binds it to the Law. This will later cause a serious crisis.

Blessing in the institutions of the settlement period. The two great institutions characterizing the life of sedentary Israel both correspond to God's continuous action: kingship and the cult. The king and priest as mediators were already presented in the context of the history of the mediator (see above pp. 73ff.). However, the institutions as such are also to be included in God's continuous activity which corresponds to that continuous, fixed institution. This is shown particularly in two features common both to kingship and the cult. In the sedentary cult as well as in the static institution of kingship it is primarily a matter of the welfare of the land and of the people in the land, here politically, there religiously. The other feature, the continuous nature of God's activity in these two institutions, is represented in the respective offices, passed on in both cases from father to son. The anointing of the king corresponds to the consecration of the priest in that both bestow an enduring character.

Blessing in kingship. Three essential features show how kingship fits into the context of God's continuing activity.

1. Kingship is universal just as blessing is universal. There has been kingship all over the world (ThB 55, 291-308). The uniqueness of this form of rule consists first in the fact that in it the familial function of the father has been united with the political function of the ruler of the people. This accounts for the fact that in dynastic kingship the king is king with his family, and the continuing character of kingship is made possible by the birth of the son. This transferal of familial continuance, as seen in the genealogies, into political continuance has given the ruling form of kingship its world-wide significance.

2. This transferal also establishes the sacral character of kingship. The relationship of the king to the deity can be viewed in various ways, from the divinity of the king to a merely functional relationship. But the king always has some sort of relationship to the diety. Kingship as such is sacral or possesses sacral consecration. This is based on the fact that in the early period (still recognizable in the patriarchal stories), when there were no cult mediators, the father performed the function of mediator; he offered the sacrifices and conferred blessing. This sacral consecration is such an inseparable part of kingship that it is preserved in vestiges to the present.

3. Just as the father is the representative of his family and at the same time is responsible for its preservation and welfare, so also the king for his people. Thus the king is the mediator of blessing and is responsible for the welfare of his people. Beyond that, the greatness, name, and splendor of the people is represented in the greatness, name, and splendor of the kingship and is viewed as an effect of God's blessing. This is shown particularly by the portrayal of King David. Wars of aggression now become possible for the sake of the greatness and name of the people represented in the king. On the

other side, it also makes possible a form of kingship such as that seen in the reign of Solomon, which includes forced labor and stark social contrasts.

These three essential features of kingship can explain both. It acquired the high political and religious significance for the people Israel after the settlement in the promised land. This and, on the other hand, the threat to Israel emerging from the receding of the old traditions of God as the savior of Israel, reflected most strongly in the prophets' critique in their announcement of judgment—upon individual kings first and then upon Israel itself represented in that kingship.

Blessing in the act of worship. With the transition to settled life comes the adoption of the form of worship that corresponds to this lifestyle, a form for which blessing acquires central significance. God's work of blessing, the gift of grain, wine, and oil (Hos. 2:8; Deut. 7:13), includes the agricultural festivals which Israel inherited from the settled people. Even after they have been "historicized" in Israel, i.e., even after they have been connected with the acts of God in history, they still remain festivals in the course of the year which celebrate sowing and harvest before God (e.g., Ps. 67). The life of the farmer who depends on the blessing of fertility passes in the natural rhythms of the year which find expression in the religious festivals.[18]

Only from the beginning of the settled period onward did the liturgical blessing—conferred in worship at the holy place at the holy time—acquire significance for Israel. A verbatim formulation of this blessing has been transmitted to us (Num. 6:22-27):

> "Thus you shall bless the people of Israel: you shall say to them,
> The LORD bless you and keep you:
> The LORD make his face to shine upon you, and be gracious to you:
> The LORD lift up his countenance upon you, and give you peace.
> So shall they put my name upon the people of Israel, and I will bless them."

It is essential for the liturgical blessing that it consist of word and act. In the promise of blessing the act was separated from the word; in the liturgical blessing the old distribution of blessing is renewed (Gen. 27) which includes word and act as with a sacrament. In this form, as the word of blessing combined with an act, the liturgical blessing has endured through the ages and extends up into the present. The priestly blessing is conferred at the end of every sacrificial act of worship (Lev. 9:22-23); the visitors to the festivals and worship services, the pilgrims in the processions (Ps. 24) receive from the sanctuary the blessing for their house, their family, and their work. The Psalms show the significance of this blessing: The priests bless the congregation (Pss. 115:14f.; 118:26; 129:8; 134:4) or an individual (Pss. 91; 121). The blessing is conferred from the sanctuary during the processions (Pss. 24:5; 118:26; 128:5). For the entire land, for the houses and fields, for the family and livestock, a blessing was expected which meant growth, prosperity, and success. At the presentation of the sacrifices the received blessing was acknowledged as God's gift. This flow of blessing to and from the sanctuary was an essential part of the life of the Israelite farmer. The liturgical institution of the blessing is concerned with nothing other than the working of God in blessing, of which the patriarchal narratives, Deuteronomy, many Psalms, and other texts speak.

In addition to this, the basic elements of worship—the holy place, the holy time, the holy act, led by a consecrated priest, with its regular character, with the regular rhythms of the annually recurring festivals—all these elements point to the continuing working of God in blessing, described in these rhythms in Genesis 8:22.

Blessing from the exile on. There is no mention of the blessing, or hardly any, in those parts of the Old Testament that speak in a very concentrated way of God's saving (Exodus through Numbers) or judgment (prophecy of judgment). But they are looking across into a future determined by blessing. The beginning of the Exodus (Exod. 3:7ff.) and the end of the wilderness wanderings (the blessings of the seer Balaam, Num. 22—24) describe the beauty and richness of the promised land. Everywhere in the Old Testament, beauty is connected with blessing. Similarly, the prophecy of judgment also looks beyond the arrival of judgment into a changed future. The portrayal of salvation or blessing (see above pp. 61ff.) offers a description of a condition in the unknown future which will stand in contrast to the present one. The Old Testament contains a profusion of such salvation and blessing portrayals, which accumulate approximately from the exile on.

The collapse of the state and the monarchy prompts a change in the promise as well. The message of Deutero-Isaiah no longer proclaims the restoration of the state and the sovereignty; the deliverance from exile is no longer Israel's victory. The promise of blessing has now been combined with the promise of Israel's return to her country. In the middle of chapters 54—55 stands growth, increase, and flourishing in the land received by Israel again. Similarly, Trito-Isaiah no longer announces an event of saving, but a change of the conditions.

In a different way in Jeremiah the promise of blessing takes the place of the announcement of saving. In the promise connected with the purchase of the field at Anathoth shortly before the fall of Jerusalem, Jeremiah says nothing about the saving of the besieged city. He has only the minimum to announce; life shall continue in the city: "Houses and fields and vineyards shall again be bought in this land" (Jer. 32:15). In the letter to the exiles (Jer. 29:4-7), Jeremiah only sees a future for them in the line of blessing. God's working in blessing his people continues even after the collapse of the state and the monarchy.

The change in the "messianic prophecies" is particularly striking.[19] They presuppose the collapse of the monarchy and at the same time the breach of the prophecy of Nathan (Isa. 4:2-6; 9:1-6; 11:1-9; 16:5; 32:1-8; Jer. 17:24-27; 23:5f.; 30:9, 21; 33:17; Ezek. 17:22-24; 24:23f; 37:22-25; Hos. 3:4; Amos. 9:11; Mic. 4:8; 5:1-3; Zech. 9:9f.). In all these texts the salvation of a coming period is conceived as issuing from a king during the salvation period; it is a branch of the old royal house of David. Righteousness and peace rule in his realm, even the animals live in peace, and the land will be blessed through him. One feature is common to all these texts. It is never said that the coming king will conquer his empire. Rather, he will become king by birth, and this announcement of his birth already means the beginning of the salvation period (Isa. 9:1-6; taken up in Luke 2). Very little is said elsewhere as well about any specific political activity of this king. He is rather a mediator of blessing through whom a new state of blessing, of peace, and of righteousness will arrive (S. Mowinckel, 1952).

For apocalyptic the description of blessing is the typical way of talking about future salvation. In it, the announcement is absent completely. Apocalyptic can only speak of salvation in the future in a timeless depiction, where it looks beyond the apocalyptic catastrophe. The depiction of blessing is universal. With the end of history, the differentiation into nations is dropped, and God acts as in the primeval history with the whole of humanity. As the creator blessed humanity and animals, so also in the eschaton do humans and animals share in the final peace.

The problems of blessing in the book of Job. The most urgent theological problem after the exile was a question, not about the saving, but about the blessing God. Part of the wisdom literature, some of the Psalms (especially Ps. 73), and the book of Job circle around this question. The question was: How is it possible that so many godless people participate in blessing and so many God-fearing people have to suffer and do not prosper? Two quite different answers have been given to this question. One is the answer of Job's friends: God blesses only the God-fearing, and if there is hard suffering and a lack of blessing, the sufferer must have sinned gravely. Job, however, cannot accept this answer. He knows that his friends' talking misses his real suffering, and that he cannot find consolation with them. In addition, he counters them by pointing out that experience does not support their doctrine (Job 21). At the end God confirms that Job, and not his friends, was right (Job 42:7). The friends' strict doctrine of compensation cannot be supported. Psalm 73 stands on Job's side, while the many proverbs dealing with the righteous and the godless and their fate represent the doctrine of compensation. The problem is determined in the post-exilic period by the collapse of the monarchy and the cult which embraces the communal life. The individual could feel sheltered in God's blessing in these institutions; any separation from this worship meant a threat to existence. When these walls no longer stood, the "godless" could also find good fortune and success without paying due homage to Yahweh. This led to the temptation which asked about the good fortune of the godless.

In conclusion, the reference to blessing in the Old Testament means that the relationship to God embraced humanity in the span of existence from birth to death. It includes growth and maturity, the increase and decrease of powers, recovery and strengthening, hunger and plenty. Further, it means the person in the community, from marriage and the family to all the differentiations of community life, in his or her work, in economic life with all its problems. A person as a member of the people of God is also always a member of these broader spheres of human existence.

Blessing, which has its origin in the blessing of all life forms by the creator, is given to a person as a living being with all other living beings together. The relationship between God and man is quite consciously expanded by means of this blessing beyond his membership in the people of God to include his membership in the human race and beyond that with all living beings. The acknowledgement of the uniqueness of God's activity in blessing means that God is not just concerned with human "salvation," but rather with the person in the full richness of his potential and needs, as a creature among creatures. Precisely when one sees the actual center of God's activity in his saving deeds, as does the Old Testament, this center acquires its horizon in God's all-embracing activity in blessing.

Additional words associated with blessing. The concept of peace stands quite close to that of blessing in the Old Testament.[20] Just as blessing denotes God's continuous action, so also is peace a concept of state or condition, *Šalom* is a status; it can never designate an act of saving. In this it corresponds to the Latin *salus* and the German *Heil,* which are also terms designating states or conditions. This is shown clearly by the fact that all three words, *šalom, salus,* and *Heil,* have and still do serve the formation of greetings. That is why it is an extremely unfortunate development that *salus* became the translation of *soteria* and *Heil* the translation of *salus* understood in this way. Neither the Latin *salus* nor the German *Heil* can designate the process of saving. There thus emerged the unclear term *Heilsgeschichte,* meaning the history of God's saving acts. Similarly, the difference between saving and blessing was no longer seen. The term *Heil* could now encompass both saving and blessing, and people no longer noticed any difference between the two.

Accordingly, the Hebraic *šalom* has also been misunderstood. First of all, in later language use (including German), peace from the very beginning became an antonym to war (or strife). This understanding implies that peace comes about through an act, the act of concluding a peace or the act of reconciliation. This, however, is a modified conception which as such, although only rarely, also occurs in late strata of the Old Testament. In the rest of the Old Testament *šalom* is a statal term designating the quality of soundness or wholeness of a human community. It does not just emerge through a conclusion of peace or a reconciliation, but is rather there wherever there is human community. This quality of wholeness or soundness also includes well-being or welfare in the physical sense, something shown especially by the use of the word of greeting. Since being whole or sound—which is what *šalom* intends—embraces the entire person, any talk of "peace of the soul" is a fundamental misunderstanding of the biblical word. When the poet of idealism points to a contrast between "happiness of the senses and peace of the soul," the biblical *šalom* embraces them both. The Joseph narrative gives the best explanation of what the term means in the Old Testament. It also shows that *šalom* always means people in community; an "inner peace" confined to the individual is not what the Bible means by this word.

However, in the Old Testament *šalom* from the very beginning means that things are in order between God and his people, thus there cannot be a relationship of salvation unless the divine relationship is intact. The contrast between judgment and salvation prophecy shows this side of the term particularly well: "Saying, 'Peace, peace,' when there is no peace" (Jer. 6:14). The prophets of salvation proclaim a peace which suppresses or ignores the people's serious transgression against God. That cannot be *šalom*.

The whole group of passages in which *šalom* is used in reference to the future should then be understood from the perspective of this usage. This promised peace plays a significant role in the prophecy of salvation, particularly from the exile on, and presupposes the breach of peace which is gathering in Israel's defection from God and which took place in the judgment announced by the prophets. As we saw, the language of blessing is dominant in these words which speak of the promised peace. This future peace is described as a state or condition, extended into the universal. In this later period one can also speak of "peace with God," seeing that the previous breach of peace was caused by Israel's disobedience.

The conceptual field of blessing also includes words associated with protecting and preserving, which develop the blessing in Numbers 6 just as does peace. In the patriarchal narratives, the concept of God's accompaniment especially belongs here, then the many contexts of God's protecting and preserving in the Psalms, e.g., Psalms 23 or 91. God's accompaniment in protection and preservation lets us recognize yet another unique characteristic of God's activity in blessing: It is not experienced in acute, momentary events, but rather in a quite simple fashion in continuing, quiet certainty: "for thou art with me." It thus has its place in the prayer accompanying daily life, in the morning and evening prayer, before commencing or concluding a journey, and so on.

The conceptual field of blessing also includes words associated with success and prosperity.[21] This includes all the contexts in the Old Testament in which we can translate with "good fortune" or "fortunate." The term "good fortune," which we have secularized, is contained in the Old Testament in the words for blessing, such as *'ašre*.

Creation and Blessing in the History of Religions and in the Old Testament

One of the differences between saving and blessing is that God's saving and judging occur only once and only at this place. This history of God's saving and judging with his people Israel has the characteristics of unconditional singularity and unconditional uniqueness. We need to keep in mind, however, that the individual elements of the saving or even judging process are not singular and not unique. In religions we quite frequently encounter a god who saves his people, or a people who petitions for deliverance or to whom it is promised, and so on. The uniqueness is nothing but the history which has occurred but once, the history which led from the Exodus to the deliverance from Babylonian captivity, from the deliverance based on compassion with the suffering people to that based on forgiveness.

God's activity in blessing, on the other hand, is based on the blessing bestowed on humanity within the context of creation. Here we can assume from the very beginning that the blessing is not confined to Israel, because all are creatures of God. Thus the same thing holds true for blessing as for creation. They participate in the history of God's saving and judging to the extent that they are in some way securely and tightly attached to that history. To the extent that they are bound to it only loosely, or not at all, religious-historical parallels can always be found.

If one inquires concerning creation stories and creation motifs in the broad field of the world's religions, one is overwhelmed by the wealth and richness a person of our time finds.[23] Here one encounters something common to all humanity. This common element, the element uniting all humans, will always be stronger than any particular form to which one might attribute uniqueness. If one looks at the first eleven chapters of the Bible, one encounters this common element at every step. There is hardly a motif in Genesis 1—11 one would not encounter again somewhere else, and indeed not only in the high religions surrounding Israel, the religions of high Near Eastern culture, but beyond that in the religions of the entire world, particularly primitive religions. One has to experience the effect of the hundreds of flood stories hitherto collected from all over the world in order to perceive in utter astonishment how the biblical flood story stands in an enormous context of countless voices, all of which have told of the flood. The petty attempt is then silenced which would prove that only one's own flood narrative is good and correct, while all the others are bad or false. The astonished joy is much greater, the joy which recognizes that there are parts of our Bible in which the element common to all of humanity is stronger than that which separates them.

One can clarify this in the following way. The New Testament Gospels have a prologue which connects the Christ event with what has gone on previously. It is different in Matthew, Luke, and John. In John the Christ event is associated with primeval history or creation, in Matthew with the history of Israel by means of Jesus' genealogy, and in Luke 1—2 with the Old Testament as a whole. In a similar fashion, the history of Israel in the main part of the Old Testament receives a prologue in Genesis 1—11 which connects it with human history. This accounts for the fact that this prologue also speaks about the things we hear said by other peoples concerning the beginnings of primeval history.

The other side of this is the variation the primeval history undergoes by being inserted in front of the history of Israel. It can be seen best in Genesis 1. P places creation into a series of seven days and thus gives this creation the character of a process—extending in time and divided into periods—which moves toward a goal, as suggested in Genesis 2:1-3. He accomplishes this by placing the creation of light at the beginning and thus subordinating the category of space to that of time. In this way he establishes a firm connection between creation and history. Both elements are thus equally balanced and equally significant: the participation of this story of the beginnings in universal human references to those same beginnings, and the uniqueness of combining this with the reference to God's singular history with Israel.

The same holds true for blessing. Because the blessing is given to all living things, it has universal character. Thus we encounter something like the deity's blessing outside Israel as well as in many places in religions. All over the world this threefold fertility is associated with the divine. In all parts of the history of religions, an essential part of the act of worship serves the preservation, renewal, or strengthening of the power of blessing, of the power of the fertility of the body, of the earth, and of the herd.

Furthermore, it is those three great institutions which are ordered under God's activity in blessing and which are distributed throughout the earth: the family, the settled cult, and kingship. In the cult and in kingship Israel participates in that which is cult and that which is kingship in the whole world. The element of uniqueness here is again the connection between God's activity in blessing and the history of God with his people, which has the character of singularity. Let us recall once more the three great transitions in the history of the people of Israel:

1. In the transition to settled life the blessing is inserted into Yahweh's historical activity: Genesis 12:1-3 and Numbers 22—24.

2. In the transition to the state, the kingship and high cult (= settled

cult), both of which by nature are ordered under God's activity in blessing, are the institutions in which various and strong connections with God's historical activity emerge (creed, festivals, Psalms, kings as saviors, king and prophet).

3. In the transition to cult congregation because of the collapse, the blessing as promise for the future is again connected with history.

Thus both the singularity and uniqueness of the history of God with his people in the one and the relationship to other religions in the other aspect of God's activity receive their due respect.

PART IV

God's Judgment
and God's Compassion

Sin and Judgment, the Prophecy of Doom

Sin and Judgment

Sin in the Old and New Testament. Both the Old as well as the New Testament speak about sin, and in both sin has something to do with what happens between God and human beings. In both the Old as well as the New Testament the talk about sin is of central significance, and in both there is a profusion of common elements in that talk about sin. One speaks, for example, about the punishing or committing of sin, of confessing or regretting sin. The impression thus arises that the Old and New Testaments mean essentially the same thing by sin. Thus it is that in the exegesis of the Old Testament, one speaks about sin as if it were the same thing of which the New Testament speaks and as if one might speak in the same way about it as one does there.

In the Old Testament there was originally no general, comprehensive concept of "sin." There are various designations for various processes: to trespass (*ḥatah*), to distort (*'awōn*), and to rebel (*paša'*), in addition to others.[1] They are not summarized in a general term "sin." This is different from the New Testament, where the general term *hamartia* (sin)[2] is dominant. An additional difference emerges from the first: In the Old Testament human trespass is presupposed, and belongs to human existence as such; therefore primeval history speaks about it. Aside from this, one speaks about a transgression which occurs in a particular relationship between God and a particular group of people, between God and his people. We must now discuss this difference in more detail.

Sin in primeval history. The primeval history speaks of man as a being limited in its possibilities.[3] He is limited by death and by the fact that he transgresses, distorts or rebels. Human limitation here is just as impenetrable as the limitation of death. There are none without failings. If now man is understood as God's creature, then these limitations also belong to his relationship to God, just as they do to his relationships to others and to his own existence as a self. One can then speak of this relationship to God in no other way than by including this limitation. God has to intervene against sin because it has a hindering, disturbing, and destructive effect on human existence, on community, and on the relationship to God. The "bad conscience," a general human phenomenon, shows that something like this is necessary. Thus we hear about sin or human transgression already in the primeval history. This brings to expression the fact that transgression, which we call sin, is a part of human existence. No religion, no world-view, and no societal order can change that. Indeed, this is unchangeable in both respects: the fact that limitation belongs to human existence, and the fact that it can endanger somebody or something, and is thus dangerous itself. This is the basis of the judicial order belonging to all human community—which is larger than a family—an order which is thus just as universally human as human erring. Beyond that, the basic elements of judicial order are the same all over the world and throughout history.

It is the intention of the Yahwist in his narratives of guilt and punishment in Genesis 1—11 to depict human transgression in its many varied possibilities in order to make clear the impending danger to humanity in these possibilities. In his astonishingly broad insight here he has recognized the basic possibilities, the sin against God and against others, the possibility of individual and of collective transgression: the transgression of the individual against the creator in an act of disobedience which threatens the relationship of trust between God and his people (Gen. 3); fratricide, which robs another of his life and thus endangers the community as a whole (Gen. 4); the despising of one's parents, which endangers the sound relationship between the generations and thus the tradition (Gen. 9:20-27). To this is added the possibility of collective sin in the crossing of the border .into the superhuman (Gen. 6:1-4; 11:1-9), which threatens man in his existence as man and can lead to the corruption of a whole generation (Gen. 6—9) and become the cause of great catastrophes.[4]

With sin in the multiplicity of its possibilities, the Yahwist wants at the same time to point out the multifariousness of the threat to human existence and to humanity. He makes no distinction here between what we call sin and what we call crime. In our terminology the disobedience against God in Gensis 3 would be a sin, the fratricide in Genesis 4 a crime. But in the Old Testament sin and crime are differentiated neither by terminology nor otherwise. The development has been such that theology and the church deal with sin, the state or society with crime; but this distinction is not supported by the Bible. Biblical reference to human limitation by transgression, which endangers the person in his existence as a self, in his social context, as well as in his relationship to God, encompasses that which we call sin and that which we call crime. No theologically established distinction exists between the two.

At the same time, the narratives of guilt and punishment in primeval history point out an important distinction in the reaction of God the creator to human transgressions. On the one hand God intervenes as judge, as portrayed extensively in Genesis 3 and 4, where this judicial intervention corresponds precisely to the basic elements of the profane trial, which itself can be found universally in the institution of courts: discovery of the crime—hearing—defense—sentence—and carrying out of the sentence. It is God the creator who in the worldwide institution of the independent court opposes transgression and restricts evil. On the other hand the flood story in Genesis 6—9 shows a different reaction of God to human transgression. The flood is an act of God's judgment for the hybris of a whole generation which has grown beyond all limits (Gen. 6:5a, 7a, J), but at the end of the flood the creator declares solemnly that such a destruction shall never occur again (Gen. 8:21): "I will never again curse the ground because of man, for the imagination of man's heart is evil from his youth." In this decision at the end of the flood, the creator promises the preservation of the world in spite of all human inclination to evil. God wishes to preserve and keep humanity as it is. Next to the reaction of judging intervention against human transgressions, we now find patient tolerance of man *in spite of* his inclination to evil. God will not in every case intervene as judge against the evil doing of a person or of a group. He can also bear it, tolerate it without intervening. This accounts for the fact that a great deal of evil occurs among people without the intervention of human or divine punishment. Jesus says likewise: "For he makes his sun rise on the evil and on the good, and sends rain on the just and on the unjust" (Matt. 5:45).

Sin in the history of God's people. From sin as a human phenomenon, as human transgression which is part of human existence, we have to distinguish the sin of the people of God and its individual members in the mutual relationship of Israel to its God. The same words are used here in part, but there is a fundamental difference. Just as in a marriage between man and woman, fidelity or infidelity presupposes a condition of belonging together in the relationship to God, which began with an encounter. It is thus essentially different than being evil outside this kind of commitment. It is a great mistake to equate general evil with disobedience against God, which is possible only in a history with God. The Old Testament does not just say in the context of God's history with Israel that all men are subject to transgression—that they are sinners—but rather says this in the primeval history as well. It also holds true outside Israel's particular history with its God.[5] What is new here is that every possible transgression has already been preceded by something, namely, all the good things Israel has experienced with God. It is also preceded by the Yes of the people of God, a decision or a vow (Josh. 24) to remain loyal to this God. It is sufficient to point out one word which makes this connection clear: the word "forget." It is often used by Jeremiah in his accusation. The transgressions of the people of Israel which lead to his accusation all point to this special element only found in this history with God.[6] It is that special element in the directions God gave to his people. God commanded his people to go a certain way; these instructions are articulated in the commandments and laws. In the admonition to obedience permeating all of Deuteronomy, Israel is reminded that disobedience is sin—sin which separates it from God.

These transgressions of Israel can only be understood in close connection with her history, and they are thus also a historical phenomenon and as such subject to change. In contrast to the concept of sin in the Western Christian tradition, in which sin has become an unhistorical, timeless phenomenon, the sin of the people of God has been taken so seriously that it decisively determined that history. It thus begins already in the founding event in the book of Exodus in the episode of the golden calf. Israel's history with its God is like an incline. The guilt of Israel before God grows to such an extent that it leads to his intervention against his own people in judgment. Precisely this is the nucleus of the message of the judgment prophets: the announcement, based on an accusation, that God will punish or even destroy his own people.

Prophecy is not the only place where Israel's guilt is seen in the context of its history. In Deuteronomy, remaining in the promised land and the continuing flow of blessing are made dependent on the obedience of the people. This expressly presupposes that Israel's obedience is possible and that therefore the relationship between God and his people can remain intact. Here, too, Israel's sin is not something which exists of necessity because Israel is by its very nature a sinful people. On the contrary, a good and intact relationship between God and his people is presupposed at the beginning. Similarly, in the review of the Deuteronomic history the idolatry of the kings of Israel and Judah, which causes God's judgment, is not everywhere the same. David and a few other kings are exempt. The Deuteronomic history also shows this incline which led to catastrophe. Things are different in Ezekiel. In his historical portrayal in chapters 16 and 23 he explains Israel's history from the beginning onward as a history of transgression and apostasy.

Sin and punishment in the life of the individual. In the section "The Creation of Human Life—Man as Creature" (see pp. 94ff.), we spoke about the sin of the individual in contradistinction to that of the group. Here, however, the emphasis is on the person as a creature—that eventually means all people. Disobedience against God (Gen. 3) and transgression against one's brother (Gen. 4), however, also have independent, essential significance in the history of the people of God. What we notice here is that one speaks in extremely different ways about the sin and guilt of the individual in various contexts and epochs. We will clarify this from the perspective of three text complexes.

1. Sin and guilt play only a minor role in the patriarchal stories in Genesis 12—27. They do not speak about any sin against God.[7] Transgression against one's brother, however, is a dominant motif in the Joseph story in Genesis 37—50. It is the point of departure in chapter 37 and is carried through up to the last chapter (50). It is not a matter here of the relation guilt-punishment, but rather entirely of the relation guilt-forgiveness. This is important because guilt-forgiveness has its origin and actual home in the family sphere. Of course, punishment can also become necessary in this sphere, but punishment in the family sphere is something essentially different than punishment as a public process. It is accompanied by love, as is often pointed out in the Proverbs (e.g., Prov. 23:15f.). This finds linguistic expression in the fact that there is no independent word for "punish" in Hebrew.

2. Both the lament Psalms of the individual and the Psalms of praise of the individual also speak particularly about sin and forgiveness as well as about sin and punishment. The relation sin-punishment can only be understood against the background of their prehistory in magic, where

the evil deed of itself drew forth evil consequences in the so-called deed-consequence context. This extremely old magical conception is so deeply rooted in humanity that traces of it have been preserved everywhere, even into turns-of-phrase such as "that comes from the fact that." In the Old Testament, too, one encounters this conception often and in myriad forms. One speaks about a "sphere of action which causes fate."[8] In Israel's religion, just as in all religions with personal gods, God's punishment replaced the self-efficacious act, even if the older conception lived on next to it.[9] Against this background we can then see how God's punishment for a transgression is experienced as a diminution of being, thus as sickness, loss, or some other kind of misfortune. In the lament Psalms of the individual this is the cause of the lament. Forgiveness, as the remission of such punishment can accordingly only be experienced as an increase of being, as the reestablishment of well-being. The understanding of the human in the Old Testament knows of no forgiveness which is merely intellectual or spiritual, but must rather have an effect on the entire person. This also accounts for the fact that not every Psalm of lament contains a plea for forgiveness. An affliction can be caused by guilt, but it by no means has to be.

3. This changes precisely in the later period, after the exile. Only in this later period does the doctrine of compensation appear, which says that every diminution in being—without exception—can be traced back to guilt. God thus rewards the pious in their situations and punishes the sinners in theirs, as all can see and verify. We find this doctrine of compensation in the large complex of proverbs about the pious and the sinful. These proverbs do not belong to Israel's early wisdom, but rather to a late stratum in which the originally secular wisdom has combined with a kind of piousness also presupposed in the friends' speeches in the book of Job. One can say that the old, magical conception of the act-consequence relationship has reawakened in this strict doctrine of compensation by combining God's activity with the verifiable act-consequence context. Psalm 73 and the book of Job are testimonies to the fact that not everyone accepted this kind of rigid doctrine of compensation.

Sin and forgiveness. The Old Testament speaks about the forgiveness of sins differently in different contexts.[10]

We notice first that the Old Testament does not everywhere speak in the same way about sin and God's forgiveness. Thus in the lament Psalms we find those in which the person speaking to God combines his plea for God's help with a plea for forgiveness, and those in which this is not the case. Some laments contain a confession of sin, while others do not. The forgiveness of sins is not a part of every encounter with God. This is particularly the case in the patriarchal stories, which portray a relationship between the patriarchs and their God in which there is almost no mention at all about sin against God and God's forgiveness.

In the Joseph story sin and forgiveness are a dominant motif in the narrative, but as an occurrence between people, and not—or only at a distance—between people and God. But precisely this narrative unfolds something which is essential for the understanding of guilt and forgiveness in the Old Testament. It shows that sin or guilt can only arise where there is an occurrence between two or more parties. The transgression breaks the *šalom* (peace), the intactness of a community, and shows itself in the suffering of at least one member of that community. Sin or guilt in a community always causes suffering. This understanding differentiates itself in a fundamental way from an individualistic-abstract understanding of sin in which the entire weight lies on the individual consciousness of sin.

The Joseph narrative also shows something essential for forgiveness. Forgiveness has its time. It does not occur in the automatic sequence guilt-admission-forgiveness, but is rather woven into the history of the community. The hour must come—often much later—in which the admission of guilt and thus its forgiveness is made possible. This corresponds to the forgiveness pledged to Israel. The admission of guilt must first traverse a long path before the hour of forgiveness comes.

From this we can differentiate the sinfulness which is discovered or which overwhelms one in the encounter with the holy. This sinfulness can thus be designated as impurity, as in the calling of Isaiah (Isa. 6:5): ". . . for I am a man of unclean lips, and I dwell in the midst of a people of unclean lips." That is also why the removal of this sinfulness is an act of cultic cleansing (Isa. 6:6-7). As regards origin, this is a different procedure. Cleansing or purificiation is not forgiveness, and a person can only admit or confess an act which one has done, not a condition of impurity.

What Isaiah experienced corresponds to the cultic penitential ritual. Cultic cleansing or purification and the affirmation of the forgiveness of sins—originally two essentially different procedures—merge in the cultic ritual of penitence. The penitential act, combined with sacrifice, takes the place of the direct statement of forgiveness. To the confession of sin (Lev. 5:5) is now added the act of penitence (Lev. 5:6), consisting of the offering of a sacrificial animal. Here it is the priest, the cult mediator, who effects the penitence for the sin (Lev. 5:6). It is hardly thinkable that the two can occur without being related. If we think of Psalm 103, we can assume that the cultic act of penitence and the personal experience of forgiveness stood in a lively mutual relationship. This mutual relationship can even be seen in the word-choice, when the plea for the forgiveness of sins in Psalm 51:2 reads:

> Wash me thoroughly from my iniquity,
> and cleanse me from my sin!

The possibility also exists, however, that the institutional penitential process becomes dominant. This is suggested by the fact that, in the post-exilic period, many sacrifices which earlier had a different function were transformed into penitential sacrifices and brought about a large increase in penitential sacrifices. This is also suggested by the establishment of the great day of penitence (Lev. 16) in the post-exilic period. The ritual of penitence was apparently highly significant in Israel's later period. The danger was that the ritual of penitence became entirely separated from history, and forgiveness was no longer possible without the institution of the cult and priests. Here the post-exilic period corresponds to the pre-Reformation period in which God's forgiveness was also excessively institutionalized and had to a large extent lost the connection with the personal process of God's forgiveness.

The Prophecy of Judgment

The Meaning of Prophecy for Israel's History[11]

There has been a phenomenon like prophecy—taken in a very broad sense—in many religions. There has even been a form of prophecy that shows similarity in its very wording to the prophecy of Israel, the prophecy of Mari by the Euphrates.[12] Prophecy in Israel has predecessors or roots in the figure of the seer, the ecstatic, and the Man of God, which are similar in a great many religions.[13] But only in Israel has there been this succession of prophets from Amos to Jeremiah and Ezekiel, who through this long period of time have steadfastly announced the intervention of a god against his own people in judgment. The prophecy of judgment is the most noticeable religious phenomenon in a particular stage of Israel's history, the stage from the beginning to the end of the monarchy (even though it also has a pre- and post-history). In a history of Israel's religion as well as in a history of the people and a history of Israel's literature, the prophecy of judgment occupies the most important position in this stage next to kingship. The theology of the Old Testament, too, can show the theological significance of prophecy in no other way than in the context of this phase of history.

This means first of all that the significance of prophecy in Israel can be seen only in the broader historical context in the middle between the preceding and following phases. In the second place, it means that that can only be seen as the history of the prophecy of judgment, within its own structure and divisions, to the extent these can be ascertained. Third, the history of prophecy as a whole and in its subdivisions can only be understood in its relationship to simultaneous processes and conditions in the other spheres of the life of the people, the political, social, cultic, and cultural spheres, all of which occur in the accusations of the prophets. It is not the task of a theology of the Old Testament to present the individual prophets in their speaking and activity, and then to glean from this sequence of individual prophetic figures a history of prophecy. The beginning question must rather be: What happened in prophecy as a whole between God and his people, and what did it mean in the history between God and his people as a whole? There are no problems in systematically summarizing and presenting the prophets in this way, since this history's content and language have so much in common.

Prophecy in Israel can only be understood in the middle between what came before and afterwards. What came before: The prophecy of judgment must be seen in close connection with Israel's beginnings, the deliverance of Israel from Egypt and the guidance through the wilderness, which only then made Israel a people. Israel obtained its very existence as a nation by God's acts of saving; if Israel turned away from this God, it would lose the foundation of its existence. Here the theology of the Old Testament links up directly to the part which deals with the saving God and history. The prophets appeared because Israel had threatened its own existence by turning away from its God. Their accusations and announcements of judgment were concerned with Israel's existence. Thus the saving God is now the judging God; the judgment announced by the prophets is the *necessary* continuation of the saving working of God. Because it is necessary for the history of God with his people, it is already inserted into the Pentateuch—in the history of saving—in the episode of the golden calf (Exod. 32—34). In the face of his people's apostasy, the savior must become the judge. In a hidden sense, this judgment is aimed at the saving of Israel—through and after the judgment. God's acts in saving and judging belong closely together.

This announcement of God's judgment stands in the middle between the announcement of God's saving before and after. This ought to be ascertainable in the nature of judgment prophecy. Its dominant language form is the announcement of judgment based on accusation. It thus has two parts: It announces what is coming, something which itself is based on the present state of affairs. The prophetic accusation, which points to this present condition, also points out a threat to Israel within it. It is a threat in any case, since the foundation upon which Israel's life stands is threatened by the errors or transgressions which are the content of the accusation: "They have abandoned me, springs of living water." This destruction announced here is not, however, mere fate, but is rather Yahweh's own act as punishment. The two-part structure of the announcement of punishment expresses this.[14] Since, however, this announced destruction is God's own intervention, it is based on God's overall activity and plan. God wants to extract Israel, his people, from the threat to its existence. The proximity of God's judging to God's saving activity can be seen here as well.

Within the history of prophecy we see the same thing again. There the section of judgment prophecy is framed by salvation prophecy before and after. Before: At the beginning of the monarchy the prophets serve the existence and support of kingship, even though this is combined with a critique of that kingship (Nathan). Prophecy is here still associated with the charismatic leaders, as the prophetess Deborah shows. Afterward, judgment prophecy becomes salvation prophecy (Ezekiel), or salvation prophecy links up with judgment prophecy (Deutero-Isaiah).

The Stages of Judgment Prophecy

We encounter this kind of prophecy in the Old Testament in two stages and two kinds of tradition. Up until Amos we hear about the prophets from the historical books, and from Amos on they become so significant that they form their own independent tradition. This indicates a heightening of the significance of prophecy. What is peculiar is that the prophets before Amos also had circles and pupils. But only from Amos onward did the prophets' pupils consider the collection and transmission of the prophetic words to be important.

This corresponds to a difference in content. Only from Amos onward is the announcement of destruction directed to the whole people; previously this was not the case. This accounts for the necessity of the special transmission of the prophetic words, separate from the historical accounts. It was now a matter of Israel's existence, as well as of the validity of God's word. There is also a third difference: Prior to Amos the judgment was announced to individuals, particularly to the king; the king is responsible for his people. The execution of an innocent person (Ahab and Elijah) endangers not only the king, but the people as well. Prior to Amos the king could be made accountable, according to the understanding of sacral kingship. After Amos this was no longer adequate. Now the prophets attributed responsibility to the people, something which was also highly significant politically. From Amos onward the prophets broke out of the conceptions of sacral kingship which said that the king represents the people, and they directed their accusations to the people as a whole. By doing this they attributed a significance to their people which went a step beyond sacral kingship.

These differences, seen together in both sections, show the growth of the significance of prophecy during the history of the monarchy. From individual voices of individual prophets, prophecy itself becomes a movement which is determinative for the history of Israel. The announcement of God's judgment on his own people acquires consistency through the sequence of prophets. It becomes unmistakably loud and creates a tension which along with the tradition of prophetic words has a lasting effect. It comes to its strongest expression in the scene from Jeremiah 36, the burning of Jeremiah's scroll by King Jehoiakim. This growth of tension also accounts for the fact that the prophets who announced God's judgment fell into an increasingly difficult and exposed position. This, too, is shown by the scene in Jeremiah 36.

In the period from Amos to 587, we can again differentiate two stages: the activity of the prophets up to the fall of the Northern Kingdom in 722, and their subsequent activity in the Southern Kingdom. We find here, however, not only the distinction between a typically northern Israelite and a typically Judaean prophecy but even more clearly a profusion of connections and cross-relationships. The Judaean Amos is active in the Northern Kingdom. Jeremiah, active in Jerusalem, comes from the northern Israelite Hosea and represents typically northern Israelite traditions. The prophecy of Amos, which refers to the Northern Kingdom, is later received in Judaea.

The Judaean Micah stands closer to Amos, who is active in Israel, than to the Judaean Isaiah. Even more connections could be shown. Although Isaiah represents a pronounced Jerusalem tradition and Hosea a purely Northern Israelite tradition, prophecy on the whole forms an astonishing unity in its fundamental features in spite of all the diversity. After the land acquisition and Deuteronomy there is no other religious phenomenon in Israel which is as pronouncedly pan-Israelite as judgment prophecy. It made an extremely significant contribution toward keeping Israel a unity in spite of the political division into a Northern and Southern Kingdom.

A third distinction can be made between the judgment prophecy from Amos up to King Josiah, and the generation of prophets whose activity extends up to or beyond the catastrophe, i.e., Ezekiel and Jeremiah. The particular significance of this final generation resides in the fact that the prophet's life can now no longer be separated from his word. This is only suggested in Ezekiel, but in Jeremiah we hear extensively about it in the Baruch account. This marks a change in the transmission of prophecy. The history of the prophets themselves as a story of suffering becomes an integral part of the history of prophecy. We then need to differentiate three stages in the development of the prophetic tradition. In the first, we have reports about the activity of individual prophets in the context of the historical presentation. In the second the prophetic word becomes the object of an independent tradition. In the third the history of the prophets themselves as a story of suffering is added to the prophetic word. If one follows this line further, it is continued in the servant songs and in the New Testament Gospels. The constituent parts of the Gospels show a clear correspondence to the structure of the book of Jeremiah: words of the prophet—words with the situations in which they were spoken—history of suffering of the prophet.

The Meaning of Prophecy for Israel's Life

The various spheres of the life of the people are all mentioned in the accusations of the prophets. Concerning this, we first have to point out that the accusations of the prophets are not concerned with individual sins. Neither are they concerned with a general, abstract condition of sinfulness, but rather in every case with transgressions which endanger the existence of Israel as Israel. This threat is normally different in different situations. It emerges from the historical-political, economic, cultural, and religious-cultic circumstances, and changes whenever these change. This historic character is clearly manifest in the prophetic accusation. It changes from one prophet to another and also within the same prophet from one period of his ministry to another. The richness of prophetic accusations directs itself to all the essential areas of life in Israel at that time, to the political, the social (including economic and cultural life), and the realm of the relationship to God.

The *political* accusation is missing entirely in Amos and Micah. Hosea in particular accuses the kings and leaders. The political accusation is pronounced and unique in Isaiah. First it is hybris (ch. 2) which injures God's majesty, then the dependence on political power (Isa. 31:1f.). Jeremiah's accusation directs itself against the separation of political decisions from the will and word of God. In Ezekiel we occasionally hear the political accusation, but it is not particularly developed. In the epoch prior to the prophetic writings, the activity of the prophets was related especially to the kings, and most of the prophetic words were directed to a king. We can still see that the original task of the prophet was to support and confirm the kingship. Gradually, however, the word directed against a king steps into the foreground. It raises an accusation wherever a king allows idolatry, wherever he supports it, wherever he transgresses against the traditional rights of God (Nathan, Elijah, Jeremiah), or wherever he disdains the word of God which has come to him (Hosea, Isaiah, Jeremiah). Here the institution of kingship, originally alien to ancient Israel, acquires an extremely watchful accompanying element of warning and reprimand. Gradually this opposition between king and prophet is heightened to the point of persecution, imprisonment, and execution (Uriah) of prophets. On the other hand, not one of the prophets ever took even the smallest step against a king. The prophets have nothing to put up against the kings except their words and, when necessary, their suffering. Hosea goes the furthest in his condemnation of the institution of kingship (Hos. 7:3; 8:4); but here, too, one finds not a trace of any outcry to eliminate it. Some of the prophets had a good understanding with the ruling king for a time (Isaiah, Jeremiah); and they only raised an accusation when a specific state of affairs made it necessary. A king no doubt was affected by the prophet's word and gave in to him (2 Sam. 12) more often than the documents suggest. An acknowledgment, albeit unwillingly, can be seen in the story of Jeremiah's suffering when a king even asks the prophet whom he has restricted for advice (Jer. 37:3-10).

The social accusation (including economic and cultural life) is dominant in Amos and Micah, and Isaiah likely raised this issue in his early ministry. It is not frequent in Jeremiah, although it is raised with great emphasis in the temple sermon (Jer. 7:1-15). It is missing entirely only in Hosea, whereas in Ezekiel it appears particularly in chapter 22. Only recently have scholars recognized that the traditional rights, handed down from the early period, are extremely significant for the prophets precisely in view of the social accusation. Whereas one earlier saw the impulse for it in the high ethical concern of the prophets, it is now recognized as more important that the traditional laws of God are reawakened by the prophets. An essential part of their commission consisted of reestablishing the validity of God's law, which was entrusted to Israel, in the face of all sorts of breaches and disrespect for the law. This is what happens with Nathan (2 Sam. 12), Elijah (1 Kings 21), and quite often in the prophetic writings. One example is Jeremiah's temple sermon, in which a series of commandments is cited which corresponds to the Decalogue. It also happens in the accusation against the corruption of the legal system, particularly in Amos (beginning with the Israel section in 2:6f., further 5:10-13, 14–15, 24; and 8:4-7). It is also Isaiah's accusation in the song of the vineyard (Isa. 5:1-7). However, even when no formal legal breach occurs, the prophets raise an accusation against the rich, the high, and the powerful, who employ their power in order to oppress the poor and small; Amos 2:6f.:

> "because they sell the righteous for silver,
>   and the needy for a pair of shoes—
> they that trample the head of the poor into the dust of the earth,
>   and turn aside the way of the afflicted."

Isaiah accuses the rich (Isa. 5:8f.):

> Woe to those who join house to house,
>   who add field to field. . . .

Micah 2:1-3 reads similarly. In connection with this we often find the accusation against a life of luxury which stands in stark contrast to the distress of the poor, the widows, and the orphans. The prophets' intervention here for the poor, the oppressed, and the weak, against the powerful, the high, and the rich, is all the more serious because it is a speaking in the name of the God who wanted all to have an equal share in the promised land. In addition, we see here the function of the prophets insofar as this kind of intervention for the socially weak was originally a part of the task of the kings, as shown by a great many documents from the sphere of sacral kingship.[15] The prophets say nothing against the fact that there are poor people and rich people. They do, however, say that the oppression and exploitation of the poor by the rich is sacrilege against Yahweh, the God of Israel.

Accusations in other spheres also dealt with worship. However, one peculiarity of prophetic accusation is that the turning of pious men to God—subjectively sincerely intended—could in certain situations be accused by the prophets of not being genuine, or of being corrupted. This accusation appears in an even more pronounced fashion when it stands against the background of a later view in which one spoke in a strongly generalizing way about Israel's defection from its God. This is what happens in the review of the exile in the Deuteronomic history; and in the Deuteronomic redaction of the book of Jeremiah it seems as if this was also Jeremiah's accusation. It is extremely significant that a summarizing, general term is used from the distance of a subsequent review. The defection from Yahweh to other gods, however, is a dominant accusation only in Elijah, Hosea, and Ezekiel. For the rest, this accusation is concerned not so much with massive idolatry as with the worship of Yahweh, the God of Israel, which is no longer genuine. We encounter this accusation against a corrupted worship in most of the prophets: in Amos and Hosea, Isaiah and Micah, in Zephaniah, Jeremiah, and Ezekiel, and in retrospect in Deutero-Isaiah (Isa. 43:22-28). This accusation, like no other, accompanies the entire history of prophecy on into the post-exilic period, where we still encounter it in Trito-Isaiah and in Malachi.

It is probably the accusation most typical of the prophets of Israel. It presupposes not only that they acknowledge their people's worship, but also that in it they see the center, the heart of the people's life. How else could we explain the passion with which accusation is raised precisely at this point. It is truly astounding that such words, directed apparently against the worship service, could be spoken in the name of God, and that at least some people heard, preserved, and handed them down. Nowhere do we sense as we do here that the prophets were deadly serious about what they had to say, and that at that time, there were some who also sensed that. It is a matter of the nucleus of worship at that time: the temple, the sacrifices, the festivals, the altars, the priests. The accusation does not even spare the holy event itself—for the sake of the sanctity of this liturgical event!

Accusation is raised against the sacrifice (Amos. 4:4-5; 5:21-25; Hos. 5:6f.; 6:6; 8:11-13; Isa. 1:10-17; Jer. 14:17; Mic. 6:6-8) because the sacrificial offering had become a lifeless activity in an institutional sacrifice business, and had lost its original meaning as the living response to the living God. This is how Deutero-Isaiah explains it in retrospect (Isa. 43:22-28): *these* sacrifices have not reached the living God at all! This is precisely what Isaiah (1:10-17) means when he throws the following contrast up to his generation: Your hands, which offer the sacrifice, are stained with blood. And Amos means the same thing when he says to those offering the sacrifice:

> "They lay themselves down beside every altar
>> upon garments taken in pledge;
> and in the house of their God they drink
>> the wine of those who have been fined." (Amos 2:8)

Accusation is raised against false temple service (Hos. 8:14; Mic. 3:9-12; Jer. 7:1-15; Isa. 66:1-2) and services at altars (Amos. 3:14; 9:1-4) because, as Jeremiah explains in the temple sermon (Jer. 7:1-15): The temple is made into a "den of robbers" when the people try to secure their possessions there which they have acquired in sacrilege against God.

Accusations are also raised against the priests (Hos. 4:4-11; 6:9; Mic. 3:11; Jer. 2:8; 5:30; 6:13; 20:1-6; 23:11), but not because priestly service as such is condemned. It is because the priests neglect their most important task: to point out the correct path during the time of threatening apostasy; "you have forgotten the law of your God!" (Hos. 4:4-11).

The prophets neither condemned their people's worship on the whole, nor did they condemn any of the constituent parts of the worship service. However, it is not enough to say that they only opposed the poor state of worship during their own time. Rather, they raised accusation because the worship of their time did not perform the function intended: to be the place where the living God encountered his people as they really were, on the decline into the abyss. The prophets raised accusations against the worship service of their time because it did not correspond to reality.

The prophets considered the worship service to be just as necessary as the rest of the people thought. Their accusation served a cleansing, reflecting, and reawakening of worship. Prophecy ceased after the exile (except for some echoes); the worship service continued to exist.

Finally, within the context of the relationship to God, we still need to mention the accusation of the prophets against false salvation prophecy, particularly in Jeremiah. His encounter with Shemaiah (Jer. 29) shows the threat of a salvation prophecy which announces salvation or peace where this announcement was obviously based on national hope. Here, too, however, we need to remember that the prophets of judgment never condemned salvation prophecy as such, but rather only its misuse.

Prophecy's Relationship to History

The accusation of the prophets was spoken into their own present. The overview just seen can correct a deeply rooted misunderstanding concerning prophecy which asserts that the function of the prophets was to predict the future. In Israel this was the function of the seer; announcement is something different from prediction. The announcement of judgment in the prophets of Israel is primarily the uncovering of a state of affairs in the present (the accusation) which necessarily results in God's intervention. The prophets announce a future event, but it is an event which is the result of present conditions. One should point out here that the talk of this future event is relatively monotonous, and has an incomparably smaller scope of variation than does the accusation itself. A collection of all the announcements of judgment would show only a few different kinds of judgment types. This itself shows clearly enough to what a large extent the prophets consider themselves not only to be sent into the present with their commission but also to be commissioned precisely for that present generation.

The historical relatedness of prophecy also includes, however, the fact that their announcement involves not only the future and the present but also the past. The announcement of the coming judgment can only be seen against the background of what has already happened up to this day between God and his people. This is particularly the case in the Israel speech of Amos (2:6-16), and in the series of indictments of neighboring peoples (Amos 1—2). Only the accusation against Israel is expanded by means of the motif of contrast: "Yet I destroyed the Amorites before them. . . . Also I brought you up out of the land of Egypt. . . . " This motif of contrast is the most important and most frequent means of expansion of the prophetic word of judgment. We encounter it from Amos to Ezekiel in all the prophets (e.g., in Hos. 9:10-13, 11 in almost every passage; Isa. 5:1-7; Jer. 2:1-13; Mic. 6:1-4; Ezek. 16 and 20). This recollection of history in the contrast motif links the past to the present by holding those addressed before their own history, i.e., before God's activity concerning them in that history. The accusation can be effectively raised only against this background. Israel is addressed concerning that which it has itself experienced, but has now "forgotten" (Jer. 2:11). The abandonment of Yahweh and his words acquires its significance through this forgetting which makes the entire previous history meaningless. This is how the image of marriage, of infidelity, and of adultery is intended into which Hosea, Jeremiah, and Ezekiel formulate this occurrence. God's decision to destroy his own people is not based on individual sacrileges, but rather on the denial implicit therein of all that God has done for his people (Isa. 5:1-7), and thus on the casting off of one's own history.

A concluding word can yet be said concerning the addressee of the words of the judgment prophets. For the most part, they directed themselves to their own people. The message they had to deliver was a message of God to his people Israel. The majority of the words of the judgment prophets was directed to the people as a whole. One must remember here that no prophet ever actually spoke to the entire people. No prophet ever had the opportunity to speak to the representatives of the entire people, as when they were assembled, for example, at the diet at Shechem (Josh. 24) or as the king might do any time. Those who heard the words of the prophets were always few in number, sometimes very few. Jeremiah's temple sermon (Jer. 7 and 26) shows how these words could nonetheless be directed to the entire people and how they could function as such. This sermon was directed to a chance assembly of temple visitors, but it was immediately understood and evaluated as having been directed to the entire people. Only in this way can one understand the preservation and transmission of so many prophetic words. They were words directed to Israel and concerning Israel.

In given situations the prophets could also direct their words to groups: to priests, princes, the powerful and the rich, the judges, and the court. We need to remember that these groups are always intended in their association with the whole of the people. The words to them are thus actually intended for the people in one (or several) of its constituent parts.

The prophets of judgment rarely direct themselves to individuals, and do so actually only when this person has a function concerning the whole, as is the case with the words of Amos to the priest Amaziah (Amos 7) or Isaiah's words to the palace steward Shebna (22:15-25). It is certainly possible that there was a judgmental prophetic ministry directed to individuals as well (Jer. 16 might suggest this). However, it has not been handed down to us.

The prophetic word directed to nations outside Israel, the oracles against foreign nations, has an important function. As the announcement of disaster (not judgment!) against Israel's enemies, it is of significance in the early period within the context of salvation prophecy. In the prophetic writings it occupies a position shown in the special collections of oracles to the nations (Amos 1—2; Isa. 13—23; Jer. 45—51; Ezek. 25—32; Obad., Nah., Hab., Zeph. 2:4—15) in which, however, we mostly find collections of sayings from different periods. In Nahum, Habakkuk, and Joel, this type of oracle is placed into a liturgical framework. It is typical for the judgment prophets that they are able to change an announcement of disaster to a people outside Israel into a word of judgment. This is the case with Amos, who bases the judgment over the peoples upon their misdeeds (Amos 1—2); and particularly with Isaiah, who announces judgment upon Assyria because the Assyrian power is not content with being a tool in the hand of God, but rather falls into hybris by trying to win and destroy by means of its own power (Isa. 10:5—11).[16] This is a manifestation of the universalistic thinking of the judgment prophets. Yahweh as the savior of his people is the Lord of history. He is able to carry out his plan with Israel by means of other nations. But now these foreign nations also fall into the sphere of Yahweh's judgment. This strand continues in Deutero-Isaiah when Yahweh also lets Israel's deliverance from the Babylonian exile be carried out by a foreign people and its king, Cyrus. In the post-exilic period there is a distinction made between those oracles to the nations in which final destruction is announced to the nations outside Israel, and those in which salvation is prophesied to those same nations for the end time. In the final stage the oracle to the nations turns into apocalyptic.

The Language of the Prophets

The historical relatedness of prophecy is shown finally in the fact that each prophet speaks his own language. In this overview, this has receded into the background because those features common to all prophecy were to be emphasized. However, it is also an essential feature of prophecy that the language of each individual prophet is a singular one in spite of all similarities. That is, it is the language of a specific, singular person at a particular time and at a particular place, nurtured with certain traditions, and with its own view of reality and its own circle of experience. Here again we see the difference between God's activity in saving and judging and his activity in blessing. The latter coins a static language in its portrayal of what happens, a language with a firm vocabulary and the same, recurring turns-of-phrase as in Dueteronomy and the Priestly Code. God's judging, which characterizes the activity of the prophets, is historical and thus coins a historically contingent language, indeed a thoroughly profane language which allows us to recognize the individual prophet in his singularity. It is fascinating—and scholarship has concerned itself intensively with this—to encounter in each of the prophetic books an individual person in all his uniqueness, whom God has called to be his messenger. There is Amos, whom God called away from his herd and who brings into his prophecy the language of the circles in which he grew up (H. W. Wolff, *Amos' geistige Heimat*, 1964). There is Hosea, whose personal fate in his marriage serves the proclamation of his message. And there is Isaiah, the dignified citizen of Jerusalem who grew up in the traditions of the Jerusalem temple, traditions we encounter in his prophecy as the Zion traditions. The Judaean farmer Micah, who belongs to approximately the same time and place, is nonetheless totally different from Isaiah in his language and thinking, with his passionate concern for the small against the large. And there are, also contemporaneous, two prophets from a priestly family, Jeremiah and Ezekiel, but how completely different are they in language and thought? In view of this obvious disparity of language, thought, and tradition from which they come, it is all the more astonishing that each in his own way was a messenger of God with the same message. The callings show this in a particularly distinct fashion. The calling belongs, as we saw, to the historical, saving-judging activity of God: Moses is called, as are the charismatic leaders and the prophets. Things are different for the priests and kings, who hand down their offices to their sons. There is, however, no fixed schema of calling. In Amos we hear only that it happened (Amos 7:15, also 3:3-8), while the calling of Isaiah (6), Jeremiah (1), and Ezekiel (1—3) happened in completely different ways. In Deutero-Isaiah a calling is only alluded to in 40:6-8, while in Hosea and Micah, among others, we encounter no story of the calling at all. This, too, corresponds to the historical contingency of prophecy. There is no schema for the calling of the prophets.

God's Compassion

God's Compassion with Individuals

In its talk about God, the Old Testament contains a very peculiar feature which makes God's actions at a certain point appear very human. As opposed to other contexts, which emphasize the holiness of God in contrast to all that is human, here a human emotion is attributed to God: the emotion of compassion. The Hebrew word for this, *rhm, rhmjm,* actually means "mother's womb"; accordingly, the compassion of the father for his child (Ps. 103) can become the image of this divine compassion. It is often associated with an "inconsequence of God," i.e., this divine compassion frequently appears where a totally different reaction from God would be expected. This is why this divine compassion appears so human.

One can follow the manifestations of this divine compassion through the entire Old Testament, from the expulsion from the garden in Genesis 3, where God makes skirts for man and woman so they need not be ashamed, to the book of Jonah, in which the retraction of the announced judgment upon Ninevah is explained in the following way:

> "And should not I pity Nineveh, that great city, in which there are more than a hundred and twenty thousand persons who do not know their right hand from their left, and also much cattle?" (Jonah 4:11)

We would need to collect on the one hand those passages in the Old Testament which deal with such manifestations of divine compassion, and on the other the terms, both verbal and nominal, which express this divine compassion linguistically.[18] Instead, I will offer here a brief exegesis of Psalm 103, which deals with this divine compassion. This Psalm belongs to the descriptive Psalms of praise (or hymns), which are characterized by the praise of God in his majesty and in his goodness. The imperative call to praise frames the Psalm in verse 1-2 and 20-22. The one side, God's majesty, is only alluded to in one verse (vs. 19). The entire rest of the Psalm (vs. 3-18) consciously and one-sidedly praises God's goodness. This praise is introduced in verses 3-5:

> 3a: who forgives all your iniquity,
>   b: who heals all your diseases,
>   4: who redeems your life from the Pit,
>   5: who crowns you with steadfast love and mercy.

In verses 6-7 there now follows an expansion which points to God's activity with his people, in verse 6 in the social sphere and in verse 7 God's working in history. In the main section which follows (vss. 8-18), the two sides of the introduction in verses 3-5 are developed:

8–13: God's mercy in forgiveness (development of vs. 3a)
   8: the framework: God's mercy
   9: God's wrath does not stay
  10: God does not forgive according to our sins
11–12: but rather his goodness is boundless
  13: the framework: God is compassionate like a father
14–18: God's goodness is stronger than our limitations (development of vs. 3b)
  14: God knows that humans are mortal
15-16: human mortality
17-18: the eternity of God's goodness

In the transition from the imperative call to praise to the main section, the Psalm poet says, ". . . and forget not all his benefits." This corresponds to verse 9: "He will not always chide. . . . " The person addressed here knows of God's anger, and the poet has no intention of contesting God's activity in wrath. But he makes a distinction. God's activity in wrath is limited; God's goodness knows no boundaries (vs. 17).[19] Thus to the call to praise, he adds the command: "forget not . . . ! " The experiences of God's goodness are the stronger ones. The same is true of sin and its forgiveness. If God compensated man commensurate with the way he sins, then one might despair. But here, too, God is inconsistent; his forgiving goodness is immeasurable. One might even say that the entire Psalm deals with the incomprehensible excess of God's goodness. Precisely because of this excess, which is not exhausted by conceptual definition, it can only be the confession of those who have experienced this excess of mercy in their own lives. Every sentence in this Psalm is spoken in the face of God's anger, and every sentence stands against the background of experienced suffering as well as the experience of guilt and its consequences. In the face of this reality—which is by no means glossed over—the Psalm praises God's mercy, which is still that which is stronger, that which is enduring: ". . . and forget not all his benefits." The descriptive praise of God wants to praise God in the entirety of his being and activity. That is why God's saving and blessing action is summarized in verses 4-5, and in verse 3a and 3b his forgiving and healing.

Another summarizing element inheres in the fact that the Psalm is, to be sure, the praise of an individual, though God's activity with his people resounds in verses 6-7. God's compassion, however, embraces all of this. Just as in the history of the people of God, we find mention of God's compassion with those who suffer as well as with those who have transgressed. Both also are found together here in the praise of God by an individual—an astonishing agreement.

We encounter *God's compassion with the individual* in all parts of the Old Testament, the historical books, the prophetic books, the Psalms, and wisdom. It embraces both God's activity in saving and in blessing; his compassion can manifest itself in both. Three complexes should particularly be pointed out.

1. In the patriarchal narratives, the "God of the fathers" is the God who protects the small group, leads it, and supports it in every way.[20] This stems from the unprotected, constantly threatened lifestyle of these groups, which do not yet have any sort of power themselves. The protection of their God, his accompaniment, and his intervention have to mean something different than they do for those human groups which have built up a powerful instrument for their own protection, security, and support. Jacob's prayer is characteristic for the patriarchal stories. It brings to expression this dependency on God's compassion (Gen. 32:9-11):

> "O God of my father Abraham and God of my father Isaac, O Lord who didst say to me, 'Return to your country and to your kindred, and I will do you good,' I am not worthy of the least of all the steadfast love and all the faithfulness which thou hast shown thy servant. . . . Deliver me, I pray thee, from the hand of my brother Esau, for I fear him, lest he come and slay us all, the mothers with the children."

The particular piety of the patriarchal period, for which God was simply the compassionate God, has been taken up into the history of the people of Israel (even the wording of this prayer of Jacob is the later version of an older, much simpler and briefer prayer). The patriarchs remained alive in Israel with this characteristic trust in God's accompaniment and help, as we encounter it in so many patriarchal narratives. In the historical books there is often a story about the personal fate of one of the characters involved, and very often these stories remind us of the patriarchal narratives, as does the story of Hannah. In his compassion, God answers her plea for a child (1 Sam. 1-2). The other two complexes which say something about God's compassion also play a part in this narrative.

2. The one complex is personal prayer, lament, and praise of the individual. Not only do they form an integral part of the Psalter, we also encounter them in the historical and prophetic books. Psalm 103, interpreted above, can speak for this entire complex. We will only make a few additional comments here.

These Psalms of the individual are truly not "cult formulations." They are rather the testimony of simple people throughout a long series of generations who have themselves experienced what they are talking about here. In them, experiences of God's compassion are fixed and preserved which say more about the God of the Old Testament than any theological reflection could.

3. The same holds true for the other complex, which speaks a language which is at least as immediate as that: the giving of names in ancient Israel.[21] A great many names of praise have come down to us, each of which expresses what a small group of people felt during the occasion of a birth of a child, and what they wanted to bring to expression in the name-giving. A few examples will suffice. One believed to have received a gift from God in this child, and so named it *ntn* (Nathan); one expressed the joy at the birth in the name Baruch, "be he praised!"

God's Compassion with His People, the Prophecy of Salvation[22]

Just as *the prophets were messengers of God's judgment,* so also are they the messengers of the saving, healing, forgiving God who brings about a turn of events. God's judgment and God's compassion are in the Old Testament the elements of a history; one cannot bring them together into a static relationship. That is why we encounter God's judgment and his compassion in the words of the prophets in an active, changing relationship which never comes to rest. Judgment prophecy is preceded by a period of salvation prophecy in which we also find words of judgment. With the exile, this salvation prophecy replaces the judgment prophecy. However, the deliverance from exile does not bring about a salvation period in which God's anger and judgment no longer exist. Even the judgment prophets were never just messengers of doom; they, too, occasionally spoke oracles of salvation. Nonetheless, it is a special kind of situation in which one of these judgment prophets speaks a word of salvation, as does Isaiah in chapter 7 to King Ahaz.

These words of salvation never invalidate the announcement of judgment, i.e., never in the series of judgment prophets from Amos to Jeremiah and Ezekiel. The language of compassion appears with particular clarity in the two prophets who stand nearest the catastrophe: Hosea (Northern Kingdom) and Jeremiah (Southern Kingdom). The language of compassion is directly connected with that of judgment in Hosea 11:8:

> How can I give you up, O Ephraim!
> How can I hand you over, O Israel!
> My heart recoils within me,
> my compassion grows warm and tender.

Here, too, the same inconsistency: Compassion breaks through in spite of the announcement of judgment! In Jeremiah we find something similar (alluded to already in Isa. 1:2-3) in the peculiar motif of God's lament which is connected with the announcement of judgment, e.g., Jer. 9:10-12, 17-22. God suffers under the judgment which he must bring upon his people. Corresponding to this, in the visions of Amos we can see the transition from compassion to judgment (Amos 7:1-9; 8:1-3; 9:1-6). In a time of national distress, the prophet as intercessor pleads for God's compassion, and in the first two visions (Amos 7:1-3, 4-6) this is granted. In the three subsequent visions, however, this compassion is denied: "I will never again pass by them!" (Amos 7:8; 8:2; 9:4). The announcement of judgment takes the place of God's turning towards Israel in compassion. This announcement of judgment thus emerges wherever the people's guilt has grown to such proportions that God can no longer forgive them. Still, God's compassion is not extirpated; it is only withheld until it breaks through again after the judgment.

Precisely this is the message of Ezekiel and Deutero-Isaiah; it can now be a message of comfort again (Isa. 40:1-11). As in the visions of Amos, the lament of the people in need is presupposed. It is the many-sided lament after the collapse (e.g., Isa. 40:27) to which the message of the prophet, in the form of the salvation oracle, comes as the divine answer to the lament. And it is, once again (as in the first two visions of Amos), the answer of divine compassion (Isa. 40:28-30; 41:8-16; 43:1-7). But in this new compassionate turning of God toward his people, a turn bringing the time of judgment to an end, a difference must be noted in comparisons with former demonstrations of God's compassion. This new turn is only possible together with, and on the basis of, forgiveness. The forgiveness of the guilt which had accumulated during the time of the announcement of judgment has to be explicitly stated and has to be pronounced immediately to the people of God. Compassion without forgiveness would have no meaning in this situation; it could not bring about a real change. There can only be a change when the relationship between God and his people becomes intact again, and that is only possible through forgiveness. That is why the message of comfort in Deutero-Isaiah is, in the initial words, immediately based upon the announcement of forgiveness (Isa. 40:2): "Cry to her that her time of service is ended, that her iniquity is pardoned." The complete agreement of the two exilic prophets in this is important. Ezekiel also assumes that the restoration of the people (Ezek. 37) will be combined with a cleansing of the people from their sins (Ezek. 36:16-38).

With this we have to compare what has been said about God's compassion to his people at the beginning of Israel's history, at the beginning of the book of Exodus 3:7f. In this case, it is pure compassion for those who suffer: "I know their sufferings" (Exod. 3:7). There is no question concerning how this distress came about. No history has taken place and no guilt has accumulated. God's compassion turns itself toward the suffering creature, just as his compassion turns toward the child dying of thirst in Genesis 21:17, and just as in the Gospels Jesus is moved by the suffering he encounters: "It grieved him."

Both therefore have their place, their meaning, and their necessity: God's compassion which turns towards the suffering creature and God's compassion on the basis of forgiveness which heals a broken community. It is of great significance for the Old Testament's talk about God that God's compassion can be the one or the other; the one is not exhausted by the other.

The history of salvation prophecy encompasses an extremely varied and diverse complex which until now has not been adequately disclosed.[23] The history of the promise sketched in above (p. 61) with the three basic forms (salvation confirmation, perfective; salvation announcement, future-oriented; salvation portrayal, future-present) are all presupposed in what follows. In this we need to emphasize a peculiarity of salvation oracles in the Old Testament which differentiates them from the words of judgment: The salvation oracle needs no justification. It is sufficiently grounded in the distress whose alleviation the salvation oracle announces. We never encounter a form corresponding to the two-part word of judgment in which the announcement of saving is based on the positive behavior of those addressed. Here again, we see the dissimilarity. God's judgment needs a reason; his compassion does not.

For the history of salvation prophecy, we can employ the same historical divisions as for judgment prophecy: from the early period to the beginning of written prophecy; from Amos to the fall of Jerusalem; the exilic and post-exilic periods.

Many strands come together in the span from the early period up to the beginnings of written prophecy, and only one of these is the early salvation prophecy. At the beginning stands the complex of promises from the patriarchal narratives. These promises do not really belong to the patriarchal period, but rather link the patriarchal history with the history of the people from a later perspective: the promises of land possession, of blessing, and of descendants. In Deuteronomy they are fused with the Exodus promise and transformed into conditional promises. The beginnings of popular sayings also belong in this early period, sayings in which Israel or a group of tribes is promised the defeat of their current enemy.

All the judgment prophets come from salvation prophecy and still show some relationship to it. We have already spoken in the presentation of judgment prophecy about the salvation words we often encounter in individual judgment prophets (see above, pp. 127ff.). The perfective confirmation of salvation is totally silent in the period of judgment prophecy. When we do encounter the announcement of salvation, it is partial and limited. The portrayal of salvation or blessing is not really a prophetic genre. In the early period it is the language form used by the seer for his vision of the future, and in the later period the language form of the apocalyptic. It is possible that the written prophets used this form now and then, though a later origin is usually suggested. This is the case with the typical salvation portrayals in Isaiah 2 = Micah 4 and Isaiah 11:1-10 with the expansion in verse 11f. as well as with Amos 9:11-15[24] and Micah 5. To this, we can add a whole series of salvation addenda to prophetic words of judgment. It is particularly characteristic of the salvation portrayal that the transformed future reality transcends the present reality in various ways. The temple mountain will be higher than all other mountains (Isa. 2);[25] there will be peace for all humanity as well as for the animals (Isa. 2:4; 11:6f.). The salvation portrayals can in part be quite old. However, whether they belong to the various prophets themselves or have been subsequently added to the prophetic collections, they belong to another strand of tradition than that of the prophetic word. During the period of judgment prophets' ministries, we find in addition to them a salvation prophecy in which the earlier salvation prophecy is carried on. It was often connected with the royal court (1 Kings 22) or with the temple.[26] We only know of it through the polemic of the judgment prophets (Jer. 28), and it is thus possible that its effect was broader and for a time even more positive than appears to be the case in the polemical utterances of the written prophets.

The collapse in 587 confirmed the announcement of judgment of the prophets of the eighth and seventh centuries. Wherever it confronted the judgment prophets, the one-sided salvation prophecy of this epoch showed itself to be a deception and seduction of the people. If after this collapse, prophecy was still possible, it could only be a salvation prophecy standing in the succession of the pre-exilic judgment prophecy. This is the case in Ezekiel and Deutero-Isaiah. Ezekiel was himself a judgment prophet up to the collapse, and the confirmation of pre-exilic judgment prophecy by history is an integral part of Deutero-Isaiah's proclamation. The uniqueness of Deutero-Isaiah's proclamation resides in the fact that a great many strands of references to God are united in it as a new whole. This new whole is the word of God directed to Israel in the hour after the fall into the depths, a word announcing deliverance from these depths.

The situation into which Deutero-Isaiah's message comes is so similar to that in the book of Exodus that the prophet can portray this deliverance as a new Exodus. The coherency of Old Testament theology, of that which the Old Testament says about God, is shown best by these two cornerstones. In the hour of need and oppression at the beginning, Israel encountered Yahweh as its savior; in the depths after the collapse, Yahweh is announced to it as its savior. This correspondence goes even further. Just as in Exodus 3:7f. the promise of deliverance is linked with the promise of blessing, so also does Deutero-Isaiah's message link the promise of blessing after the return in chapters 54—55 with the promise of deliverance. This is not, however, simply a matter of repetition. The long intervening history, in which Israel has accumulated serious transgressions, demands the connection of saving with forgiveness.

The two strands of God the savior and God the creator come together in Deutero-Isaiah's message. From past worship, the prophet awakens the universally broad praise of the creator for those who despair and who are tired, the creator who is still at work today (Isa. 40:12-31): "He does not faint or grow weary." As creator, however, he is also the Lord of history before whom the nations are "like a drop from the bucket."

The two strands of prophecy and worship come together in Deutero-Isaiah's message. This is shown on the one hand by the strong influence of the language of the Psalms on the formation of his message; it can be recognized at every point. In the text just cited, Isaiah 40:12-31, we recognize the structure of the descriptive Psalm of praise which praises God in his majesty (vss. 12-26) and in his goodness (vss. 27-31). This profusion of Psalm motifs in Deutero-Isaiah is explained by the fact that the first worship services after the collapse were lament services. Deutero-Isaiah takes up this lament of defeated Israel and cites it in many different ways (e.g., 40:27). Now, however, he can counter the lament with the long silent hymn of praise. The many songs of praise permeating his work show just how strongly his entire message is characterized by praise (Isa. 42:10-13; 44:23; 45:8; 48:20-21; 49:13; 51:3; 52:9-10; 54:1-2), which already prefigure the response to God's saving intervention. We often encounter them at the end of larger sections. No Old Testament text complex shows as clearly as does Deutero-Isaiah how word and response belong together in any Old Testament talk about God.

The two strands of prophecy and worship also come together in the special form of the salvation word in Deutero-Isaiah, the "salvation oracle" (named and defined by J. Begrich; Isaiah 41:8-13, 14-16; 43:1-4, 5-7; 44:1-5). By linking up to the liturgical confirmation of hearing, the prophet makes the announcement of God's turning toward Israel—which has already commenced—the center of his salvation word: "For the LORD has redeemed Jacob" (Isa. 44:23); the prologue already makes this clear (40:2): "Cry to her that her time of service is ended, that her iniquity is pardoned." By beginning this confirmation of hearing to the individual with the cry "fear not," the prophet recalls the worship services in which humanity, for many generations, experienced the propitious turn of events in a situation of distress. Beyond that, it is important for the history of promise that all three basic forms (see above pp. 61f.) come together in Deutero-Isaiah's message: the prophetic confirmation of salvation (together with the confirmation of forgiveness), the future-oriented announcement of salvation in the announcement of liberation, and the future-present salvation portrayal in the promise of blessing in chapters 54—55.

The two strands of judgment and salvation prophecy come together in Deutero-Isaiah's message. This occurs particularly in the form of a judgment speech against Israel (Isa. 43:22-28; 50:1-2; 42:18-25), in which it is a matter of Israel's past transgressions. Here Deutero-Isaiah confirms the message of the judgment prophets and places himself among them: God had to let that judgment come upon his own people.

However, Deutero-Isaiah understands himself to be an immediate successor to the judgment prophets in another sense as well. In the judgment speeches directed to the nations and their gods (Isa. 41:1-5, 21-29; 43:8-15; 44:6-8; 45:20-25), he sees the real proof of God's deity in the continuity of his activity beyond historical catastrophes. That which the judgment prophets predicted has come. Since he himself has announced the catastrophe, he remains at work beyond it. That is why the salvation word now issued is dependable.

Finally, we recognize in the prophecy of Deutero-Isaiah a connection, not with the laws or law, but with the commandments. When in the discussion of the commandments we found that the small group of the first to the third, or even the first and second commandments were particularly significant, Deutero-Isaiah now confirms this. The polemic against the gods of the nations in the judgment speeches includes the emphatic, frequently repeated assertion that God is *One* (Isa. 44:6, 8):

> "I am the first and I am the last;
>   besides me there is no god."

(Cf. also Isa. 41:4; 43:15; 45:5, 6, 21; 46:4; 48:12.) This statement must be understood within the context of the prophet's understanding of history: The continuity of God's activity in history, the dependable connection between his words and his deeds, proves that he is One. The prohibition of images preserves for God the freedom in which he alone is the sustaining one from the beginning of the history of the people all the way to its old age (Isa. 46:4). The God who cannot be cast into any sort of image—that God can also remain the sustaining one in catastrophes. The prohibition of images and likenesses also includes any conceptions men might make of God. A conception of God is always only a limited one. God, however, remains God, even if conceptions of him are broken.

As an addendum, let us here compare a feature in the prophecy of Ezekiel. Here, too, two strands come together which were previously separate: prophecy and worship. But for Ezekiel it is not the language of the Psalms, which is virtually missing, but rather the priestly language, particularly the language of sacral law.[27] This accounts for the fact that out of Ezekiel's circle of pupils, an outline for the new, cleansed worship service was added to his prophecy, an outline which is viewed as determinative for the future. These two prophets have much in common, but it is also understandable that their effect in the post-exilic period went in different directions.

Aside from a few exceptions, we no longer encounter the unconditional announcement of judgment after the exile; there are only isolated echoes, e.g., in Malachi. The post-exilic prophets speak primarily in a conditional fashion about the coming salvation which is bound to the obedience of the people of God; this, too, is only an echo of prophecy. The pre-exilic cultic prophecy is carried on by Haggai, Zechariah, and in a great many individual passages. It is characteristic of post-exilic prophecy that its predominant element is salvation portrayal (e.g., Trito-Isaiah). Specific historical events are for all practical purposes no longer announced at all.

This also holds true for the so-called messianic predictions. To be sure, they begin in Haggai and Zechariah with the announcement that Zerubbabel will be the king of the salvation period; but this announcement is not fulfilled. The others are promises of blessing from the future king who will bring justice and peace (Isa. 9:1-6; 11:1-10; Mi. 5; Jer. 23:5-6; 33:15-16; Zech. 9:9f. and elsewhere). They recall 2 Samuel 7 and old historical promises of a king (Gen. 49:10-12; Num. 24:17) and agree that the king of the salvation period never becomes king through war and victory, but rather through birth. They are far removed from the reality of a historical kingship.

We find a noticeable contrast in the post-exilic popular sayings. Words stand there in sharp juxtaposition which on the one hand announce the destruction of the nations by Yahweh, as in Isaiah 65; and on the other that the eschaton will also bring salvation to the nations, as in Isaiah 19. The same inclination is shown by a series of oracles to the nations or addenda to such oracles in Jeremiah 45—51. Isaiah 45:20-25 is particularly important in this context. After the world power Babylon has collapsed, the nations are invited to Yahweh's salvation:

> "Turn to me and be saved,
> all the ends of the earth!"

Here we see the universalism which has God's activity in all humanity in view.

God's Judgment and God's Compassion at the End: Apocalyptic

The apocalyptic texts in the Old Testament are: Isaiah 24—27, the night visions of Zechariah, Zecheriah 1—8, also Zecheriah 12—14; and in Trito-Isaiah, certain sections such as chapter 66 are considered apocalyptic texts. The same is true for a series of scattered texts in the prophetic books, particularly Ezekiel 38—39 and Joel 2—4. The most important and most typical text is the Daniel apocalypse. The main body of apocalyptic texts is post-canonical, and is collected in the Apocrypha and Pseudepigrapha. They are normally attributed to figures in primeval history or the early period such as Enoch, Abraham, Moses, Elijah, and others. Apocalyptic extends into the New Testament in the apocalyptic sections of the Gospels and in the Apocalypse of John. I will limit myself here to the apocalyptic texts in the Old Testament.

Apocalyptic and Prophecy[28]

Prophecy is always concerned with the present, past, and future at the same time, apocalyptic predominantly with the future. Prophecy announces an event in the future, e.g., the death of a king, the fall of the Northern Kingdom, the fall of Jerusalem, or the return from exile. The present, into which the announcement is issued, as well as the future hour in which what is announced arrives, both belong to this history. Apocalyptic does not announce an event in the future, but rather develops a picture of it (the apocalyptic is a seer). This other future, however, no longer belongs to history; it is beyond history.

Prophecy takes place within the horizon of the history of the people. It speaks of other nations only in their relationship to the history of the people Israel. Apocalyptic takes place within the horizon of human history and cosmic history. The great empires have special meaning for the apocalyptic drama, and it is a matter of the fate of humanity. Here in particular lies the intellectual-historical significance of apocalyptic to which K. Löwith has drawn our attention (*Weltgeschehen und Heilsgeschichte*). What apocalyptic announces is, indeed, the end of history. The particular history of God with his people also ceases with the end of history and flows once more into the history of humankind and the cosmos. In this respect, apocalyptic corresponds to primeval history, where it is also a matter of humankind as a whole and the world as a whole (Gen. 1—11). Only these final occurrences, about which apocalyptic speaks (Rev. 4—5) will show again that God is the creator and Lord of all humanity, and that he is also the Lord of world history. In primeval history the complementary relationship between creation and flood (see above p. 88) already prefigures apocalyptic. Only primeval history and the end history know of a world catastrophe.

Typical of apocalyptic is the periodization of history, characterizing and determining an incline from the present world-historical situation up to the coming kingdom of God, God's commencing reign over the entire world. This is especially the case in the book of Daniel. Precisely this periodization serves to juxtapose world history, which is hastening to its conclusion, and the coming reign of God as the other, new eon which stands in absolute contrast to the present (NT). This periodization is often associated with a drama of struggle for the acquisition of final world (Rev. 12—14). The anti-divine powers are conquered in a final, colossal battle (Joel 3; Zech. 13; Ezek. 38f.), and, after that, God assumes his royal reign. This apocalyptic drama is characteristic of the atmosphere of apocalyptic speech. In this drama, God's judgment and God's compassion also conclude their perpetual change and interchange in history, and the last judgment takes place; God's activity as judge comes to an end here. God is now exclusively the compassionate God for those who are saved from this final judgment. His compassion has the last word.

This juxtaposition of a coming and the present eon also results in the fact that the understanding of God in apocalyptic is to a large extent transcendent, much more so than anywhere else in the Old Testament. This transcendent conception of God can already be recognized in the night visions of Zechariah; the seer cannot understand the visions he sees. An *angelus interpres* comes to him and explains them (just as in Revelation). God is the one reigning in distant majesty. As the Lord of humanity he will reveal himself only in the future kingdom. Here apocalyptic stands in massive contradiction to prophecy. A dualism emerges particularly in the doctrine of the two eons, which comes from Parsism and is actually alien to the Old Testament. The negation of the world is also based on this doctrine of the two eons. The entire world is judged anti-divine and must thus be destroyed. The new eon demands a new world.

The basic concept of apocalyptic concerns an end occurrence encompassing all of humanity and bringing God's judgment as well as God's compassion to an end. It is an independent continuation of prophecy and independently corresponds to primeval history. Nonetheless, there is something archaic in its stylistic eclecticism, its imagery, and its ideas. The eclecticism of this imagery is, however, impressive. In apocalyptic, the post-exilic theology once again gives the impression of magnificent flight. We must see, however, that the immediacy and realism of prophecy in it has disappeared. The apocalypses are characterized through and through by reflection and demonstrate a strongly visible literary character.

In the last decade, apocalyptic has played a significant role in the interpretation of the New Testament (E. Käsemann). This interpretation is to a large extent based on precisely this reflective and literary character of apocalyptic. However, this view of apocalyptic cannot yet be the last word. We still lack a thorough disclosure of apocalyptic from the perspective of the entire Old Testament, a disclosure which would include adequate tradition-historical differentiation. The new attempt to understand apocalyptic essentially as determined by wisdom, or even as a product of wisdom, is also too one-sided. It is possible to speak of wisdom elements in apocalyptic, but the emergence of apocalyptic out of wisdom is impossible. Wisdom lives and thinks in the present; it is concerned as little with history as with the future. However, this orientation toward the future is indeed the essential element of agreement between prophecy and apocalyptic, a fact which is fully confirmed by the late prophetic writings which show the transition to apocalyptic.

The Theological Significance of Apocalyptic

The most important feature here, the one linking extremely varied apocalyptic texts, is probably that view of history in which history itself as a whole comes to an end, and with that end God's reign begins. In its own turn, this reign includes the saving and restoration of Israel as the people of God, or of the pious members of this people, even if in a reality beyond the present. This is how it is portrayed in various ways in Isaiah 24—27; Ezekiel 38f.; Zecheriah 12—14; Joel 2—4; and in the book of Daniel.

This vision of the apocalyptic is what first makes possible a conception of world history in the full sense of this word. In this hastening toward the end, one discovers something which links and unites the vastly different histories of different nations and empires. The history of the nations becomes world history. This unified conception of world history is shown particularly well by the book of Daniel. In it we find the ingenious attempt to portray the sequence of the four world empires—the Babylonian, Medean, Persian, and Greek—as a totality held together by the downward inclination; and to portray this in the figure in Daniel 2, which consists of four integral parts, and in the sequence of the four animals in Daniel 7. It acquires its theological aspect in its position within God's plan, in which the history of humankind is predetermined. The number *four* here serves as a designation of totality.

This kind of astonishing conception was likely possible only in the wake of the conceptions of history which preceded it in the Old Testament, those of the Yahwist, the Priestly code, and the Deuteronomic history. In contrast to all these conceptions in which history is conceived on the basis of the singularity of Israel's God as opposed to the mythical theogony, the apocalyptic writer in the book of Daniel lets a trace of mythical thinking emerge once again: A heavenly struggle, in which the Angel Michael fights for the people of God, corresponds to the war between the nations.

The basic apocalyptic feature is this hastening of human history toward an end struggle in which those powers hostile to God are overcome and God saves his people or those faithful to him. Precisely here is where the new eon, God's eternal reign, breaks in. This basic feature differentiates itself from the proclamation of Deutero-Isaiah in that Israel's deliverance from the Babylonian exile means the extraction of power from Israel. This difference can also be seen in the fact that in Deutero-Isaiah and Ezekiel the saving is based on forgiveness, while in apocalyptic the establishment of the new kingdom of God is not associated with forgiveness. Neither does apocalyptic show any trace of a continuation of that strand from the history of prophecy which is concerned with the suffering of the mediator. Perhaps this difference is part of the reason Jesus' parables speak in such a totally different fashion about God's royal reign than does apocalyptic.

PART V

The Response

The Response in Words

Introduction

One side of what takes place between God and humanity is response. Contrary to the opinion that prayer and offering are works initiated by humans, the Old Testament understands them both as response. There would be neither cult nor prayer if it were not for the acts and words of God. However, it must be said with equal emphasis that the acts and words of God cannot remain unanswered. God acts and speaks in order to elicit a response, both in action and in speech. What happens in the Old Testament has the form of dialogue. A typical example from the Old Testament is the first commandment in its dialogue structure "I-thou." Another example is the double meaning of the verb *berek,* which in the direction from God to man means "to bless," and in the reverse direction "to praise." A typical example from the New Testament is Luke 1—2, where what happens between God and humanity is accompanied at every point by human response, as shown by the songs of praise running through this chapter (cf. Deutero-Isaiah).

The Call to God in the Old Testament

We ask first about the response in words. It would seem that we ought to ask about prayer in the Old Testament, since according to our understanding the response to God in words is prayer. But there is a difference here which allows one to employ the term *prayer* in the Old Testament only with caution. In its oldest strata, the Old Testament knows no term for prayer; the term emerges only in the post-exilic period. The call to God here is not yet a process separate from the rest of existence, a process needing a special designation. One simply says: I will call or speak to God, or one uses one of the specific words such as praise, lament or appeal, to seek or ask God. What is decisive for this other understanding of that which we call "prayer" is that it is a reaction to something which happens. That is why one cannot praise and lament at the same time; the Psalms of lamentation and praise in the Psalter remain separate genres. Just as laughing and weeping have their own time (Eccles. 3), so also do lamentation and praise. Things change, however, when thanksgiving takes the place of praise and supplication that of lamentation. Supplication and thanksgiving can be directed to God simultaneously, and a prayer can consist of both supplication and thanksgiving. Thus the term *prayer* arose as a collective term summarizing the various kinds of call to God. This difference is of great theological significance. One can argue whether prayer is a necessary integral part of theology; some thus order it under ethics. But if this calling to God is understood as a reaction to God's action and words—a reaction which is a response—then the two belong together like word and answer. Decisive elements of what the Old Testament says about God can only be found in this response, so that it is indispensable for a theology of the Old Testament.

The history of prayer in the Old Testament. We can follow the development of prayer (in our sense) in a long process throughout the Old Testament. It can be summarized in three stages.[1] The middle stage is that of liturgical Psalms, collected in the Psalter which has come down to us. However, this middle stage can only be understood and evaluated in the middle between an early stage from which it emerged, and a later stage in which it has a post-history.

From the early stage we have extremely short cries of prayer or calls to God, immediate products of the situation in which they were spoken, e.g., Exodus 18:10: "And Jethro said: 'Blessed be the LORD, who has delivered you out of the hand of the Egyptians and out of the hand of Pharaoh.'" Or the lament of Samson in Judges 15:18: "Thou hast granted this great deliverance by the hand of thy servant; and shall I now die of thirst, and fall into the hands of the uncircumcised?" Or David's deep sigh in 2 Samuel 15:31: "O LORD, I pray thee, turn the counsel of Ahithophel into foolishness."

There are a great many such calls to God occurring in the middle of a narrative.[2] They cannot, however, be taken out of context and perhaps collected, since they are constitutive parts of the narrated course of events. This presupposes that all this really happened, i.e., that this calling to God from a situation in which it was meaningful and necessary appeared normal and natural. It requires no cultic framework, no gestures. It simply belongs to that which is said and done in the narrative.

These short calls to God come together in the second stage in the structure of the Psalms. The Psalms are compositions, composed from parts which earlier had an independent existence as such calls to God from a situation determinative for them. We encounter such calls of prayer in prose texts as the address of God, the lament, the cry for help, the supplication, the vow, the expression of confidence or trust, the cry of praise, the expression of astonishment, the relief of those rescued, the exultation of victory, and others. All these calls of prayer can without exception become parts of a Psalm. They go into the Psalms as into a form which is made into a whole.

It is this poetized form which constitutes the liturgical character of the Psalm. The Psalm's form and its *Sitz im Leben* mutually explain one another. When a person calls to God from distress or fear, the call can be quite different according to the situation at hand. He can express his fear in the plain outcry "Oh, God." Or he can break out in lament, which implies but does not mention the supplication (Samson's lament). He can speak a vow or a supplication accompanied by a vow. It can be a deep sigh or a word of trust: "Thou art with me." Each of these elements alone, in and for itself, can express the turning towards God. The composition of all these individual elements into a whole, the totality of the Psalm, emerges on the other hand from a different *Sitz im Leben:* the worship service, in which many people from many situations come together to a fixed place at a fixed time. In this poetized form, the Psalm can take up the experiences of many people, and as such a form it is suitable for transmitting these experiences further. Thus handed down from one generation to the next, it can become the expression of repeatedly new experiences in repeatedly new situations. The Psalm sung in worship stands therefore in the middle between the many experiences from which it once emerged in its various elements, and its application to new experiences into which it is taken from the worship service. The form of the Psalm corresponds to the form of settled worship, which itself is characterized by the double movement of those who go from their own homes into the "House of God," and then from the worship service back into their own homes and work. The liturgical form of the Psalms can fulfill this function for the group in which it is transmitted only if this movement is maintained from the multiplicity of daily life into the "assembly" of liturgical Psalm prayer, and then back again into the multiplicity of real experience.

The third stage is that of the long prose prayers such as 1 Kings 8; Ezra 9; Nehemiah 9. In this stage we no longer find the unity between the congregation coming together in worship and the civil community held together by state and monarchy. The Psalms indeed live on, but they are no longer adequate. That membership in the liturgical community has lost its self-evident character. The ones hold to the worship service of the Jewish congregation; the others do not. In this new situation, that lost and self-evident belonging is replaced by a conscious and reflected belonging. It finds its commensurate form in the long, reflected prose prayer in which reflection and doctrine are combined with the simple call to God. A typical example is Ezra 9.

The Psalm genre. The Psalter collection emerged in the middle stage in a long, gradual growth process. The structured "prayer" of the Psalms, which was spoken or sung in the worship service from the distance of the holy liturgy, always remained associated with the simple, spontaneous prayer call which emerged from the immediacy of life. This accounts for the fact that the two main genres of the Psalter are the Psalm of lamentations and the Psalm of praise, which are based on the reaction to that which moves people most: joy and suffering. The Psalms of lamentation are the pain which is expressed before God; the Psalms of praise of the joy which is expressed before God. They belong together in polarity, i.e., in their polar relationship they mean the totality of human existence, just as the entirety of human existence can be expressed by the word-pair "joy and suffering." Just as joy and pain are reactions, so also are lament and praise reactions in the Psalms; they are response. This can only be explained if one becomes aware of the change which occurred in the understanding of prayer, a change in which, to a large extent, thanksgiving replaced praise, and supplication replaced the lament. The polar juxtaposition of lament and praise corresponds to a stronger, more comprehensive pendulum swing. This is why lament and praise were never mixed together in one Psalm. Supplication and thanksgiving correspond to a smaller pendulum swing and can together form one prayer. What we call prayer emerged first only through this admixture.

We might ask now how praise and thanksgiving, lament and supplication are related one to another. Common to both is the difference inhering in the fact that in supplication and thanksgiving, the person is the subject: "We thank thee that. . . . " "We ask that thou might. . . . " In lament and praise, God is the subject: "How long dost thou stand afar off?"

"How wonderful are your works!" Other differences concern either the lament or praise specifically. The Hebraic verb *hodah,* normally translated as "to thank," actually means "to praise." In no primitive language do we find a special verb for "to give thanks." It was originally contained in the verbs of praise and only later developed into a specific and particular term. Rendering thanks was originally an element or mode of praise. We can still see that today in the fact that small children have to be taught to give thanks—they do not do it from their own initiative.

Lamentation differentiates itself from supplication by always presupposing a situation of distress to which it reacts. In our term "to ask or request," on the other hand, two different processes have come together during the course of time: the transitive appeal from distress (which in the Psalms is thus ordered under the lament) and the transitive request for something. The one corresponds to the Hebraic *hithanan,* the other to *ša'al.* Only from the perspective of this difference does it become clear that the calling to God in the Psalms in the polarity of lament and praise embraces man as a whole. Praise and lament belong to human existence as such, and even in secularized peoples there remain traces.

To the two main genres we can add a series of others, but these are not such that they can be considered on an equal basis. In the liturgical Psalms (such as Pss. 24 or 103) the praise of God is associated with a liturgical act. The Psalms of Yahweh's kingship (Pss. 93—99 excluding 94) are a special form of Psalms of praise just as are the creation and historical Psalms. Just as in the Psalms of praise, a motif of the lament Psalm can constitute a Psalm, as in the Psalms of trust (Pss. 23; 123, the Psalms of the godless, 14 = 53; 109), the Psalms of forgiveness (Ps. 51), of mortality (Pss. 39; 49; 109). They can be strongly characterized by reflection (Ps. 73) or associated with wisdom motifs (Ps. 37). A confession of innocence lies at the base of Psalm 139. Even the royal Psalms are not a special genre; the special element in them is only the subject.

Various groups can be distinguished in the main genres; in all these groups, however, the orientation towards praise or lament is always discernible.

The Praise of God

"The more deeply one climbs through the centuries into the breadth of the Old Testament writings, the more loudly does praise and glorification of

God resound; neither is it lacking even in the oldest pages . . . " (L. Köhler, *Theologies des AT*, 1947, 1f.). The very first chapter of the Bible shows how acknowledgment is a part of the working of God. Here it is still God himself who utters it: "And God saw that it was good." The goal of his creative acts, however, is that this recognition should come from the creatures themselves, and Psalm 148 expresses just this. In it, all creation in heaven and on earth is summoned to praise: "Praise the Lord from the heavens . . . praise the Lord from the earth" (author's translation).

Humanity is also included in this universal praise of God. The narrative of the creation of human life ends with the expulsion of Adam and Eve, who have sinned against God, from the garden and thereby from proximity to God. But the woman, when she bears a child, gives her child a name which contains praise of God. And from this first birth and name-giving there flows a stream of the same kind of name-giving; the name of the child praises the creator. This one fact, which can be verified many times over in the Old Testament—that the name of a child contains praise—already expresses clearly enough that, for the people of the Old Testament, praise of God is an essential part of life.[3] This fact alone suffices to controvert the assertion that the praise of God was an exclusively cultic process and thus confined to the cult. The Old Testament itself rules this out in that praise appears not only in the Psalms, but in all the books of the Old Testament. It belongs to the whole life of God's people, just as it belongs to the whole life of an individual. This finds convincing expression in the words of Job; his wife urges him to renounce God, and he answers her: "The LORD gave, and the LORD has taken away; blessed be the name of the LORD" (Job 1:21). This sentence is to express in this passage that Job does not use the direct call of praise *baruk;* the jussive is less immediate and means approximately. The praise of God must continue, I cannot do it now, and no one can expect it of me, not even God. But Job can see from the depths of despair outward to where the praise of God goes on in spite of this. No matter what happens in human life, praise of God must not cease. It cannot be stated more clearly that praise belongs to the entirety of human life, from beginning to end. Praising God and being a living creature belong together for the Old Testament, just as the sick king Hezekiah said after his recovery (Isa. 38:19): "The living, the living, he praises thee, as I do this day!" (author's translation).

Praise of God permeated the whole life of the Israelites; it was the natural reaction to events in which they experienced the gracious guidance of God. Therefore there is a flowing transition between the exclamations of praise in the historical books, for instance between 1 Samuel 25:32: "Blessed be Yahweh, God of Israel, who sent you to me this day!" And a similar sentence in Psalm 66:20: "Blessed be Yahweh, who did not take his mercy from me" (author's translations).

The Psalms of praise in the Psalter constitute two groups with different structures which are normally called hymn and Psalm of thanksgiving. In reality, these are two kinds of Psalms of praise. The one is an immediate reaction to a specific, unique experience of saving; the other is a less immediate, liturgical song of praise which praises God for all that he is and all that he does. The one is a narrative, the other a descriptive praise of God. Both are concerned in their own way that God is praised. Both can thus be called Psalms of praise. This clarifies the elementary correspondence between praise and lament, which characterizes not only the Psalms but the entire Old Testament as well. These designations (narrative and descriptive Psalms of praise) are also more appropriate because the verb *hodah,* normally translated as "to give thanks," can be used interchangeably in the descriptive Psalms with *halal,* which can only mean "to praise or glorify." It is not incorrect to translate the verb *hodah* in certain situations as "to give thanks" as long as it remains clear that this thanksgiving in the Psalms is an aspect of the praise of God. If one continues to speak of Psalms of thanksgiving, one should not forget that the Psalm of thanksgiving is a particular way of praising God.

Praise of God within the context of events (the narrative Psalm of praise). This Psalm genre is particularly characteristic for the way the Old Testament speaks about God. We spoke at the beginning about the fact that narrative praise of God belongs to the accounts of saving (Exod. 15), and it is no accident that the Song of Miriam (Exod. 15:1-21) is probably the oldest song handed down to us from ancient Israel. Similarly, we encounter the narrative praise of the individual not only in the Psalms but also in the narrative books in virtually the same form (see paragraph above). The historical creed (see above, p. 46) also has the structure of narrative praise, i.e., the saving act which established the people of Israel received its response in the narrative praise of God. In this structure we thus find a firm connection between Israel's worship and its history, the history of the people of God and the life history of individuals. We find a confirmation, cast in language, of the uniqueness of Israel's relationship to God as a mutual exchange which takes place in a living fashion and ever anew between God and humanity, humanity and God. In Israel's religion there was neither an absolutizing of the cult nor of doctrine. The relationship to God remained a living exchange throughout history, characterized by ever new experiences within changing life. The Psalms of praise of the people as well as of the individual reflect this so directly that they have maintained their power of expression to the present day.

The Psalms of praise of the people have not been transmitted to us in the Psalter. We encounter them rather in the historical books (Exod. 15:1–21) in the specific form of victory songs, Judges 5, and alluded to in Psalms 124 and 129, and as integral parts of liturgy in Psalm 118:15, 16. In Psalm 124 one senses the relieved joy of those rescued:

> Blessed be the LORD,
>   who has not given us
>   as prey to their teeth!
> We have escaped as a bird
>   from the snare of the fowlers;
> the snare is broken,
>   and we have escaped!

This Psalm expresses how the Old Testament understands "freedom" (with the subject people). There is no word in Hebrew for freedom, since it is implied in "life." Life includes freedom. Instead of the term *freedom*, the Old Testament uses verbal references to losing and winning freedom, as shown by Psalm 124 as well as Psalm 126:1-3, in which a Psalm of praise of the people still echoes. Since there is no nominal term for freedom, there is no lofty or rapturous talk of freedom at all such as we find characteristic of every type of idealism. All the more intensively, however, are the loss and gain of freedom experienced and brought to expression in lament and praise before God.

The narrative Psalm of praise of the individual (Pss. 18; 30; 34; 40:1-12; 66:13-20; 92; 107; 116; 118; 138; Jonah 2; Job 33:26-28; Sir. 51; Wisd. 15:1-6; 16:1-15, continued in the *Hodajot* = Songs of Praise, one of the manuscripts found in Qumran, IQH), of all the Psalm types, has the most firmly established structure. It can, however, as we saw, extend far beyond the Psalms:

> Proclamation (with introductory summary)
> Report of Distress and Saving:
> I called—he heard—he rescued
> Praise of God and/or renewed Vow of Praise

Within this structure we find anchored that which in the preceding discussion was called polar correspondence of lament and praise, since the account of distress and saving includes the lament which raised itself up to God from that distress. However, not only are praise and lament firmly connected within the structure, but also the verbal encounter in which the change occurs: I called—he heard. This reflects the experience out of which these Psalms emerged, an experience which is never cut off. It continued on in Christianity and became an integral part of Christian piety:

> I called to God in my need:
> My God, answer my cry!
> Then my helper helped me from death
> and let my comfort increase. (*Evangelisches Kirchengesangbuch Nr.* 233).

By listening closely to this group of Psalms, we hear most clearly what is meant in the Psalms by the praise of God and why it is a narrative praise. Psalm 40 begins:

> I waited patiently for the LORD;
>   he inclined to me and heard my cry.
> He drew me up from the desolate pit . . .
>   and set my feet upon a rock . . .
> He put a new song in my mouth,
>   a song of praise to our God.

and similarly at the end of Psalm 30 (vss. 12-13):

> Thou hast turned for me my mourning into dancing;
>   thou has loosed my sackcloth
>   and girded me with gladness,
> that my soul may praise thee and not be silent.
>   O LORD my God, I will give thanks to thee for ever.

In both Psalms we find not only the saving, but in exuberant language also the responsive praise described as having been effected by God. This presupposes a firm, indissoluble connection between God's act and the praise responding to him. Perhaps we can understand this connection better if we translate according to the images in Psalm 30: "thou hast made me glad," as in the Christmas carol: " . . . then you, my salvation, came and made me glad." The praise of God is nothing other than the natural expression of such joy.

This type of praise of God is, of necessity, characterized by verbs. Someone who experienced God's dependability or aid speaks about it to others (Ps. 66:16):

> Come and hear, all you who fear God,
> and I will tell what he has done for me.

(Cf. also Ps. 40:10f.). The designation "narrative praise" is therefore more suitable than "Psalm of thankgsiving." In Israel's worship the basic form of speaking about God is not the statement but rather the narrative or report. The listeners participate in this kind of narrative:

> O magnify the LORD with me,
> and let us exalt his name together! (Ps. 34:3).

Genuine, living joy wishes to communicate itself, and wants others to be glad with it. In the narrative praise we find a basic form of proclamation which needs neither office nor commission, since it is characteristic of narrative praise that it occurs spontaneously, as the passages cited above from Psalms 30 and 40 make clear. The impulse to speak about God in these Psalms does not stem from thinking or knowing, nor from tradition or a commission, but comes from the heart which has experienced God's help. Here lies the source of the praise of God.

> *Excursus: Death and Life in the Psalms.* In many of these Psalms the rescue is described as one from death, and the threat of death as the effect of the power of death.[4] When the person who has experienced God's help can say: "Thou hast delivered my soul from death," this is no exaggeration; it demonstrates a different understanding of death than our own. Death is understood here as a power invading life. It is death which attacks the living during the threat. It is death which in sickness robs the sick person of power. This encounter with death echoes in the experience of saving. Death is thus not primarily that moment when things are "done," the exit, but rather the power encountered in the life of an individual which is after that individual's life. The *living* person experiences the power of death. This is what is meant when the person rescued says:

> > The snares of death encompassed me;
> > the pangs of Sheol laid hold on me;
> > I suffered distress and anguish.
> > Then I called on the name of the LORD . . .
> > Thou hast delivered my soul from death. (Ps. 116:3-4, 8)

This understanding of death results in one's thoughts of death not being fixed on the moment of the end. Those who speak this way are acquainted with death and its power from their past; they have also experienced that God is stronger than death and can liberate them from its power.

Accordingly, life is also understood differently. The king who has recovered from his sickness says: "The living, the living, he praises thee, as I do this day!" (Isa. 38:19; author's translation). Life is a full, intact, free, happy life. Mere physical, verifiable being alive is not yet life. This is how King Hezekiah's exclamation is to be understood: The joy of life of the recovered person is the liberated joy of one who has experienced God's help; it is thus a joy which turns to God in a totally spontaneous fashion.

The praise of God within the cult (the descriptive praise of God). In these Psalms God is praised with regard to the fullness of his working and his being, and includes both his saving and blessing activity. This is the praise specific to worship, whose subject is primarily the liturgically assembled congregation. In addition, we also encounter descriptive praise of God of the individual. The transition from the narrative to the descriptive praise of God, recognizable in the transition to nominal statements, is already shown by the narrative Psalms of praise. They show clearly how these statements characterized by nouns emerge from the verbal ones. In Psalm 30 the two sentences in verse 5a read:

> For his anger is but for a moment,
> and his favor is for a lifetime.

They are an immediate echo of the experience of which the Psalm speaks. The same is true of Psalm 116, which is narrative, but from whose narrative there emerges a sentence concerning God's being:

> Gracious is the LORD, and righteous;
> our God is merciful. (vs. 5)

Psalm 40:5 shows with particular impressiveness how a continuing reflection on one's own experience expands out of the experience of an individual:

> Thou hast multiplied, O LORD my God,
> thy wondrous deeds and thy thoughts toward us;
> none can compare with thee!

One senses that these words of descriptive praise of God have grown from experience. The examples taken as a whole show that the nominal references to God have emerged from the verbal ones.

One peculiarity of descriptive praise of God in Israel as compared with Egyptian and Babylonian divine hymns[5] is that it does not list a series of predicates of God which simply praise him, but concentrates rather on a fundamental statement which in many Psalms constitutes the center of the praise. Psalm 113 shows this in exemplary fashion; in its center we find the sentence (vss. 5, 6; author's translation):

> "Who is like the LORD our God,
>> in the heavens and upon the earth?
> who is seated on high,
>> who looks far down . . . ?"

The two statements belong together in polarity and as such determine the entire Psalm. The Psalm is introduced by the imperative call to praise in verses 1-3. God is seated on high (vss. 4-5) in order to be able to gaze into the depths from where the suffering people look up pleadingly to him, in order to be able to help them (vss. 7-9). He is able to see into the deep because he has enthroned himself in the heavens, from where he is able to see all things and avert all suffering. The structure of this Psalm shows that, behind it, there stands the experience of those who have experienced God's looking into the deep.

Aside from this ascertainable basic motif of God being praised in his majesty and in his goodness, the structure and development in the descriptive Psalms of praise is much more free and varied than in the narrative ones. The one side, praise of majesty, is developed in a series of Psalms such that this majesty manifests itself in his activity as creator and as Lord of history, as in Psalms 33 and 136; cf. Job 9/10 and 12. The praise of the creator can be made independent in the creation Psalms (Pss. 8; 19a; 104; 139; 148; Amos 4:13; 5:8f.; 9:5f.), the praise of the Lord of history can be made independent in the historical Psalms (Pss. 135:8-12; 136:10-22; 105; Exod. 15).

A typical feature of Israel's Psalms of praise is the imperative call to praise, with which the majority of the Psalms begin and which sometimes characterizes the entire Psalm (the imperative Psalms such as Pss. 100; 148; 150). It is a cultic summons to praise, in many cases probably spoken or sung by a priest (as in Neh. 9:5f.); it is based, however, on the summons to join in the gladness, a summons emerging from the narrative praise (such as Ps. 34:3). In the hymn this summons tends to be expanded. Kings, nations, and indeed all creatures are summoned to praise. Because God is so great and marvelous, the call to praise must go out to everyone and everything. Psalm 148 is astonishing and of high theological significance. The subject of the praise of God is expanded, as is customary, to include all creation, "from the heavens . . . from the earth." In this, the kings stand relatively close to the worms. This casts a spotlight on a side of the Old Testament relationship to God which Christian theology has hardly noticed. The fact that God is the creator does not mean in the Old Testament that a statement is being made concerning a process in the distant past, but rather an aspect of present reality. This aspect is so weighty that it comes to splendid expression in worship. To speak of God means to speak about the universe; a God only concerned with human salvation would not be the real God. This call to praise directed to creation can also point out an aspect of praise of God in the Old Testament in its relationship to the New Testament concept of faith. It would not be possible in a cultic song to summon all creatures to believe in God, since faith is a strictly personal process. All creatures can be called to praise because it is a much wider concept. It brings to expression that joy of existence which can be attributed to all creatures—one does not need human language for it (Ps. 19:3: "There is no speech, nor are there words; their voice is not heard"). This joy of existence alludes to their meaning for existence: turned towards the creator. When Paul speaks of the "groaning of creation" in Romans 8, he is referring to the other side, the suffering of creation in the present world age. Both, however, necessarily belong together, the call to praise to creation and the groaning of creation. In this sense, lament and praise also include the creatures. A text corresponding to Psalm 148 is chapters 38—41 in the book of Job, God's speeches in which God refers Job, as a creature, to the whole circle of creation in which everything has its place.

The "hymnic participles" (F. Crüsemann)[6] constitute a special type found only outside the Psalter which thus represents an important documentation of the praise of God outside the Psalter. It consists of praising participles, as are characteristic of non-Israelite hymns, as well as the concluding sentence: "The LORD is his name," with which the God of Israel takes the place of the other gods (Amos 4:13): " . . . he who forms the mountains, and creates the wind . . . who makes the morning darkness, and treads on the heights of the earth—the LORD, the God of hosts, is his name!"

The significance of the genre of the descriptive Psalm of praise points beyond the Psalter; it forms an important element in the book of Job and in the prophecy of Deutero-Isaiah.

The praise of God in the Psalms does not speak additively, lining up one statement of praise next to the other, but rather in an explanatory fashion which develops the one basic polar statement which characterizes God's entire being. This is shown by a structure which we encounter in a series of Psalms of praise and which the author of the book of Job takes up. The one side of the statement in the middle of Psalm 113 (vs. 5f.), which speaks of God's majesty, is developed in Psalm 33 such that in verses 6-9 God is praised as creator, in verses 10-12 as Lord of history:

> "By the word of the Lord the heavens were made . . . " (vs. 6).
> "The Lord brings the counsel of the nations to nought . . . " (vs. 10).

The author of the book of Job picks up on this structure. In the first speech sequence, Job's first speech (chs. 6—7) is characterized entirely by lament. In the second (chs. 9—10), and the third (chs. 12—14), he picks up the motif of the praise of God's majesty from the friends' speeches (Job 5:9—16, Eliphaz and 25:2—3, belonging to ch. 8, Bildad) and develops it in the second speech (chs. 9—10) as praise of the creator, separately of the world (9:4—13) and of humanity (10:3-17). He develops it in the following speech (chs. 12—14) as the praise of the Lord of history (12:10-25). The fact that we encounter the same structure in the development of praise of God in the Psalms as well as in the book of Job shows to what a large extent the praise of God is theologically determined as a response in Israel. From this praise of God we learn that God's being as such is understood in the polarity of majesty and goodness. We learn that God in his majesty manifests himself in both nature and history, a fact which thus presupposes a close connection between both spheres.

The theological significance of praise of God in Israel, however, goes even further. In the first exchange between Job and his friends, the author of the book works out—in the motifs of the praise of God—the contrast between Job's theology and that of his friends. For the friends, praise of God is something like a declaration. It says how God is: If God is praised in his majesty, then this is meaningful in that it establishes God's majesty and greatness. For Job, on the other hand, this praise of God is a process between God and his people. He therefore asks: What does it mean for humanity if God is praised in his majesty? The motif thus acquires new meaning. Job relates the praise of the creator to lament by speaking of God's activity in creation and in history such that he also includes God's destructive activity and thus the incomprehensibility of this majesty and greatness.

In a completely different way, praise of God in its given structure is, in the prophecy of Deutero-Isaiah, one of the most important elements of his proclamation. Isaiah 40:12-31 especially shows this. Deutero-Isaiah reminds his people in exile of the praise of God familiar to them from worship before the collapse. Behind the composition of Isaiah 40:12-31 stands the structure of descriptive praise of God. God is praised in his majesty (vss. 12-26) and in his goodness (vss. 27-31). The praise of God's majesty is developed: He is the creator and the Lord of his creation (vss. 12-17) and the Lord of history (vss. 18-24). Here, too, praise of God is associated with lament; to the despondent and despairing (vs. 27):

> Why do you say, O Jacob,
>   and speak, O Israel, "My way is hid from the LORD,
>   and my right is disregarded by my God"?

The prophet announces to them the help of their God (vs. 29):

> He gives power to the faint,
>   and to him who has no might he increases strength.

By awakening in them the former praise of God, the Lord of creation and history (vss. 12-24, 28), he tells them that God still keeps that possibility open in spite of Israel's defeat:

> The LORD is the everlasting God,
>   the Creator of the ends of the earth.
> He does not faint or grow weary,
>   his understanding is unsearchable.

The appearance of the same structure in the praise of God in the Psalms, in the book of Job, and in Deutero-Isaiah shows that in the Old Testament the call to God is an integral part of theology. Through the centuries, the structures into which the fundamental statements about God are cast are formed in this address to God. Theology in the Old Testament has the form of dialogue—speaking of and to God belong together.

The Lament

Significance and characteristics of lament in the Old Testament. As is the case with praise of God, lament also has its place in the historic creed in Deuteronomy 26:7a: "Then we cried to the LORD the God of our fathers." Lament is a part of the overall process of saving. If a theology of the Old Testament attributes fundamental significance to the deliverance from Egypt, then the lament must also have significance, the cry of distress which is followed by God's helping intervention. From beginning to end, the call of distress, the cry out of the depths in the Old Testament belongs to what happens between God and man.[7] If the lament has had little or no significance in the theology of the Old Testament until now, then this has two causes. First of all, one has not been sufficiently aware of the fact that the lament for the dead and the lament of affliction—which in modern languages are no longer terminologically separated—constitute two distinct phenomena in the Old Testament and in antiquity in general, with two different words.[8] The lament for the dead looks backward, the lament of affliction looks forward; it is turned toward life and cries for an alleviation of the affliction. The lament of affliction is directed toward God; the lament for the dead is a secular form (e.g., 2 Sam. 1). The other reason is that the lament, separated from prayer, lost its original meaning in the course of a long development and thus acquired a negative accent. The lament became mere complaining, moaning, and was thus the opposite of a courageous or believing posture. When we express praise by saying "he never complained," or when a proverb exhorts "learn to suffer without lamenting," this means something different than does the lament in the Old Testament. The lament was separated from prayer and was no longer understood as a call to God, so of necessity it degenerated, since its real meaning was the appeal to God. Recently, things have begun to change. In experiences of the present, the lament has been rediscovered in the original Old Testament sense.

The call to God out of deep distress accompanies Israel through every stage of its history, from the lament from bondage in Egypt to the laments of the people and mediator in the time of the wilderness sojourn and in the period of struggles for the land (Judg. 2:15f.): ". . . and they were in sore straits. But when they cried to the LORD. . . ." Thus it goes again and again in times of distress up to the collapse at the end of the state of Israel and Judaea, in the lament songs Psalm 89 or Isaiah 63/64. The fourth book of Ezra especially shows how the lament lived on in the later catastrophes. In addition to the lament of the people, the lament of the individual is also present and can be followed through the entire Old Testament. In the many lament Psalms in the Psalter it is a matter of this cry from the deep (Ps. 130): "Out of the depths I cry to thee, O LORD!"

In order to measure the significance of the lament and the role of lament texts in the Old Testament, we must also include the laments in prose and in the prophetic texts. Corresponding to the three stages of prayer (see above p.

154), three stages can be differentiated in the case of the lament: the short lament of the early period (Gen. 25:22; 27:46; Judg. 15:18; 21:2f.), the lament in the poetized form of the Psalms, and the lament in prose prayers from the later period (Ezra 9: Neh. 9). We can recognize these three stages of the lament throughout all the writings of the Old Testament. The short laments of the early period have been transmitted in narrative and reporting texts as a part of what is narrated or reported, beginning with the lament of Cain in Genesis 4, the lament of Abraham in Genesis 15, and the lament of Rebekah in Genesis 25. The laments in the form of poetized lament Psalms are not confined to the collections of the Psalter and the songs of Lamentations. We also encounter them in the prophetic books (the laments of the people in Jer. 14f.; Isa. 63f. and the laments of the individual in Jer. 11—20).[9] Beyond this, the lament of the people is an important motif in the proclamation of Deutero-Isaiah, the lament of the individual a supporting motif in the book of Job.

This overview can show that the lament in the Old Testament has an essential role to play in what happens between God and humanity. The meaning of the lament is based on the Old Testament understanding of man. We find human existence only within the limits of mortality and error. His existence includes the danger accompanying these limits. It should and it can come to expression in the lament. Just as it belongs to human existence that a person can pour out his heart in the lament (Ps. 102:1), so also does it belong to God's existence as God that he inclines himself to this cry of distress (Ps. 113).

The structure of the lament and its three dimensions. The laments in the poetized form of the Psalms display a fixed structure which, to be sure, allows a great deal of variety, but which in every Psalm shows a fixed sequence of elements which qualify it as a lament Psalm: address (and introductory petition)—lament—turn to God (confession of confidence)—petition—vow of praise. This structure contains an incline. There is not a single Psalm of lament that stops with lamentation. This shows that the lament functions as an appeal. It is not concerned with a portrayal of one's own suffering, nor with self-pity, but rather with an alleviation or turning of that suffering, since the lament appeals to him who is able to turn the affliction. The transition is already evident in the fact that the lament flows into petition (this sequence is not reversible!), and also in the fact that every lament Psalm, without exception, goes one step beyond lamentation. This is often indicated by a "but" (*waw adversativum*),[10] which introduces a confession of trust or some similar statement. At the conclusion of the Psalm, the transition is shown particularly by a vow of praise which anticipates God's intervention or already issues into praise of God (especially in Ps. 22).

The structure of the lament Psalm includes a division within the lament. The lament has three dimensions. It is directed towards God (God's complaint or a complaint against God), towards other people (complaint against an enemy), and towards the lamenting person himself (I-lament). This threefold division is demonstrated in brief form in Psalm 13:1-2:

> How long, O LORD? Wilt *thou* forget me for ever?
> How long wilt thou hide thy face from me?
> How long must I bear pain in my soul,
> and have sorrow in my heart all the day?
> How long shall my enemy be exalted over me?

In an expanded form this determines the structure of Psalm 22. Verses 2f. read: thou God; verses 7f.: But I . . . ; verses 12f.: the enemies. (A summary of further examples is given in ThB 24, 1964, 280 passim.) It is also found in Job's laments, where it determines the structure of the concluding lament in chapter 30. In these three dimensions the whole of human being comes to expression. Not only is the lamenter personally threatened, but also his standing in the community and his relationship to God. The threefold character of the lamentation shows an understanding of humanity in which the existence of an individual without participation in a community and without a relationship to God, is unthinkable. The existential relation is unthinkable without the social and theological relation. It presupposes an understanding of humanity in which theology, psychology, and sociology have not yet been separated from each other. This corresponds exactly to the account of the creation in Genesis 2 and in the book of Job, in which the drama of the suffering individual unfolds in these three dimensions, between God, Job, and his friends. They form the basic framework for the Old Testament understanding of humankind.

Equally important is the consistent differentiation in the Old Testament concerning the subject of the lamentation: The lament of the people and that of the individual exist side by side throughout the entire Old Testament. These are two different spheres of existence in which human suffering is experienced both here and there, and these experiences of suffering are also different here and there. The two spheres of experience are equally important for the relationship between God and his people, and neither a theology limited to the relationship between God and the individual, nor one limited to that between God and his people, corresponds to people as they really are. The lament is equally important for the Old Testament as the language of the suffering of the individual as well as of the community. This is shown in exemplary fashion by the juxtaposition between the prophecy of Deutero-Isaiah, in the lament of the people, and the book of Job, in which the lament of the individual experienced its continued theological development.

The motif of lamentation in Deutero-Isaiah and Job. The proclamation of Deutero-Isaiah is built on the lament of the people. The collection of lament songs suggests that after the destruction of the sanctuary, the worship service of those who remained was continued only as a lament liturgy. Psalm 89 and Isaiah 63/64 also show the significance of these lament liturgies. The lament of the people here acquires an eminently important function for the continuity of Israel's relationship to God after 587. This defeated remnant has the opportunity to bring the pain and shame of the catastrophe before God. Since, on the other hand, the lament as such looks forward, it contains the possibility of calling again to God. Deutero-Isaiah's salvation proclamation could link up with these lament liturgies, which certainly took place among those who remained in the land as well as among those expelled. He proclaimed the successful hearing after the lament.

The lament of the people acquired its function in the later catastrophes of the Jewish people, as shown impressively by the fourth book of Ezra. Today we can still see something of its positive power in the function of the Wailing Wall in Jerusalem.

The book of Job[11] is something like a grand fugue based on the central motif of lament, among others. Here it is the lament of the individual and is a matter of personal human suffering. The turn in the book of Job is the successful hearing of the lament. By means of the lament, the author of the book of Job has presented his understanding of God and of humanity, and he did this in the face of the theology of his time as represented by Job's friends. That theology was based on the doctrine of requital, according to which a hard, difficult fate must be the consequence of serious sin, since God is righteous. Job admits that he has sinned just as others have, but he cannot admit that he has committed so serious a transgression as the friends presuppose in view of the heavy blows which have struck him. Job knows that his suffering is not punishment, and now he can no longer understand God. Job does not, however, counter the doctrine of requital with another doctrine. He can only hold to God in lamentation, the God he no longer understands. With Job the lament acquires the most extreme possibility of that function as appeal: He holds to God against God. Despair which turns itself against God also receives its language in the lament, which yet links it with God as a complaint against God.

The book of Job speaks of a man who holds fast to God in and through all the depths of suffering. It is this holding to God, a holding in mortal despair and mortal loneliness, which actually concerns the author of the book of Job. The message of the book is that this is possible. The author recognizes and concedes that serious suffering has the power to separate a person from God. From this he concludes that this despair should come to expression. The author of Job wants to return to the language of suffering, to the lament, its vitally important task and its dignity. Even in the complaint against God, the author says at the conclusion that Job spoke correctly about God.

For Job, God is hidden, he is silent, and he is distant, as is also said in the lament Psalms. The Reformation theologians speak of the hidden God, the *deus absconditus*. The Old Testament has a slightly different expression for this:

"Thou art a God who hidest thyself (*'el mistatter*)" (Isa. 45:15). [12] It makes a difference whether one makes from God's hiddenness a statement of being, such that it belongs to God's essence that he is a *deus absconditus,* or whether one speaks of the possibility that God can conceal himself from a person. "A God who hides himself" is something different than a hidden God. Job in fact does not come to the conclusion that the God who has taken everything from him is a hidden God, and that he must make do with that. He experiences rather the God who conceals himself, and he appeals to him to show himself once more. And the final word in the book of Job is that God does *not* remain for Job the hidden God: ". . . but now my eye sees thee!"

The author of Job, however, always says what he has to say for the benefit of Job's companions in suffering. He is filled with a deep humanity. He knows: Suffering makes one lonely and isolated. With the figure of his Job, he wants to give to those who suffer a place, a place out of their isolation and among the others. He wants to give them meaning in their suffering. If this Job were not in the Bible, something very essential would be missing. If this man in his torment were to be missing among other men, there would be no one there who could step in for the others in a certain hour (Job 42). At the end it is Job who steps in for his friends before God. In this work, human suffering is given a dignity which shows suffering to be a necessary part of human existence. And in this, the book of Job points beyond itself.

Lament and confession of sin. In many laments of the individual and of the people, confession of sin is added to the lament, though not in all. In contrast, one series of laments contains an assertion of innocence. The lamentations of the Psalter show here a conscious distinction between suffering which is apparently caused by guilt and that for which no such guilt can be ascertained. This distinction shows that the Psalms in question do not yet know the strict doctrine of reprisal of Job's friends. This distinction brings to expression the opinion that the suffering person has the right to pour out his heart before God, aside from the question of guilt. Not every suffering person must come before God as a guilty person. There can be situations in which it is vitally important for him that precisely this suffering has not been caused by his own guilt. The lament is thus not bound to the confession of sin, just as this confession is not bound to the lament. Here, too, the decisive element is said in the book of Job: Job defends himself against the friends who want to press him into a confession of guilt.

The lament of the mediator. We have already spoken about this in the context of the history of the mediator. It is the lament of an individual which is, however, concerned with a matter of the people. The suffering lamented in it has grown from the service of the mediator. This lament begins with Moses and recurs in the lament of Elijah, then reaches its climax in the lamentations (or confessions) of Jeremiah. It reaches its goal in the suffering of the one mediator for the people in the servant songs and in the passion of Jesus.

In the Lamentations of Jeremiah,[13] the superhuman, grievous burden of the task comes to expression in laments which show both things clearly. The language of suffering, which acquired its characteristics in the liturgical Psalms of lament of the individual, and the burden of the commission, standing behind this expression of personal suffering, are shown in the three dimensions of the lament: the enemies he has made because of his announcement of judgment, his loneliness under the burden of the commission, and the silence of God, who does not appear to step in for his servant.

The lament of the mediator shows that Israel's prophets, as messengers of the judgment God had to bring upon his own people, themselves took part—as suffering individuals—in what happened to the people. The lament of the mediator prefigures the meaning of suffering for the coming history.

The lament of God. This same context includes a peculiar phenomenon which directly recalls the "inconsistency" of God in his compassion (see above pp. 138ff.): the lament of God.[14] The book of Isaiah begins with God's lament over the rebellion of his people (Isa. 1:2-3):

> "Sons have I reared and brought up,
> but they have rebelled against me.
> The ox knows its owner,
> and the ass its master's crib;
> but Israel does not know,
> my people does not understand."

The same lament recurs in the book of Jeremiah (Jer. 8:4-7). The lament of God appears in even sharper outline where it laments the judgment he himself had to bring upon his people. We encounter such laments already in Hosea (Hos. 6:4); they appear more clearly in Jeremiah (Jer. 12:7-13; 15:5-9; 18:13-17), where they stand side by side with Jeremiah's own laments. In them the word of judgment has been transformed into lament. God mourns his desolated people, the "beloved of his soul" (Jer. 12:7-13), whom he must give into the hands of its enemies. God's wrath and God's grief over his people stand closely juxtaposed in these texts. One can speak in this way only in the most extreme border situations, at the brink of the annihilation God brings over his people. This will then enable those who have been defeated to turn once again in supplication to the God who struck them down.

The Response in Action

Just as God's word and deed belong to whatever one can say about God (Ps. 33:4):

> For the word of the LORD is upright;
> and all his work is done in faithfulness,

so also does human response include both words and deeds. In both cases two polar statements stand for the whole. The formulation "response in deed" is based on the frequent situations in the Old Testament in which a deed is reported as the response to a word of God, as e.g., in Genesis 12:1-4a. The response in deed in the Old Testament first of all includes the large complex of commandments and laws in which God commands or stipulates how humanity can fulfill his will. The large complex of the worship service is also a part of response in deed. To be sure, the deeds and words both of God and of humanity come together in that worship, but as an institution, worship initially comes into view as a human activity. In all the designations for worship (*'abad, 'abodah, colere, cultus,* service, *Gottesdienst,* etc.), man is the subject, and the most noticeable phenomenon of worship is the assembly of people at one place in order to serve God. The response in deed thus involves what is generally called ethos and cult. Ethos, however, (ethics) is an inadequate term for what is meant and cannot be employed with reference to the Old Testament. As regards the relationship between both complexes "commandments and laws"/"worship service," the former is fixed in its linguistic forms; the texts of commandments and laws stand together in series of commandments and in legal collections. This is true in part for worship as well, in the cultic laws and above all in the Priestly Code. The two complexes overlap here. One part of the commandments and laws in the Old Testament is concerned with worship (in the priestly laws, the overwhelming majority). In addition to these commandments which are concerned with worship, we learn the most about Israel's worship from two text complexes. First is from the historical books, since worship is a necessary and inseparable part of history. The second is from a collection of liturgical texts, the Psalter (including the lamentations), in which an important and large part of Israel's worship—the prayer (= song)—becomes accessible to us.

Commandment and Law in the Old Testament

Commandment and law. The commandments belong first of all in the context of the word of God (see above pp. 20f.). Next to God's words of promise, they are, as words of instruction, a major part of God's word in the Old Testament. This duplicity of God's words of promise and of instruction is shown with particular clarity in the patriarchal narratives, where they of necessity belong together. They also, however, belong in the context of human response, or of Israel's response, since in these commandments and laws Israel is shown how it can respond to God in deed. When we said above that worship was an inseparable part of Israel's history, the same holds true for the commandments and laws. We know that the laws in Israel had a long history, from the Covenant Code onward, to the Deuteronomic law, the law of holiness, and finally to the Priestly Law.[15] We also know that the series of commandments emerged within historical development: The Decalogues in Exodus 20 and in Deuteronomy 5 both demonstrate signs of having arisen gradually.[16] It is then all the more noticeable and significant that the legal corpora have not been handed down in the historical books, each within its own historical context (in that case the Deuteronomic Law would have to have been transmitted in the account of the books of Kings within the context of the Reform of Josiah). Rather, they have all been ordered under the Sinai event. Only in this way could they become an integral part of the Pentateuch, the Torah. In the emergence of the Old Testament this is one of the most important places in which a theological point-of-view was given priority over the historical. The traditionists made a conscious decision to order the commandments and laws under the Sinai event, even though these same traditionists were fully aware of the temporal-historical location of the individual legal corpora. The difference between the theophany in the Old Testament and the epiphany is that the former has its goal in a word of God. Exodus 19 is followed by the Decalogue in Exodus 20 with the Covenant Code in Exodus 21—23. Exodus 24:15-18 (the theophany in P) is followed by the Priestly Law in Exodus 25f. The theophany at Sinai is in the Pentateuch an integral part of the founding event, the event which establishes Israel. The word of God issuing from this theophany to his people Israel becomes God's commandments (Exod. 20, the Decalogue) and God's law (Exod. 21—23 and the following legal corpora). This was an expressly theological decision which attributed to God's commandments and laws an overwhelming significance for his people Israel. This significance, however, can only be understood within the broader context in which the Sinai theophany follows upon the deliverance from Egypt. God's saving activity is placed unconditionally before God's commanding. The commandment following immediately upon Exodus 19 brings this to unmistakable expression: "I am the LORD your God, who brought you out of the land of Egypt, out of the house of bondage. You shall . . . " (Exod. 20:2f.).

This prevents the law from being separated from God's saving deed and absolutized. Because God encountered Israel as savior, he commanded to it his will. Acting according to God's commandments and laws is response. Israel's worship at the transition to settled life is based on this Sinai theophany. The majesty of the Lord belongs to the God revealed at Sinai. The new relationship of Lord and servant emerges which is distinct from that of the period of wandering. The Lord enthroned at the holy place reveals his will in commandments and laws. The people declare themselves ready to serve this Lord, as the representatives of the people attest at Shechem (Josh. 24).[17]

One needs to differentiate between this imposing theological conception standing behind the ordering of all commandments and law to God's revelation at Sinai, and the process spanning Israel's entire history, the process of emergence and growth of the commandments and laws as an integral part of the historical development of the people of Israel. This ordering of the commandments and laws to the Sinai revelation is a relatively late occurrence. The history of the commandments and laws from Israel's beginnings to the emergence of the basic structure of the Torah should be considered in the same way as the final stage. When considering both the development of the commandments and laws and the finished Torah, we are confronted with a difficult question for the theology of the Old Testament. Throughout the entire Jewish and Christian tradition, this large complex has been understood, interpreted, and evaluated theologically from the perspective of *one* concept, that of the Law. Commandments and laws (of various sorts) were subsumed under the concept of the Law. The Old Testament texts, on the other hand, show us a clear and unequivocal distinction between commandments and laws. This distinction manifests itself in three ways.

1. First as regards form. The commandment or prohibition is a single statement in which God speaks directly to the people: "Thou shall not. . . ." The law consists of two statements, an assumed situation and a determination of the consequences: Whoever does this and that—such and such a thing will happen to that person. The commandment is a direct proceeding between God and people, and in this regard corresponds to a commandment to depart or a direction to follow, as we encounter them in the narrative context (e.g., Gen. 12:1). In contrast, the law is not a direct word of God. In every case it is tied to human institutions, since the determination of punishment as well as the civil-legal consequences both require some agency to execute the punishment.

2. A distinction in the manner of transmission. The commandments are transmitted in commandment series which had their *Sitz im Leben* in worship. The direct address could only be meaningful if it was indeed issued as an address through a cult mediator, the priest, to those assembled in the

worship service or at a festival. The laws were collected in legal corpora which were put together from individual groups of laws intended for a specific area, e.g., slavery laws. These laws involving secular areas were originally transmitted within the context of the legal institutions. The difference between the manner of transmission is clearly visible in the Old Testament texts. In the Sinai narrative, only the Decalogue in Exodus 20 is the word of God coming to Israel from the divine mountain. The Covenant Code, which originated separately from it after the land acquisition (Exod. 21—23), was added subsequently. Accordingly, the Decalogue as God's commandment in Deuteronomy 5 is placed clearly before the law following in chapters 12—26.

3. A third distinction follows from the form. The commandments are direct and immediate words of God as address, and have their place in worship. The law is tied to human institutions through its two-part form. The laws within the legal corpus of the Old Testament are thus much more subject to change than the commandments. The laws were dependent upon the community forms and their changes. The laws about slavery, for example, were bound to become inoperative when slavery was done away with; the laws for sacrifices, when the temple was destroyed. The commandments of the Decalogue, however, are not subject to such changes. Commandments such as "thou shalt not steal," "thou shalt not commit adultery" still stand today. The commandments in the Old Testament have also undergone change, as has been shown by research into the Decalogue, but these never have the proportions we find in the changes in many laws. It is no accident that the commandments of the Decalogue could be taken over by the Christian church.

One can only conclude from this distinction that commandments and laws do not have the same theological significance in the Old Testament, and that the ordering of the commandments under the concept of law cannot be supported by the Old Testament as a whole. It was only subsequently, at a later stage, that the laws were explained as God's word. This in turn is based on the fact that in the period when the summary term "Law" emerged, the law in the legal collection characteristic for this later period, in the Priestly Code, was overwhelmingly related to worship. As liturgical law, related to the sanctuary, to sacrifice, and the service of the priest, it was understood as the word of God. The distinction between commandment and law then receded entirely. It is thus understandable that "Law" became the primary concept which also included the commandments.

This concept of Law, embracing both commandment and law, then played an especially important role in the New Testament in the antithesis between two paths of salvation, the salvation attained through the Law and that given in Christ, in the work of Paul and of John. In the Old Testament itself the Law is never understood as the way to salvation. The adherence to the commandments and laws can indeed be designated as the condition for the acquisition of God's blessing, particularly in Deuteronomy, but never as the condition for God's saving. Rather, the ordering of the commandments and laws to the revelation at Sinai *after* the deliverance from Egypt shows that they are intended as a response to God's saving deed.

Beyond this, the differentiation between the commandments and the laws gives to God's commandments a function which only they, not the laws, have; it is the function of instruction. It is based on the fact that the commandments are issued as direct address. When the person praying in Psalm 119 asks: "Teach me, Lord, your path, that I may walk in your truth," he means God's commandments in this function. The supplicant shows here that he is directed to this guidance; it is necessary to his path. But this also means: God's guidance cannot be replaced by promise; the promise cannot step into the place of guidance, the one is as necessary as the other. This is just as much the case for the New Testament as for the Old. The gospel can step into the place of the "Law" if one understands under "Law" a way of salvation opposed to the gospel. The gospel cannot, however, replace God's guidance, which occupies a necessary position next to the salvation message. This is then the case in the gospels as well as in the apostolic letters. That guidance is not exhausted by the gospel, but rather emerges from it. This is shown in the New Testament letters by the structure common to them all: The paraenesis follows the proclamation or teaching section of the letter. In the Gospel of John this corresponds to the sequence of departure speeches (John 13—17) following upon the section in chapters 1—12. They are characterized by the *kaine entole,* the new commandment (John 13:14). In the Synoptic Gospels Jesus' commandments and guidance are an essential part of his activity in words. This suggests that in the New Testament, as well, one differentiates strictly between commandment and law, and that the commandments are not affected by what is said of the Law as the way of salvation which has been overcome.

History of the tradition of commandment and law in the Old Testament. A brief outline of the history of commandment and law in the Old Testament can only point out a few essential lines. A comprehensive history would have to take three points into consideration: (a) the terminology, its meaning, and its function; (b) the history of the tradition of commandment and law in the oral and written stages; (c) the understanding of commandment and law in the epochs of Israelite history.

Concerning (a): As to these terms, in general we encounter them initially in the stage of collections, whereas previously commandments and laws are usually introduced by a verb of speech or a specific verb such as "he commanded" or something similar. The early stage knows only the specific term corresponding to the situation, whether verbal or nominal. The middle stage, for which Deuteronomy is characteristic, mentions several terms in succession: "the commandments, statutes, and laws." Only at a later stage does the general concept "Law" develop under which the specific terms are now subsumed. The term *torah*, embracing various termini and thus various procedures, emerged only in the final stage of commandments and laws.

The most important termini are *ḥoq, mišpaṭ, miṣwa.*[18] The denominative *miṣwa* (from *ṣiwwah*) is an order or commandment issued in a limited situation and valid only for that situation. In the commandment series it is a commandment valid for all time. *Ḥoq* (verb *ḥaqaq*) is the determination or stipulation coming from a ruler or leader. *Mišpaṭ* is the legal statement or legal decision issuing from legal proceedings. The legal statements and the stipulations of a ruler together make up the law; *ḥoq is the apodictic, mišpaṭ* the casuistic legal statement. In contrast, the word *torah* actually means guidance (the etymology is uncertain), but seldom occurs in this specific meaning (e.g., Prov. 1:8). If *torah* has become the all-encompassing designation for commandments and laws, this is perhaps based on the fact that God's instruction for the wandering group (Gen. 12:1), which preceded all the commandments and laws, was viewed as fundamental for them all. A *metabasis eis allo genos* took place, however, when the Hebraic *torah* was translated as Greek *nomos,* which is actually the law of the *polis,* the political law. This had to lead to serious misunderstandings.

Concerning (b): Commandments and laws belong to different spheres of life and are thus transmitted in different ways. The commandment is a personal process, represented by A → B; the law has an objective character, represented by A → B ← C (where C is that stipulated by A, which is then followed by B). Concerning the commandment, one needs to ask about the personal relationship between A and B; concerning the law one needs to ask about the sphere for which it is valid. In the commandment, A commands B; in the law, A gives a law or stipulates something which is then followed by B (or not followed). One can only obey a commandment, not a law. In the inscription at the pass at Thermopylae, " . . . as the law ordered," the law has been subsequently personified.

The *commandment* as we encounter it in the Decalogue has two preliminary stages. In the patriarchal narratives God's instruction is issued directly to one of the patriarchs or matriarchs (Gen. 12 and 16). We do not yet encounter any commandments or commandment series here; instruction rather comes into a certain situation in which it is necessary. In the period of the wilderness sojourn, the instruction comes through a mediator who receives it for the entire wandering group and then delivers it to them. But here, too, the instruction is completely situation-bound—there are not yet any fixed, perpetually valid commandments here. Commandments with perpetual duration and laws valid for the entire community become necessary with the transition to settled life. However, whereas the laws initially serve the order of the community and are essentially secular and oriented towards the legal system, God's instruction is carried on in the commandments, though it is now no longer situation-bound. It now has the tendency to be valid for everyone and for all time.

The majority of the commandments are negating. When a commandment (e.g., the one concerning parents) occurs both in positive and negative form, the negative—the prohibition—is always older than the positive. This is based on the fact that in the settled form of life of the early period, the behavior of the individual in the community was so firmly embedded in invariable life structures and in the structure of the community (custom: "one does not do that") as well as in life with God, that there was in general no need for God's special instructions. The commandments or prohibitions here have more the function of pointing out the limits of behavior which may not be transgressed without seriously threatening the community. In the commandments of the Decalogue, elementary human existence is protected from danger. They are concerned with the intactness of human community in the settled form of life. To this extent, the commandments of the Decalogue are not instruction for daily activity—since this is not necessary—but they are instruction for the moment of threat to the community by the breach of the limits set up here. The liturgical *Sitz im Leben* of the commandment series shows this function: Wherever the commandments are spoken in the worship service by a priest, directed to the congregation assembled for worship and to every individual in direct address, God's instruction occurs, directed to the threat to the community.[19]

The collection of commandments into small and large series took place step by step. The earlier series consisted of two or three commandments, and then grew up to ten or, at the most, twelve. This limitation points to an oral mode of transmission and to the *Sitz im Leben* in worship.

The development of the Decalogue from smaller series can still be seen in the comparison between Exodus 20, 23, 34, and Leviticus 19. The initial commandments of the Decalogue have predominant significance. The first commandment, with its prohibition of images, forms the nucleus. We encounter these first commandments in the parallels Exodus 20, 23, 34, and then in Leviticus 19. Various groups of commandments were then added to these fundamental commandments from the earlist period on: in Exodus 20 community commandments, in Exodus 23 and 34 liturgical commandments (Lev. 19 mixed forms).[20]

The structure of the Covenant Code shows that the traditionists were aware of the distinction between commandment and law. They lined up laws or legal stipulations (Exod. 21—22:19) and commandments (Exod. 22:20—23:29 with additional formations) together. We encounter commandments only in the second part of the Covenant Code (Exod. 22:20—23:19). A. Alt[21] did not see, in his standard differentiation between casuistic and apodictic legal statements, that the traditionists of the Covenant Code reckoned casuistic and apodictic to the one, commandments (with additional formations) to the other group. By making "statute" the overriding concept for both (instead of "Law"), he obfuscated the fact that the decisive distinction is that between commandments and laws. The commandments and prohibitions have nothing to do directly with legal statutes; they are not legal statements.

The *laws* have their original *Sitz im Leben* either in a stipulation or determination of a ruler (1 Kings 2:36f.) or in a legal statement coming from a legal proceeding. In both cases this origin is secular. The law does not have an originally religious function. On the other hand, every law presupposes civil or social institutions.

The collections of laws, the legal corpora, are developed for these institutions or in connection with them. They emerge in two steps. The first is the summary of stipulations concerning an individual legal area, such as the slavery laws (Exod. 21f.) or the property offenses. In this first stage, civil and criminal law are still separated. The second step is the summarization of all the laws necessary for the community. The legal corpora, as they developed throughout Israel's history, reflect the changes in communal forms characterizing this history. The Covenant Code in Exodus 21—23, developed after the settlement of the tribes in Canaan, shows the acquisition of Near Eastern legal culture, which became necessary with the transition to agriculture.[22] This also includes the sedentary worship service with the annual festivals oriented towards agricultural periods. That is why the stipulations for the annual festivals belong to this legal corpus. It shows the tight, fixed relationship between all spheres of life in the early period.

This is not fundamentally different in the Deuteronomic Law (Deut. 12—26), which developed in the course of the period of kings. Religious commandments and stipulations for worship form a unity with the commandments and laws concerning the protection of families, the land and people and quite generally of one's neighbor. What is new and different in the Deuteronomic Law is above all that a special emphasis is put on the preservation of Israel's uniqueness and its religion in connection with its history. The law is to serve this preservation of Israel's uniqueness above all by demanding the concentration of worship (ch. 12) and sharply guarding against the intrusion of others, primarily the Canaanite religion (ch. 13). In this the Deuteronomic Law reflects the threat to Israel during the period of kings. It was threatened with the loss of its identity under the pressure of its surroundings, something we also learn from the prophecy of the time and in retrospect from the Deuteronomic history. The other peculiarity of the Deuteronomic Law is its strongly visible social orientation, which corresponds to the simultaneous social accusation of the prophets.[23]

The Holiness Code in Leviticus 17—26[24] forms the transition to the later period, a code in which the various spheres of life are still fused, but in which we find a noticeable turn towards the predominance of the cultic sphere even into the choice of language. The pervasive leitmotif, "You shall be holy, for I the LORD your God am holy" (Lev. 19:2 and elsewhere), shows the gradual transition from a civil community to a liturgical congregation.

This transition has been completed in the Priestly Law (Exod.

25—Num. 10 P).[25] Here for the first time Israel's laws are for the most part cultic laws, and here for the first time worship has become the predominant life sphere. Whereas in all previous laws liturgical and secular laws were mixed and only those liturgical stipulations appeared which were important for the people, the Priestly Law is a liturgical law in the full sense that worship in all its elements characterizes this law. The Priestly Law deals with the holy place (Exod. 25—27) together with the holy accoutrements of worship (Exod. 25; 27; 30—31; Num. 15), the holy time (Exod. 14; 31; Lev. 16), the holy acts, the sacrifice (Lev. 1—5), purification (Lev. 11—15; Num. 19), blessing (Num. 6), vows and tithes (Lev. 27; Num. 30), sacrifice and festivals (Num. 28—29) and other procedures (Num. 5—6), and with holy persons (Exod. 28f.; Lev. 8—10; Num. 3—4; 8).

If one considers the history of the legal corpora in the Old Testament, there emerges an important point concerning the relationship between commandment and law in the Old Testament. First, as regards the relationship between commandment and law: The laws demonstrate a strict and unmistakable orientation toward history. The law must change with the changes in history, something shown already in the various addenda to individual laws. In Israel there was never *the* law as a timeless quantity. The ordering of all laws to the revelation at Sinai is a subsequent theological statement and did not eliminate the historical changes in the laws. This history reflects the way from the unity of all spheres of life at the beginning to gradual differentiation and at the end to a separation of the liturgical congregation. The "law" is therefore something different in the Covenant Code than in P. In the Covenant Code the center of gravity still lies entirely in the secular realm, and the majority of law has an unconstrained secular character. In Deuteronomy (and in the Holiness Code), the secular and holy spheres are of approximately equal significance, while in the Priestly Law the laws refer almost exclusively to the sacral sphere. If one designates the profusion of laws as *the* law of God, this means different things in the different stages of the history of the law. This is not the case with the commandments. Here, too, there are changes, but things stand differently with them. The changes occur on the periphery in the number and kind of the law added to the nucleus. The nucleus, however, the first and second commandment (one can also include the third), has not changed throughout the entire history of the tradition of the commandments and commandment series. These two commandments say something to Israel which is decisive and unchangeable for its relationship to God from the hour of initial encounter with this God all the way to the end. However, even the community commandments of the Decalogue which have been added to this nucleus have changed only minimally. God and the neighbor belong together here just as in Genesis 3 and 4 and then again in the proclamation of Jesus. Nothing can change this.

The First Commandment and the prohibition of images. Among all the commandments and laws of the Old Testament, none has had such profound significance as the first commandment of the Decalogue along with the prohibition of images, which is closely connected with it.[26] We saw above how these two commandments form the nucleus of the Decalogue. The relative clause expanding this first commandment: ". . . who brought you out of the land of Egypt, out of the house of bondage," is an integral part of this commandment. However one might explain the origin of the first commandment, it grew out of Israel's encounter with the saving God. Because Israel encountered Yahweh the saving God, it decided to serve him alone (Josh. 24). Considered within the history of religions, this connection between the first commandment with Yahweh as the God of history can be explained in the following way: It is characteristic of the conception of a pantheon that what happens is primarily an event among the gods, as is shown by the myths and mythical epics of Babylonia, Egypt, and Ugarit.[27] The commandment to serve only one God, on the other hand, means that this one God with his whole being is concerned only with his creation and his people. There is no inter-divine action for him. The fact that he is *one* God and that he is the God turned toward history—these are only two sides of the same fact.[28]

Considered theologically, the first commandment meant for Israel that it could bring all the spheres of its existence into relationship with this one God, that in all life situations it was dealing with this one God. The oneness of God had its strongest effect on the relationship between the two spheres of nature and history. After the settlement in Canaan, Yahweh as the God of history became the God who bestowed the blessing of the land upon his people and the God from whom they could expect nourishment, clothing, the security of dwelling, and protection. The oneness of God thus made possible a continuity of historical consciousness which withstood all changes, breaches, and catastrophes. Because Yahweh was one, the past, present, and future all belonged inseparably together for Israel. The future lay in the hands of him who had guided and preserved his people up to the present and who answered in the present when they called to him. It is therefore by no means accidental that this special emphasis of God's oneness, of God's singularity, is found in both the Old Testament books which reflect the two greatest changes in Israel's history: Deuteronomy (6:4) and Deutero-Isaiah (43:10f. passim). Deuteronomy reflects the transition to settled life, and Deutero-Isaiah the political collapse and its consequences. In both radical changes it was seen that Yahweh, the *one* God, bridged them both.

The prohibition of images stands in close connection with the first commandment. This God who remained the same through all the changes and transformations does not allow himself to be bound to images which seek to depict him. Because he is and remains free in his action and words, he is not permitted to be fixed by men onto something visible and concrete. This prohibition of images also prohibits God from being tied down to a concept of God which one might be able to fix in conceptual terms or even in a conceptual system. Neither can one speak in a figurative sense of an "Old Testament conception of God" or of the "prophetic conception of God" or something similar. God cannot in any way be tied down to an image or concept. The prohibition of images expresses the fundamental insight that the God of the Old Testament cannot be objectified; this God can never, in any way, become an object, not even an object of human thought and reflection. The prohibition of images confirms the fact that the Old Testament speaks of God in the form of dialogue.

In no other Old Testament passage has this sense of the prohibition of images been so profoundly understood as in the proclamation of Deutero-Isaiah, 46:1-4:

> Bel bows down, Nebo stoops,
> > their idols are on beasts and cattle;
> these things you carry are loaded as
> > burdens on weary beasts . . .
> Hearken to me . . .
> who have been borne by me from your birth,
> > carried from the womb;
> even to your old age I am He,
> > and to gray hairs I will carry you.
> I have made, and I will bear,
> > I will carry and will save.

Deutero-Isaiah has seen that only in the great catastrophes does it first become apparent what the worship of images means. In the historical catastrophes the divine images must be borne away on cattle; they thus reveal the whole impotence of the gods they represent. The uniqueness of the God which is not bound to an image, however, shows itself in the fact that he is able to carry a people through a catastrophe: "I will carry you even to your old age and to gray hairs." The God not bound to an image or concept is thus able to make possible the continuity of his people's history: "I have done it and I will do it."

Worship

Individuals can serve God insofar as they acknowledge God as their Lord in daily life, follow his instructions, and keep his commandments. They can also serve him by doing him honor in worship, at the holy place and at the holy time. This is the specific sense of the phrase "to serve God," or "worship service" in the biblical[29] and in many other languages. To the extent that worship is a human institution, this designation is justified; however, it does not adequately cover all that transpires in worship. This worship brings rather the relationship to God, in its reciprocity, to institutional expression. In the Old Testament as well as elsewhere worship is a reciprocal exchange between God and his people (this is also how Luther's famous definition formulates it: "that God may speak to us in his holy word and we to him in prayer and song of praise"). Something happens from God to man and vice versa. On both sides this reciprocal exchange includes both action and speaking, and it occurs at a special place and at a special time. As such it is a holy event, separated from daily life, and as such it requires a mediator of the holy, the priest.

Though this also characterizes worship in the Old Testament as generally as possible, this definition, too, must still be subject to limitations. Israel's worship, characterized as such, was established by the theophany at Sinai. Here for the first time, on the way through the wilderness, the group liberated from Egypt experienced the holy place, the holy time, and the word of God coming to them from the theophany. Moses becomes the mediator of the holy in this event (Exod. 19 and 24:15-18). What is established here is the worship characteristic of the settled form of life. However, there has already been talk of worship events previously, in the patriarchal narrative and in primeval history. There are both preliminary stages and a post-history; worship has a history.

The history of worship in the Old Testament. a. Worship as belonging to humanity. In the primeval history in Genesis 1—11 we encounter two passages containing a gesture of worship: the sacrificial offering of Cain and Abel, and Noah's sacrifice after the flood. With this, the traditionists tell us that gestures of worship have been a part of human existence since the beginning of humanity, and that there has never been human community totally void of something like worship. Worship is a universally human phenomenon. This has in the meantime been confirmed by the history of religions. In the two passages mentioned, two basic types of liturgical gestures have been chosen which have remained determinative for the history of religions as well as for Israel's worship, two fundamental types as regards the motivation for sacrifice. In Cain and Abel's sacrifice it is a matter of the primitial sacrifice of the first-born or first fruits,[30] which is concerned with the blessing of the yield of human work, the blesssing for the fruit of the earth or the fruit of the beast. The first-born or first fruits are offered as thanks for the gifts of blessing and simultaneously as a petition for further blessing. In Noah's sacrifice, Genesis 8:20-22,[31] it is a matter of rescue from mortal danger. After surviving the danger, the person saved begins life anew with his eyes on the savior who has preserved him and to whom he now entrusts this newly acquired life. Both these motifs have remained determinative for worship up to the present. It is God's activity in saving and blessing which is celebrated in worship, and accordingly there is the worship service circling in the rhythm of blessing (the annual festivals) as well as the worship service based on special occasions.

b. Worship in the patriarchal narratives. We also encounter liturgical action and speaking in the patriarchal narratives.[32] It is essentially different from worship in the sedentary form, primarily in the fact that the cult is still fully integrated into the life of the small familial group. It is not yet a separate sphere of life. That is why this form of early cult must be distinguished from the cult of the settled period, the official cult. The holy place is not yet made by hand; it is the mountain, the rock, the tree, the spring. These, too, are special places, but not yet in the sense of a place actively separated off. Rather, they are special places for the life of the wandering group, as the patriarchal narratives show. These also contain stories about the founding of sanctuaries, such as Genesis 28, but such stories already belong to the transition to settled life.

There was as yet no holy time. Special events in the life of the group were celebrated in festive fashion, such as changing pastures[33] (on which the Passover is based), or the birth, naming, or weaning of a child. There was not yet the mediator of the holy. The father receives God's instructing word, the father and mother receive the promises, and the father bestows blessing. Only rarely do we encounter sacrifice as a holy act, and when we do, it is prompted by a special occasion. There was not yet any regular sacrifice. The same holds true of prayers, which occurs as part of a particular situation (Gen. 12; 15; 32), and lament and praise are also still pre-cultic. We also encounter pre-cultic rites such as blessing (Gen. 27). It is important for this early form of cult that it as yet knows no distinction between worship and idolatry; there is no cult polemic.

c. Worship in the settled period. The first great caesura is the transition to settled life. With it there emerges the form of worship described at the beginning, the form which is the most widely distributed in religious history and which is the most enduring. In its main features it is common to a great many religions. The specifically Israelite element in the worship established by the Sinai theophany is that this divine revelation occurred on the way from Egypt into the promised land, and that it followed the encounter with the saving God and was this God's revelation, the God who had intervened for his people in the hour of greatest need. That is the theological significance of the insertion of the Sinai pericope into the account of the deliverance from Egypt and the journey into the promised land. This accounts for the fact that Israel's worship always remained closely associated with history.

The Sinai event (Exod. 19—34) established Israel's worship. In contrast to the patriarchal stories, the people is now the subject of worship. The theophany establishing worship is thus no longer that before an individual (the narrative of the burning bush, Exod. 3, marks the transition), but rather before the people. It thus requires a mediator of the holy, something extensively established in Exodus 20:18-21.

The narrative in Exodus 19 contains the basic elements of the holy act. The first is the holy place where God appears (cf. Gen. 28). The mountain cloaked in clouds, on whose heights God appears, represents the sanctuary; the sanctuary is the place of encounter with God. The second is the holy time, the stipulated time which makes possible the preparation for that encounter with God by means of purification. The third is the mediator of the holy, to whom alone God speaks after he has made his way alone to God. The people waiting below hear God's words through the mouth of the mediator; it only perceives the accompanying manifestations of the divine appearance. The fourth element is the gesture of acknowledgment or response of the people to the word of God proclaimed to them by the mediator.

In the usual interpretation of Exodus 19, the goal of the theophany is either the Law or the covenant or both. Both of these, however, were only subsequently attributed to this event. It is possible that the commandments or, as the nucleus of the Decalogue, the first two commandments, originally belonged to the Sinai narrative. These commandments are then the word of God which was directed to his people from the revelation, a word which for just this reason remains liturgical address. The covenant is not established in Exodus 19, but rather in the later narrative Exodus 24:3-8. The covenant does not belong to the establishing event itself, but is rather its later interpretation (see above pp. 42-45).

The real significance of the Sinai narrative lies in the establishment of the settled worship service. A further text complex also belongs to this establishment: the sanctuary narratives in the patriarchal narratives. These are (in contrast to Exod. 19) etiological narratives in which the acquisition of a Canaanite sanctuary, such as the sanctuary at Bethel in Genesis 28, is legitimized by having Yahweh appear to one of the patriarchs there. In the patriarchal sanctuary narratives, however, it is not Israel's worship as such which is established, but rather always only the taking over of a Canaanite sanctuary for the Yahweh-worship. Only from this perspective does the significance of the Sinai narrative first become totally clear: The establishment of Israel's worship in the settled period does *not* take place through a divine revelation at one of the Canaanite sanctuaries, but rather out there, on a holy mountain in the wilderness which belongs to the type of sanctuaries of the early period to which Yahweh does not remain bound. Here, too, the fact is expressed that Yahweh is primarily the God of history.

All the fundamental elements of worship emerging from the theophany in Exodus 19 are associated in Israel with history: the holy place by the fact that Sinai remains a locale along the way, and the God appearing there remains the coming God ("God comes from Sinai," Judg. 5:4-5); the holy time by the fact that the annual festivals are historicized (see below, pp. 208ff.); the mediator of the holy by the fact that Moses is simultaneously the leader during departure. The responsive acknowledgment of the people by the fact that the praise of God's great deeds becomes an integral part of worship. This association of worship with history, an association already prefigured in the Sinai event, results in the simultaneous celebration in Israel's worship of both God's activity in saving as well as blessing. Both are equally significant and of equal import for worship. It is then impossible to characterize worship in Israel one-sidedly from a cyclical (S. Mowinckel and others) or a historically determined understanding (M. Noth, G. von Rad). Israel's worship combines the cyclical and linear understanding of time (see below pp. 208ff.). It is the blessing and, at the same time, the saving God who is celebrated in Israel's worship. The uniqueness of worship in Israel resides in the fact that both are combined.

d. The second important caesura is the beginning of kingship, which introduces a new period for Israel's worship. Sacral kingship everywhere gives liturgical significance to the king. The sanctuary of the royal city becomes the royal sanctuary (1 Kings 6—7); the priests become servants of the king, and the king himself acquires liturgical functions. In a moment of distress he can bring the people's lament before God (Isa. 37), and he can bless the people and pray for the people (1 Kings 8), just as the prayer for the king is a part of worship (Ps. 20; 21; 72). All the more significant then is the account of the ark narrative, in which King David brings the ark to Jerusalem and thus links the old sanctuary with the new and thus the old historical tradition with the worship service in the royal city (1 Sam. 4—6; 2 Sam. 6). The worship of the royal sanctuary is concerned primarily with God's blessing for the king and people. With the ark, the traditions of the saving God of the wilderness period acquire a fixed place in the worship of the period of kings. In the following period, worship is threatened by kingship, as witnessed by the prophets and the Deuteronomic history. There are, however, attempts by kings to reform worship (Hezekiah, 2 Kings 18; Josiah, 2 Kings 22—23). The kingship made worship possible in the splendor and luster of the royal sanctuary (Solomon's building of the temple). Because of the dependency on royal politics, there developed a serious syncretistic threat (e.g., under King Mannaseh). This worship also collapsed with the monarchy.

e. The third caesura is the exile, introduced by the destruction of the temple and the cessation of sacrifice. After the catastrophe worship consists only in gatherings for lamentations, as shown by the lament songs. In the course of the exile there then develops—probably initially among those exiled—a completely new type of worship by word with prayer and readings as its main constituents. The synagogue worship emerges from this, and in it, many features of the early cult come to life again. Above all, the family now regains significance for worship after the collapse of the state. This type of worship by word will later become determinative for worship in early Christendom.

In addition to this, however, the renewal of temple and sacrificial worship is prepared during the exile by two great configurations. The outline of Ezekiel (Ezek. 40—48), the priestly prophet, builds a bridge from prophecy, with its message of judgment for Israel, to the new beginnings of worship after the catastrophe. In spite of all the criticisms leveled at the contemporary institution of worship by the prophets, Ezekiel's plan for a new worship is the one sure and strong sign showing that even judgment prophecy never opposed worship as such, but rather even contributed to its renewal.

The Priestly Code is not an outline of a future worship service, but rather a historical work which developed at the turn of the exile and presents the history from the establishment of the world onward. The astonishing and admirable thing about this work is that, through the presentation of the beginnings, it lays the foundations for renewal for its defeated people. The author of the Priestly Code does this such that worship is placed in the middle of these beginnings.[34] God's goal with his people was from the very beginning—this is already prefigured in Gen. 1—the establishment of worship in the promised land and its center, the Jerusalem temple. We have already seen (see above, pp. 183ff.) how P concentrates the law revealed at Sinai on worship. Beyond this, however, the author of the Priestly Code considers the divine revelation at Sinai on the one hand to be the goal to which everything points which has happened since the beginnings. On the other hand, this Sinai revelation enables him to show in the most extreme concentration and in the most reflected manner what worship is. What we encounter in the old sources in Exodus 19 in a narrative fashion, concerning the elements of cult, is in the P-parallel (Exod. 24:15b-18) systematically concentrated as the course of the holy event:

15b: The cloud covered the mountain
16a: and the glory of the LORD settled on Mount Sinai
16b: and the cloud covered it six days; and on the seventh day he called to Moses out of the midst of the cloud.

17: Now the appearance of the glory of the LORD was like a devouring fire on the top of the mountain in the sight of the people of Israel.
18a: And Moses entered the cloud, and went up on the mountain.
18b: And Moses was on the mountain forty days and forty nights.
25:1 The LORD said to Moses, "Speak to . . ."

The goal of this procedure is the commission God gives Moses in Exodus 25:1f.: "And let them make me a sanctuary, that I may dwell in their midst." This is the goal, the dwelling of God among his people, to which the theophany proceeding leads, divided into two parallel, partial processes: coming—remaining-word; coming—remaining—word. In the middle of these partial processes in the parenthesis in verse 17, the appearance of the *kabod* is described, whose appearance is the concern here. The coming of the mediator of the holy to the mountain corresponds to the coming of Yahweh's glory to the mountain from above. The entrance into the sanctuary or into the holy of holies corresponds to the theophany. The word coming from the theophany acquires its *gravitas* through the two-fold remaining, the stillness of the stipulated holy time. This is the difference between the word issuing from the theophany, the liturgical word, from the word issued into a historical situation (see above pp. 25ff.), which does not require this background of solemn stillness. This solemn stillness is what gives the liturgical word its particular character.

In this stylized presentation of the theophany at Sinai, P thus gives the basic framework for worship in Israel: God's appearance establishes the holy place and the holy time, the God appearing at the holy place calls the mediator of the holy and orders the holy event, "that I may dwell in their midst." This expresses the reciprocity of what happens in worship in both movements; the one movement from above, the coming of the *kabod*, continued in the movement of the mediator to the people. The other movement is that of the people's approach to the mountain, i.e., to the sanctuary, but only to a certain boundary.

The term *kabod*, which characterizes the holy event in the Sinai theophany of P, has yet another side in P.[35] It is the same glory of God which manifests itself in God's saving intervention in the hour of threat to the people on their way through the wilderness (Exod. 16; Num. 14; 16; 17; 20, P). In all the text the event is presented as a sequence of five equal acts. The appearance of the glory of God stands variously in their center (Exod. 16:10;

Num. 14:10; 16:19; 17:7; 20:6). In this way, P brackets the events during the wilderness sojourn with the theophany at Sinai. The majesty of Yahweh's activity reaches from the middle across the entire sphere of his people's historical reality. P thus brackets worship with history. In this conception of the Priestly Code, the uniqueness of Israel's worship is affirmed and preserved which characterized that worship from the very beginning. In it the God is celebrated whom Israel encountered as savior in its history and who therefore also remained the God of the history of his people even in the settled cult.

f. Worship in Chronicles. Worship in Chronicles differentiates itself in a fundamental way from worship in P in that this firm connection of worship and history, standing at the center of the entire work, can no longer be found in Chronicles. The structure of Chronicles already shows this by reducing the early history of the people to the genealogies at the beginning. The history essential for Chronicles begins only with the monarchy. The extremely extensive institutionalization of worship recognizable in Chronicles is only the other side of the extensive separation from history. The cyclical form of worship on the whole and the "official" determination of liturgical acts to the smallest detail, the strict hierarchical organization of the clergy—which becomes the determinative subject of worship behind which the liturgical congregation recedes into the background as only passive participants—this and much more shows that a fundamental change has taken place in the understanding and practice of worship. This corresponds to the decision of the traditionists: P, with its understanding of worship, became a part of the torah, while the Chronicles were not taken up into the "former prophets," but rather only into the "writings." This also corresponds to the historical fact that the worship conceived by Chronicles was not restored after the second destruction of the temple, the synagogue service took its place.

The elements of worship. Worship is a holy occurrence between God and his people. It is a special, holy event in that it occurs at a special place, at a special time, and through the mediation of specially commissioned people. On both sides, this occurrence between God and his people consists of the two basic elements, word and action. Originally they are intimately associated; in the "cultic drama" they are separated. Their relationship to one another is extremely variable, but both belong necessarily—in both event directions—to all liturgical occurrences, even where the gesture has taken the place of action. In the following presentation of these elements, one should not forget the changes prompted by the history of worship. Nonetheless, I will essentially present the elements here which have remained constants.

a. *The holy place.* For Israel the temple was never the holy place in the sense that its holiness consisted in its separation from the unholy outside world. It was understood, rather, in the strict functional sense. The special place in the middle of the land was special because blessing proceeded out from it onto the whole country, and then the blessing of the land (sacrifice) flowed back from the land to the special place of worship. The holiness of the temple was realized in the fact that the inhabitants of the land came together at special times to this special place and then returned to their homes with that which they received there. This path from the homes into the temple and the path from the temple to the homes is thus an essential element of worship: The holy place would not be holy without this movement to and from the temple. Ancient Israel's awareness of this functional character of the place's holiness is shown by the institution of processions and pilgrimages in which the way to and from the sanctuary belonged to the holy event. This functional character of the temple's holiness comes to expression in Ezekiel in a complete way when Yahweh's glory togther with the final announcement of judgment leaves the temple, to return only at the restoration of the temple for the new, cleansed temple worship service.[36]

b. *The holy time.* As in many other religions, the annual festivals in Israel were the most important holy times when families sought out the temple. These times are collected in the festival calendars, but change somewhat during Israel's history (Exod. 23:14-19; 34:18-26; Deut. 16:1-17; Lev. 23:1-44).[37] The annual festivals were taken over from the settled population during the entry into Canaan. Commensurate with the annual rhythm, they celebrate primarily God's blessing activity and are ordered according to the primary events in the natural year: sowing and harvest. Only the Passover reaches back in its origins, as the festival of changing pastures, into the nomadic period, and that is why it is traced back to the time of the departure (Exod. 12), even if it acquires new meaning here.

Since the annual festivals grew out of the agrarian economic form taken over in Canaan and not from Israel's history, they were later "historicized," i.e., events from Yahweh's history with Israel were also celebrated in them. The association of God's saving with God's blessing activity was thus also anchored in the celebration of the festivals. While they remained, sowing and harvest festivals and such were vitally important for Israel, but the association with the recollection of God's saving deeds protected the harvest festival from Canaanization. Typical for this historicizing is the narrative of the establishment of the Passover festival in Exodus 12, which associates the festival with Israel's beginnings.

Yet another development characteristic of Israel's worship is important for the history of the Passover festival. The Passover was originally celebrated in the family as a shepherding festival. With the growing significance of the temple in the country and then particularly the temple in Jerusalem, it was moved to the temple. With the destruction of the temple (perhaps even earlier), however, it once again became a festival celebrated in the family. This development shows that Israel was not unconditionally bound to the holy place as regards the celebration of its festivals.

Another development in the festivals is important for the understanding of the holy time. In the early period the festivals were directly the celebration of events in the course of the year, thus of the first sowing or the wine harvest. There was as yet no separation here into a sacral and secular part of the festival. The festivals were thus not set according to the calendar in the early period, but rather fell together with the events, for example, according to whether the wine harvest was earlier or later. Only with the separation of the cult into a separate sphere of existence did the festivals become sacral in the strict sense and thus fixed according to the calendar, so that they no longer necessarily fell together with the celebrated event.

We particularly need to mention the Sabbath, which was a day of rest from the social perspective in Israel's early period. Then, however, it was taken into the cult and from the exile on became a sign of confession. The strict observance of the Sabbath proved one's membership in the Jewish people all the way to the point of martyrdom.

Finally, we need to recall the discussion concerning the New Year's festival precipitated by S. Mowinckel's "Psalmenstudien" (II, 1922). The rediscovery of the Babylonian New Year's festival led to the attempt to postulate a corresponding festival or at least a main festival in Israel during the monarchy (a festival called "the Enthronement Festival of Yahweh" by Mowinckel). The discussion can now be considered closed. The frequent calendars handed down to us neither know of such a festival, nor do they suggest the development of such a festival. The New Year's festival emerged extremely late in Israel, only after the exile. Above all, however, the

Babylonian New Year's festival does not correspond to what we know about the Israelite festival cult.

c. *Situational worship.* The holy and as such fixed time can be differentiated from situational worship, which was highly significant in Israel. Only fully institutionalized worship runs completely according to fixed times, so that one knows in advance for an entire year when worship takes place. In contrast, fixed times alternate with situational ones in Israel's sanctuary. Here, too, we find the association of worship with history. We know this primarily from the lament Psalms, which make up a considerable part of the liturgical Psalms. If a serious threat or danger comes over the people, then a "fast" is called whose center is the liturgical lament gathering. This lament gathering cannot wait until the next scheduled worship service, but must immediately be brought to God so that he may turn the distress. In the early period these situational celebrations also included the victory celebrations with the victory song directed to God. These took place, however, at the place of victory or after the return of the army. There were still other such liturgically celebrated events which could not be inserted into the festival calendar, and which were in contrast celebrated on the occasion of the event.

But here a further addendum is necessary. The Psalter contains considerably more laments of the individual than laments of the people. This suggests that we have to pay attention to a distinction in the subject of worship. The subject of worship at the great festivals as well as at the lament gatherings in a time of national need was the congregation of the people, i.e., the people which was simultaneously the liturgical congregation. Next to this, however, the worship of the small group, the family, occupied an essential place in Israelite worship. The question can remain open concerning to what extent this family worship service took place in the temple or in the homes. It is significant, however, that in addition to liturgical proceedings in the temple which encompassed the congregation of the people in Israel, the family was and remained the other subject of liturgical proceedings throughout Israel's entire history.[38] These family services were situational in nature. They emerged from events in personal life, as shown particularly well by the Psalms of praise of the individual in the Psalter in which deliverance from mortal danger was celebrated before God. The fact that the situational worship service in Israel played a significant role next to that of the annual festivals shows the direct theological significance of worship. For Israel, the

God whom it called upon and trusted accompanied the history of the people as well as the life history of the individual in his family both in joy and suffering. Thus this contingent occurrence between God and humanity also had to find expression in the form of worship.

    d. *The mediator of the holy.* We have already spoken, in the context of the history of the mediator, about the priest as mediator of the holy event (see above pp. 79f.); this only needs to be completed as regards the liturgical function of the priest.[39] What is said in the Sinai pericope concerning this is of fundamental importance, particularly in Exodus 20:18-21. This is the basis for the fact that the priest is not called by God like the prophet, but is rather appointed or commissioned by the people to be the mediator between them and the holy God. Commensurately, the priest is commissioned for life and passes his office down to his sons. This shows that the priest is essentially the mediator of God's activity in blessing. As such, he was of greater significance than the Old Testament suggests at first glance. The priestly service extends from the settlement period in Canaan through Israel's entire history up to the time of the New Testament. Just as worship belongs to the relationship to God, so also does the liturgical mediator.

    The history of the priesthood through the Old Testament cannot be presented here. Let us point instead to one important development in this history. In the beginning, there was no priestly hierarchy in Israel. At first there was no doubt some competition between groups or families of priests, particularly at various sanctuaries, just as in other religions. An actual hierarchy, however, emerged only along with kingship. During that monarchy it did not appear very frequently, and acquired determinative significance only with the restoration of the temple after the exile, when the high priest took over some of the functions of the king. There now developed a rigorous hierarchy characterized by the divisions of the clergy and the gradations from the lowest to the highest office. It is important for the further development, including within the Christian church, to remember that the priestly hierarchy in Israel as in other nations did not originate in the nature of the priesthood itself, but rather in the stage of the history of the priesthood in which it was closely associated with kingship. The priests were thus servants of the king, royal officials. The priestly hierarchy is fundamentally and originally a political structure which was secondarily applied to the priesthood. It is not an inherent part of the priesthood as such.

In what follows, I will present the individual liturgical elements in the reciprocal event of worship in word and action.

God's action in worship. The action of God in, as well as outside, worship is primarily blessing and saving, except that here it occurs mediated by the word. Within liturgical blessing, however, word and act are indeed inseparably with and in one another, since blessing takes place in the utterance of the blessing (Num. 6:27); "So shall they put my name upon the people of Israel, and I will bless them." Blessing within worship is bestowed upon the congregation (Num. 6:24-26) and upon individuals (Pss. 91; 121), not only when the congregation is dismissed (blessing = departure greeting), but also during other occasions: during pilgrimage (ps. 122), during the harvest festival (Ps. 65), in connection with sacrifice (Lev. 9), and elsewhere. The blessing is bestowed by the priest, but the priest is here the mediator of God's blessing (Num. 6:27). As regards liturgical blessing, the entire history of blessing in the Old Testament is presupposed (see above, pp. 104ff.). When, for example, Deuteronomy speaks of a threefold blessing—of the body, the livestock, and the field—this threefold blessing is implied in the liturgical act of blessing. The blessing bestowed upon the liturgical congregation returns with that congregation into all spheres of life. Blessing is such an indisputable part of worship that the prophets never attacked blessing or the priestly bestowal of blessing in their cult critique.

God's saving activity does not take place in worship. It is attributed to the epiphany, not to theophany. Nonetheless, the word which pledges that saving—to be distinguished from the announcement of saving—does belong in the worship service. This is the so-called salvation oracle or pledge of hearing, for which the cry "fear not!" is characteristic. It performed an important liturgical function within the context of the lament of both the people and the individual. Because the fear has already been taken from the supplicant, the saving has already commenced. If an answer is pledged to the lamenter, this indicates a turn in the distress. The echo in the praise of those saved shows how great a role this pledge of hearing or saving played in Israel's worship. To the extent that the lament is associated with a confession of sin and the request for forgiveness, the pledge of forgiveness or the purification through atonement is also an act of the saving God, since with it the cause of distress can also be eliminated. In exceptional situations this saving can also take place directly in the worship service. This is by means of the divine judgment which acquits the innocent person and by means of the sanctuary's function as an asylum.

The theology of the Priestly Code in particular differentiates between the word of God in the sanctuary at the holy time and God's words in daily life (see above, pp. 16ff.). It is the word spoken in the stillness of the sanctuary to which those who have come to the sanctuary bring the willingness to hear. God's words in the sanctuary also include those words which are actually a part of God's action, of which we have already spoken. Thus both God's action and his words are present in the word of God in the worship service.

The words occurring in worship can be divided into proclamation and instruction. The proclamation of the priest includes the recollection of God's great deeds, in whatever form, the making of the covenant and its renewal (Exod. 34)—all the words in which God himself speaks, mediated by the priest. We still know very little about the liturgical acts in which this took place. Indirectly, we can also consider the proclamation occurring in praise to be part of the proclamation in worship. God's word of instruction in worship is primarily the proclamation of the commandments of the Decalogue, whose *Sitz im Leben,* as we saw, is the worship service. The significance of the Decalogue for worship is shown by the sequence of Exodus 19 and Exodus 20. The formulation of the first commandments proves how closely proclamation and instruction belong together and how they cannot be separated. This is seen even more clearly in the commandment paraenesis, as we encounter it already in the Covenant Code and then particularly in Deuteronomy. This paraenesis includes the historical recollection as one of its essential constituent parts. Typical of Deuteronomy is the causal and determinative anchoring of the commandments, which connects instruction with the proclamation.

However, God's instruction also comes directly in the answering of questions through the oracle, whose place is later taken by the priestly instruction.

In contrast, the laws were not originally a part of worship; the reading of the law in worship was introduced only at a later time.

The action and words of man in worship. As regards man, an essential part of worship is already the preparations, something not normally given adequate attention. This includes the journey to the temple, the *processio,* which is a part of the holy event. The procession is nothing other than the cultic stylization of the journey to the sanctuary. In Israel, as the journey of people to the sanctuary, this acquires its significance precisely from the fact that there can be no divine procession of gods in the sphere of the prohibition of images. It is commensurate with its significance when the journey to the sanctuary finds specific expression in a pilgrimage Psalm (Ps. 122:1):

> I was glad when they said to me,
> "Let us go to the house of the LORD!"

Preparations also include the physical, bodily preparation, which is so important that it is already a part of the account of the Sinai theophany (Exod. 19:10f.): the cleansing and washing of clothes. This holds true not only for the liturgical congregation but to an even larger extent for the priests, who put on the festive garments and "holy adornment" for the worship service. Beauty belongs to worship as an essential constituent part. It is there in the space and in the form, in the preciousness of the cultic instruments, in clothing and adornment of the priests and the congregation, in the temple music and in the beauty of the songs.

Under certain circumstances, this physical preparation also includes abstinence and fasting, particularly for the priests, but at certain occasions for the liturgical congregation as well. This preparation finally includes the procedure—corresponding to the cleansing of the body—in which one casts off all impurity before entering the sanctuary in the institution of renunciation and negative confession (Ps. 15); this gate-liturgy brings about cultic readiness. One comes before God accompanied by gestures which express the acknowledgment of God as Lord by those serving God: kneeling or prostration.

a. *Sacrifice.* The most important liturgical act is that of sacrifice. At times, it was so important that sacrifice and worship were synonymous (Lev. 9). However, worship in Israel never consisted only of sacrificial offering. A thorough presentation of the history of sacrifice in Israel is not possible here, [40] and only the most important lines can be sketched in. Our term "sacrifice" or "offering" (*offeree,* to offer) is a secondary general term which subsequently summarized extremely different procedures and phenomena. Sacrifice or offering is one of the most widespread of all religious phenomena, found all over the world and preserved through many millennia. None of the sacrifices mentioned in the Old Testament is specifically Israelite, nor are any of the sacrifice motifs. In its sacrifices, Israel's worship participates in one of the phenomena common to all religions. In the history of religions we can recognize two basic types of sacrifice or offering, both of which we encounter in the Old Testament. They are so different that they actually transcend the overriding term. The one type is the communal meal at a special time and special place, at which the deity is considered to be participating; this is the sacred meal (*zaebah*). The other type is the offering in the burning of an animal (*'olah*) or the offering of vegetable sacrifices (*minhah*) or the sacrifices of the first-born or first fruits (see L. Köhler, AT-Theologie, 171).

Concerning the two basic motifs of sacrifice, I refer the reader to what has already been said about Genesis 4 and 8 (see above, p. 31). The one is ordered under God's activity in blessing and was originally the sacrifice of the first-born or first fruits. This offering of the first part of a harvest was to effect the blessing of the entire harvest. The other is ordered under God's activity in saving. It is the praise of the saving god associated with the offering or is the petition for saving. At a later stage there is also the sacrifice as atonement, which gradually acquires dominant significance.

The history of sacrifice in a simplified fashion can be viewed in three stages. In the earliest stage, sacrifice belonged to the life processes for which it was necessary, and was still fully integrated into the life of the community. Every kind of sacrifice included the event which prompted it, something like a harvest or recovery from sickness. A slaughter was conducted as "sacrifice," and certain events in the life of the family, the group, or the individual were accompanied by sacrifice. This is how we encounter it in the patriarchal stories as well as in the Ugaritic epics or in the narrative framework of the book of Job.

The second stage is that of the inclusion of sacrifice in the cult at the holy place and at the holy time. The sanctuary becomes the only place where sacrifices can be offered, and the festivals now have their center in the sacrificial offering. This is the stage which in the Old Testament encompasses the period from the settlement to the destruction of the temple in Jerusalem, and which includes the majority of regulations for sacrifice as well as the prophetic critique of sacrifice. It is characteristic of this stage that many different kinds of sacrifice come together in the cultic sacrificial service. Each sacrifice, however, maintained its own individual character, such as, for example, the sacrifice associated with a vow. It was also characteristic that the father was the person offering the sacrifice and bringing the sacrificial produce, as shown, for example, in Deuteronomy 26.

The third stage is characterized by two opposing procedures. The one is the cultic isolation of sacrifice, which manifests itself above all in the fact that the sacrificial priest is now the exclusive subject of sacrifice. The father now only brings the material for the sacrifice, which he hands over to the priest for the purpose of actually offering it up. At the sacrifice itself he is only a spectator. This type is also characterized by the fact that the variety of sacrificial types recedes, and the sacrifice of atonement becomes dominant. The wholly determinative sacrifice motif is now the atonement effected by sacrifice. This is the stage of post-exilic sacrifice, as shown by the Chronicles as well as in the later strata of the sacrificial law in P.

This strong institutionalization of sacrifice arouses the question of whether (these) sacrifices correspond to God's will at all. This question comes to massive expression in Psalms 40, 50, and 51. Psalm 51:15-17 asserts that the true sacrifice, the one pleasing to God, is praise and a contrite heart; Psalm 50:7-15, after an extremely thorough criticism of the sacrifice of animals, declares it to be praise and lament (14—15). There was thus a piety in the post-exilic period which indeed included praise and lament, but not the sacrifice of animals. One can be sure that its way was prepared by the criticism of the pre-exilic prophets directed towards the sacrificial practices of their time.

A far-reaching change in the concept of sacrifice is, however, also shown by the fact that, in Isaiah 53, the death of the suffering servant is designated as a sacrifice of expiation ("an offering for sin," Isa. 53:10).

b. *The festivals.* What is essential for the celebration of festivals has already been discussed in the context of the holy time. We can only add here that the celebration of festivals required man's extensive participation. A thorough examination of the relationship between ritual and cult would be necessary at this point. For primitive peoples, existence is so totally determined and permeated by ritual that it is an integral part of all community life. Ritual embraces both secular and holy events. There is not yet a cult which is separated from the rest of existence. Ritual equally determines both the secular and the holy realms. In the stage of the official cult, however, the purely religious ritual separates itself out and becomes determinative for the cult; cult and ritual enter into a firm association. Since ritual is a human act, however it is organized, man's ritual action in particular belongs to the festival cult in a great many forms. This has shown an astonishing tenacity down through the centuries and millennia, and is thus much more significant than is normally recognized. Within the sphere of cultic ritual or cultic acts there are thus a great many which have outlived the stage in which they were meaningful (survivals) and have lived on without being understood. This is also closely related to the fact that often only a *gestus,* a gesture, survives from a ritual and then lives on even though it is only understood "symbolically" or not at all. Ritual and gestures recede to the extent that worship is understood rationally. Nonetheless, it is often the incomprehensible ritual or gesture which clearly defines an assembly of a group of people as a liturgical one.

c. *Man's words in worship.* This finds its dominant expression in the liturgical Psalms in praise and lament and the other speech forms found in the Psalms. The Psalms are the strongest and clearest expression of the dialogue relationship to God in the Old Testament. Man before God is the responding man. This accounts for the astonishing liveliness of the Psalter and the even more astonishing fact that it has never hardened into a fixed cult language (that it never became a survivor), but rather remained comprehensible for every new generation and could be taken over into the Christian worship service. The Psalms, however, do not exhaust people's liturgical participation in word. There is also the word which accompanies liturgical acts, such as the sacrificial speech which in Deuteronomy 26 is combined with confession. At special occasions we also find the renunciation, various kinds of greetings, words accompanying the prompting of a vow, and many others.

The Response of Meditation or Reflection

Devotion and Theological Reflection

Devotion. Man's words in worship encompass yet another important element. This makes it clear why the Hebrew *dabar* embraces both "speaking" and "thinking." The word directed to God turns into meditation or reflection. Just as for us in a close personal relationship the "speaking to . . ." is continued in a "thinking of . . ." and "reflecting on . . . ," so also in one's relationship to God, as is reflected in the Psalms. In later stages the Psalter was not only a liturgical songbook, but beyond that a devotional book as well. This is shown by the Psalms in which reflection is determinative (such as Pss. 119 or 139) as well as those in which the address to God changes into reflective passages, such as Psalm 34 or 39. Here we need to distinguish carefully between meditation (reflection) and wisdom. The two brush against one another and permeate one another in various ways, but are different as regards origin.

One series of Psalms shows a reflection on God emerging from praise or lament which, however, carries these forward in reflection. The Psalm of praise of an individual thus passes over into reflection (Pss. 40:5):

> "Thou hast multiplied, O LORD my God,
> thy wondrous deeds and thy thoughts toward us;
> none can compare with thee!
> Were I to proclaim and tell of them . . . "

All of Psalm 139 is a reflection grown from the assertion of innocence; from lament there grows a reflection on man's mortal fate (Pss. 39; 49; 90). These reflective parts of the Psalter are a sure sign that one reflected on the Psalms, that they were not "thoughtlessly" recited. They touch the individual in his innermost thoughts and continue on inside him. It should be pointed out that this reflection very often took on the form of address (as in Ps. 139). The words directed to God continued on in reflection and could also pass directly over into address again. The person doing this reflecting on God and his activity lives a life addressed to God and remains bound to this particular lifestyle. God could never become objectified in this reflection, could never become the mere object of reflection. God unconditionally remained the personal counterpart.

Theological reflection. The individual's response in action, words, and thought embraces his entire existence as a human. The link or relationship to God is not something in the Old Testament which was there in addition to other human relationships—those to one's fellow beings, to one's work, to nature, art, and so on. This relationship is only possible as the relationship of the entire person to the God who created him in his own image and in correspondence to himself. One is dealing with God in all relationships within existence, be it one's work (Gen. 2), the love of one's husband or wife (Gen. 2), be it joy in nature (Ps. 104), one's study of the world (Job 28) and questioning (Proverbs)—a person cannot extricate himself from the relationship to God.

To be sure, one can deny God this response. He can be disobedient and not show him the honor due. One can renounce God and despise his word. The great drama of Israel's history grew out of the turning away from God. But with all their sin and disobedience, with all their despisal and rejection of

God, people can do nothing to change the fact that they were created to be God's counterpart. They cannot force God, cannot on their own destroy the relationship between themselves and God. From this denial of response there emerges a new history, since God suffers from this denial, and this suffering manifests itself in a historical fashion.

This suggests that devotion in Israel, meditation on God, led to a theological reflection which emerged from what happened, what does happen, and what will happen between God and his people. This reflection thinks back over the history in which the reflecting individual stands. This accounts for the fact that theological reflection in Israel did not result in conceptual systems or doctrinal edifices, but led rather to historical writing.

At the beginning, we said that the work of the Yahwist is based on the confession of praise, the Deuteronomic history on the confession of guilt. These are the two experiences which most deeply impressed the consciousness of the Israelite people: the deliverance at the beginning and the collapse of 587. It is thus quite understandable that the two became points of crystallization for the two great historical works. Theological reflection proceeded from these two experiences, which were experiences in the history of Israel with its God, and asked from this perspective about the contexts from which they grew and in which they acquired meaning. The confession of praise and of guilt, however, belong to response. The great historical works thus grew out of response.

If one now asks how such enormous, multifarious historical works were able to emerge from this kind of theological reflection, the answer would be that this reflection took up the traditions, linked itself to these traditions and constructed from them a whole whose center was the confession of praise or of guilt. But what is a *tradition* or *the tradition for the Old Testament?* Tradition or transmission is in the Old Testament primarily and actually the process of transmission, not the transmitted material itself as the result of this process. We can best see this in the fact that the process is rendered with two verbs: a verb of giving and a verb of receiving. The beginning of Psalm 78 gives us a classic description of the process of transmission:

> I will open my mouth in a parable;
>   I will utter dark sayings from of old,
> things that we have heard and known,
>   that our fathers have told us.

We will not hide them from their children,
>   but tell to the coming generation
the glorious deeds of the LORD, and his might,
>   and the wonders which he has wrought.

As long as there was only oral transmission, it was only possible as a process within a community to which both the person giving as well as the person receiving belonged and in which both had to be present. The traditions were an integral part of this community without which they could not exist. They belonged to that which one generation handed down to the following one in order to make it capable of life. Traditions belonged to every sphere of life, to agriculture and the crafts as well as to family life, all forms of community, and to the relationship to God. The traditions were an integral part of life and were carried on in the processes of the existence to which they belonged, and the traditions ceased when the processes of the existence ceased.

Only with written documentation did traditions emerge in the sense of *traditum,* that which lies before one as tradition. Now, however, tradition differentiated itself and there emerged the various strands of tradition: that of the royal court, of the temple and worship, of law, prophecy, wisdom, and so on.

The uniqueness of the Old Testament historical works resides in the fact that from the perspective of their center the extremely varied traditions were brought together into a whole. Because one of the great experiences of the people with God stood in that center, the whole into which that experience was placed became a whole which embraced Israel's history with its God. It was thus possible for traditions from the most diverse spheres of life to be brought together in these works and fused into a unity. Thus also was it possible for the whole of those occurrences, from beginning to end, the entire life of the community and the individual with everything belonging to it, to be embraced in these historical works.

The Theological Interpretation of History: The Great Historical Works of the Old Testament

Excursus: In the introduction we proceeded from the assertion that the Pentateuch is based on the confession of praise, the Deuteronomic history on the confession of guilt. We can now see what this point of departure means. The fact that two great historical works constitute the middle of the Old Testament as holy Scripture is itself based on the fact that they both fundamentally portray an occurrence between God and humanity. The deepest experiences in Israel's history were that of deliverance and that of judgment. From this dialogue event there emerged for Israel the contexts in history as well as meaning in history. This accounts for the fact that a historical writing developed in Israel the likes of which we find nowhere else in all of oriental antiquity.

The connection between praise and historical writing is shown most clearly at the beginning, in Exodus 1—15, in a twofold manner. The spontaneous, narrative praise of God, the Song of Miriam, has only *one* event as its object. To the narrative praise of God there is added in ch. 14 the account of the same event, but now in a form which narrates the event. The prose account is added to narrative praise. Then, however, the Song of Miriam is expanded into a historical Psalm which lists a long series of events. One sees how the circle is expanded from the center, the experience of deliverance: the event by itself as an act of God—the thorough account of the event which adds how all this came about. Finally, the fusion of this one event with a series of further events, connected by the praise of the saving God who acts in the history of his people.

During the course of this growth, two expansions offered themselves quite naturally. First of all, God's judgment was added to his redemption, as exemplified in the Psalms by the proximity of Psalms 105 and 106, in the historical writing by the fact that the Deuteronomic history follows the Pentateuch. It is already given *in nuce* by the insertion of Exodus 32—34 into the history of deliverance from Egypt. The other expansion is already prefigured in the promise of Exodus 3:7f. The promise of departure is combined in the language of blessing with the promise of entry. The contexts determining the whole in Israel's historical works are thus based on the events between God and humanity.

The work of the Yahwist. The first great historical work in Israel, that of the Yahwist,[41] grew out of the combination of God's activity in saving and blessing, specifically from the insertion of Genesis in front of the national history which begins in Exodus to Numbers. The fact that J transformed blessing into a historical concept by combining it with promise is only the one side of the conception. The other is the insertion of Genesis in front of the Exodus story. This shows an understanding of history which is fundamentally different from the modern understanding, which grew out of the Enlightenment. It does *not* isolate national history, that is, political history, as *the* history per se, but rather views it as the center of two circles. The one is the circle of the "family of humanity," whose community form is the family. The other is humanity as a whole and the world as a whole. This is how J understands history: Because Yahweh as Israel's savior is at the same time the personal God and the creator of the world and of humanity, these three circles belong to history. A truly grand conception.

For national history this means not only an expansion by means of these two circles within which it moves but also a different understanding of national history as such. The activity of the creator and God's blessing participate in it to the same extent as does God's historical activity. It is thus not just a "salvation history" in the sense of a series of God's saving acts together with a corresponding series of promises. It is rather a history between God and people in which God acts not only in promises, proclamation, saving, and judgment, but also in growth and decline, success and failure, in work and in nourishment, in the soundness of the family and other community forms, in economic life and in culture. This other conception of history is shown particularly in the acquisition of mature language forms of various kinds, from primeval narratives on: the family narratives from the patriarchal period, the narratives of the wandering groups, narratives of liberation and heroic legends, local legends, narratives about sanctuaries from the period of the land conquest and many others. Only then does the transition to historical writing gradually take place during the early monarchy, writing such as Judges 9 (Abimelech) and the portrayal of the rise and royal succession of David. The work of J also emerged in this period. But J did not conceive a historical work in our sense. By carefully employing and preserving the literary forms of past epochs, he let these express themselves in their own words. The language forms which developed in the community forms of those past epochs bring to this historical portrayal a depth and authenticity which could never be attained by the leveling style of historians according to our understanding. J knows of two ways to mark historical time lapse: in historical time by means of facts and dates, in prehistorical time by means of genealogies. He does not try to put prehistory into a historical framework, but rather leaves the time framework of the genealogies for the primeval and patriarchal history, a framework which grows from God's blessing.

According to earlier understanding, the Old Testament understanding of history was characterized by a purely linear understanding of time. G. von Rad in particular has in his theology placed the Old Testament understanding of history as purely linear in contrast to a cyclical historical thinking in oriental antiquity.[42] B. Albrektson[43] has objected that we find talk of historical action of the gods in Israel's surroundings as well, particularly in Babylonia and Assyria. J. Barr[44] objects that the Old Testament does not just speak about God's action in history. Both objections are justified. G. von Rad had proceeded on the basis of his concept of salvation history, according to which God's action in history consists alone of his deeds, i.e., the acts in which he intervenes in history, either for redemption or judgment. He combined this with the purely linear understanding of time, whereby time for the Old Testament was only a linear movement toward a goal. If, however, one includes the primeval and patriarchal histories, one can no longer say this so one-sidedly. At the end of the flood in Genesis 8:20-22, time is presented in a classical formulation as time which moves in the cyclical rhythms of creation: "While the earth remains, seedtime and harvest, cold and heat, summer and winter, day and night, shall not cease." If one takes primeval history seriously as an undercurrent continuing on in history, then both elements will always belong to the movement of time: the cyclical and that moving toward a goal. Even if the time which moves toward a goal was the more important for Israel, the time circling in the rhythms of creations remains a part of it, a time without which there would be no linear time.

The Deuteronomic history. In its nucleus it is a confession of guilt. Its place is the time of the exile. There it grew out of Israel's reflection on its past, its present, and its future. It embraces the entire period of Israel's settlement and civil organization from the entry into the promised land onward. Thus Deuteronomy commences in the speech of Moses before the crossing of the Jordan.[45]

We need first to ask about the possibility of the origin of such a work. The reaction after the catastrophe among the remnant after 587 was the confession of guilt, as we encounter it, for example, in the songs of lament. This was no abstract or sterile confession of guilt, but rather contained within it the question concerning the reason, and contained the will for an about-face: How did it happen, how could it happen? The confession of guilt thus sets a process of reflection in motion which attains an astonishingly spacious view of history. Prior to the historical writings of the Greeks, not a single work emerged in all of antiquity which embraced this kind of time period and this kind of sequence of different historical epochs. Such a work can only be explained by Israel's relationship to God, in which the connection between God's words and God's acts through the centuries had led to insights and overviews regarding various contexts within history (cf. the history of the promises). The confession of guilt of the remnant which prompted the reflection "How did it happen?" was itself already a recognition of a certain context. The prophets said it, and we did not believe it. This was the first of the newly acknowledged contexts, the one extending from the arrival of the prophets' message of judgment back to the issuance of this announcement of judgment, first to the prophets of the last generation, Jeremiah and Ezekiel, then to the entire chain of judgment prophets from Amos on. Then, however, came the second, further context: the early period of judgment prophecy prior to Amos in which the prophets' accusation was directed primarily against the kings. Under the auspices of this further context, the Deuteronomist found it necessary to present the entire history of kingship in Israel, and to present it as a history of apostasy and disobedience—thus not primarily from a historical perspective, but rather from a theological one. This created a tension which dominated the entire period of kings. At the beginning of the monarchy there thus stands not judgment, but rather salvation prophecy, such as the prophecy of Nathan for the house of David, the Davidic dynasty. Through his history of the monarchy, the Deuteronomist shows why this promise had to fall to the wayside. Psalm 89, in which the complaint about the breach of this promise was raised, shows that the promise itself was not forgotten throughout the entire breadth of the period of kings. Here, too, we find reflection in broad historical contexts, the kind which made the emergence of the Deuteronomic history possible.

Now, however, there is added yet a third, further context, back into the distant past, centuries beyond the beginning of the monarchy, back to the initial entry into the land and the beginning of settled life. This third, further circle is not a result of a context prompted by a prophetic word of salvation or of judgment, but is based rather on the context associated with the keeping or neglect of God's commandments and laws. The accusation always raised against the kings is that of the "sin of Jeroboam," the deviation from the first commandment. Precisely this deviation and disobedience has a prehistory which commences with the entry into the land, the great threat of Israel's defection to other gods, particularly to the Baalim of Canaan, a defection which is the concern of the entire Deuteronomic Law.

From the reflective meditation of the confession of guilt there thus emerges an enormous context reaching from the collapse back to the entry into the land. In Deuteronomy the promise of blessing takes the place of that of redemption, but it is a conditional promise bound to the people's obedience. At the beginning of the monarchy stands another promise of blessing, this time for the monarchy and through it for the people of Israel. In the historical period portrayed by the Deuteronomist, God's blessing is added to his saving, and to a certain extent it steps into the foreground. However, the gifts of blessing for the land and its fertility became a threat, and the history of kingship belonging to them becomes a history of disobedience. This leads to collapse. Because of this collapse, reflection—itself growing out of the confession of guilt—becomes aware of these great contexts. These make this historical work possible which spans so many centuries.

The question concerning the work's intention has been discussed by M. Noth (1943), who believes it is "the actual intention of its entire presentation of history to teach one how to understand the concluding end of Israel's history as divine judgment" (109). G. von Rad assumes that the remark concerning the pardon of Jehoiachin at the end of the work (2 Kings 25:27f.) points "to a possibility where Yahweh can link up again" (Theol. I 341), and H. W. Wolff sees a call to reversal in the entire Deuteronomic history: "The work thus serves an urgent invitation to the God of salvation history" (ThB 22, 322). He sees this particularly in Solomon's prayer of temple dedication, e.g., in 1 Kings 8:33, 35: "If they turn again to thee, and acknowledge thy name, and pray and make supplication to thee in this house; then hear thou in heaven, and forgive the sin of thy people Israel." I agree basically with Wolff, but would like to carry his thesis one step further. If the nucleus of the Deuteronomic history is a confession of guilt, then this confession goes back to such confessions within the context of the lament of the people. Here it functions to serve the supplication for a turn in the distress. It makes a request for forgiveness to him who is able to turn that distress. In any case, it looks forward into the future. The reflection growing out of this confession of guilt is seeking an answer to the question: Why did that have to happen? The answer to this question resulted in an extended conception of history whose object is not just the failure of Israel and its kings, but also the high periods of Israel's history, particularly the period of David's kingship. It thus goes far beyond a mere explication of the confession of guilt. If this supplication for a new turning of God towards his people, which is intended in the confession of guilt, is viewed against the background of the entire arc from the entry into the land up to the fall of Jerusalem, then it must include the possibility of a totally new act of God with Israel. The author of the Deuteronomic history thus wants to bring his people to request from its God not only the restoration of what has been, but also a new turning of God which will bring Israel a new, different historical period. Commensurate with the confession of guilt, this will include the renunciation of much of what previously had been Israel's pride.

The Priestly Writing. The Priestly Writing (P) developed in the same approximate period as did the Deuteronomic history, yet the two have little in common. They must have emerged from completely different circles and completely different traditions. P stands closer to the work of the Yahwist, with which it to a large extent runs parallel. This parallelism with J, however, shows even more clearly that P has another conception of history. It is astonishing that two such different conceptions are possible within the one larger work of the Pentateuch. They are possible, however, because a fundamental feature of the Old Testament understanding of God stands at the center of both: in J Yahweh's activity in history, in P the Yahweh present in worship.[46]

Ancient Israel lived from two fundamental types of Yahweh's revelation: the epiphany, the coming of Yahweh to a place where his people were in distress and had asked for his coming and intervention; and the theophany, in which God revealed himself at a holy place where he was then cultically worshiped. Whereas the center of the work of J is God's coming deliverance (Exodus), the center of P is the theophany at Sinai, from which is issued the commandment to build the tabernacle, the model for the temple. Accordingly, J has to a large extent grown out of historical traditions and P out of cultic ones. We must immediately add, however, that this fusion of J and P in the Pentateuch would not have been possible if this difference had been the only determinative factor. If one looks more closely, a noticeable correspondence between the two becomes visible. P has combined a historical strand with his basic cultic one, while J has combined a cultic strand with his basic historical one. The Sinai pericope has been taken up into the work of J so that both Exodus and Sinai belong to the basic event. P has conceived his work such that it does not begin with Sinai, the founding of Israel's worship, but rather takes up the old traditions of J, so that he, too, combines Sinai and Exodus. But whereas J lets the two stand next to each other in two tradition blocks, P connects the two by means of a subtle conceptual bracket, the term *kabod,* which designates the glory of the God appearing in the theophany as well as the glory of the God who proves to be the savior of his people.[47] The association of worship and history is thus an integral part of both conceptions. However, P also follows J by placing the history of Israel, which acquires its center in worship, into the broader horizon of patriarchal and primeval history. In this way the author of P attains a conception in which the center, the founding of worship in the divine revelation at Sinai, is brought into direct connection with what happened at the beginning, the creation. With this, however, worship acquires a universal horizon in P, suggested by the relationship between the seventh day of creation and worship. The sanctification of the seventh day and God's rest on this day point to worship as the goal of history within this universal horizon.[48]

P originated around the turn of the exile. The new situation consisted in the fact that Israel, which had lost its existence as a state and was able to survive only as a liturgical congregation. P created his work in this situation. On the one hand, it places worship in the center of all history, and on the other it preserves for the new Israel, the Israel surviving as a liturgical congregation, the connection with its history, above all with its beginnings, while not relinquishing the universal horizon. The blessing bestowed by the priest in worship (Num. 6; Lev. 9) comes from the blessing with which God blessed creation (Gen. 1); worship as the goal of Israel's history comes from the sanctification of the seventh day of creation. The Law is also universally anchored in P. Everything that happens comes in P from the commanding word of God. That is the meaning of the schema permeating Genesis 1: God spoke—and it happened. In creation, God's commanding word is the source of everything that is. This commanding word of God, however, then also determines the entire history of the people of God. Thus God commands Abraham, along with his all-encompassing promise, to introduce circumcision (the pre-cultic ritual, Gen. 17). From his appearance in majesty (Exod. 24; 25) after the act of deliverance he commands the building of the tabernacle at Sinai, and in both cases the commandment is followed by the execution: "Thus he speaks, and thus it comes about." This is the real meaning of the Law in the middle of the priestly writing. Evaluations of the Law in the middle of the priestly writing do not normally pay adequate attention to the fact that in the Priestly Code it is overwhelmingly a law which orders and regulates worship and secures it for all time. This stands in contrast to the Covenant Code and the Deuteronomic Law, which draw in all spheres of existence into the Law, including the social, economic, and political. In this way, however, the Priestly Code becomes something new and different as opposed to the older laws. It serves primarily as the founding commandment given to Israel at Sinai through Moses, for the building of the sanctuary as the new center of Israel's life, a center which is to be secured, preserved, and fixed for all time by this law. It is a matter of preserving this holy occurrence and thus the connection with God for Israel. In this law, the commanding word of God which moves history acquires a form accessible to the people in Israel so that it can be carried out. The sanctuary is there to mediate this word.

Conclusion

We can ask now about the significance of these great historical works as a whole. In them we find the greatest and most significant theological accomplishments of ancient Israel. They serve to show with particular clarity what theology is in the Old Testament. There is an understanding of theology according to which all talk of God can be objectified, and according to which universal, timelessly valid statements, brought into a logical connection or system, are determinative for this talk of God. In contrast, the Old Testament speaks about God such that it says what has happened, what does happen, and what will happen between God and humanity. This can be confined to an event within the smallest possible temporal and spatial horizon, to a single experience of deliverance. It can be a composite of various occurrences within an extremely broad horizon. But one thing always remains the same: God is never abstracted to a conception of God, and there can be no doctrine of God. One can only speak about God as the one who speaks and acts. Everything one can say about God remains in the context of a reciprocal occurrence between God and world, God and his people, God and a single individual.

The uniqueness of the great historical works of the Old Testament consists in the fact that in them a profusion of extremely varied occurrences throughout long spans of time have been combined into a coherent arc of events. J and P demonstrate the broadest horizon because in them God's action and words encompasses the three circles: people of God—humanity—world. When they speak of God, they speak of the whole. This whole, however, can only be presented in the two as something which happens.

They portray narratively the fact that God is the same in all three circles and through long periods of time ("I am who I am"), and thus portray the oneness of God such that God's pledge in Genesis 8 is confirmed through the millennia, or such that God's promise comes true after a shorter or longer or even very long time: "I am who I am."

The great art of these historical works consists in its astonishing balance between constants and variables in talk about God. If these works are supposed to be concerned with real history, then change and variety must be a part of it. If God always did the same thing, there would be no history (Isa. 28). If God's action and words were definable by nominal concepts, that, too, would yield no history. The authors of these great works attain a portrayal of the variety and multifariousness of God's activity by reverently taking the language forms of the various epochs they present and integrating them into their work. They respect the portrayal of an individual event in the language of those who experienced it and leave it in its original form. They do not think according to concepts but according to events. There thus emerges a polyphony which as such is the mark of authenticity.

How is it then possible that these historical works present a coherent whole? It is only possible because God is *one* for them and because this one is involved with *everything* that happens. The unity and totality of these historical works is already given to the authors; they do not have to create it. Here lies the real meaning of the confession to the one God. Since God is one, he is not involved with gods or the divine, but only with what is created and what happens. With all his divine being he is turned solely towards his creation, his people, and individuals. Only in this way can we understand the astonishing dimensions of the historical works of the Old Testament. Because God is one, because he is the first and the last and beside him no God, his activity can embrace the totality of events in its entire multiplicity and in the entire richness of occurrences.

PART VI

The Old Testament and Jesus Christ[1]

Since we are concerned with the relationship of the entire Old Testament to Christ, we ought to start from the context of the Old Testament as a whole, the canon in its three parts. From what has already been seen, it can be assumed that this context is historical rather than theoretical. The Old as well as the New Testaments emerged from a history that actually occurred. It is then not possible to have a comprehensive concept of this relationship according to which the Old Testament deals with the Law, the New Testament with the gospel; or the Old Testament with the wrathful, the New Testament with the merciful God. A specific conceptual definition of the relationship which asks how the Old and New Testament speak about the Spirit of God, about sin and forgiveness, or about the world, retains its necessary significance, but remains subordinated to the question of what happened.

The Historical Books and Christ

Three Common, Fundamental Statements

The beginning of the Old Testament tells the story of a rescue (the book of Exodus as the nucleus of the Pentateuch). The beginning of the New Testament, in the Gospels, tells the story of a rescue. The prime declaration about God in the Old Testament, that God is the savior of Israel, persists even in the case of his relationship to the individual, as the Psalms demonstrate. Throughout the New Testament Christ is proclaimed as the savior. "There is salvation in no one else" declares the sermon of the first apostles (Acts 4:12). It is the saving God who acted in sending Christ. This, then, is a fundamental proclamation about God common to both the Old and the New Testaments. This proclamation of God as savior links the Old and New Testaments even though salvation here and there may mean something different.

There is a second statement which is also common to the Old and New Testaments: The savior of the people of God is simultaneously the creator of humanity and the creator of the world. This couches the history of the people of God in the history of humanity and the history of the world, from the creation of the world to its end. What the Old Testament says about God does not come to an end when the historical books of the Old Testament end. What the New Testament says about God does not just begin with the birth of Jesus. The activity of the creator remains the same in the Old as well as in the New Testament. What is said in Genesis 1—11 about God's relationship to the world and to humanity continues to be valid after Christ. It is presupposed by Christ when he speaks about the creator and the activity of the creator. That is why the New Testament can only speak of it in suggestions and allusions. God's history with his people cannot be separated in the Old and New Testament from the history of humanity and the world.

From this, however, emerges the third statement common to both the Old and New Testaments: Because the savior of the people of God is the creator of humanity and the creator of the world, he remains the Lord of both until the end. That is why both the Old and New Testaments speak in the apocalyptic texts about the end of human life and the end of the world as an act of the God who created them. God's activity, which began as a universal one, also ends as a universal one; to speak of God means to speak of the whole.

The Contrast Between the Old and New Testament

However, if one compares the history emerging from God's saving act in the Old and in the New Testament, a massive contrast between the Old and New Testament immediately steps into the foreground, a contrast based on the difference between God's saving act here and there. In the Old Testament, God's saving act inaugurates the history of a people which from the conquest up to the collapse is a nation based on political-military power as one nation among others. In the New Testament, God's act of salvation in Christ establishes a religious or cultic congregation void of political power, composed of followers from many peoples and similar to other cult-congregations within the Roman Empire. This constitutes an unequivocal contrast between the Old and New Testaments which must be fully acknowledged.

One can explain this difference inhering in the histories introduced by God's saving deed in the Old and New Testaments in various ways. If one understands it separated from history as that which in the Old and New Testaments is salvation, then the contrast practically forces itself on us. In the New Testament salvation is the redemption from sin and death through Christ, while in the Old Testament it is political liberation, the gift of the land, security and nourishment within the land. One can then easily conceptualize it as follows: In the Old Testament salvation consists of secular gifts, in the New Testament of spiritual gifts. When confronted with such generalizations, however, one always has the feeling that they crudely oversimplify the real state of affairs.

If one understands this contrast verbally, if one first asks what happens here and there, one must then start from what is common. In the Old as well as the New Testament God's saving act for his people stands at the beginning. The contrast in the emerging history is based first of all on the two different situations. One can carry the comparison through, however, only if one takes into consideration that only in the Old Testament, in the historical books, is the entire history of the people of God presented, and in the New Testament only the earliest beginnings of this history. We would have a real correspondence only if one added to Acts its continuation in church history.

In the New Testament we encounter the history of the people of God only in the earliest stage of the "wandering people of God," which corresponds to the stage of the former people of God in the wilderness sojourn. Here, too, we find clear correspondences. At the beginning of both the old as well as the new people of God, the message of deliverance starts a group of people on their way as a wandering people of God. Its form of existence is that of followers called away from settled existence. The wandering group which experienced deliverance from Egypt and was led on the path through the wilderness corresponds to the wandering group of disciples called by Jesus, who similarly followed him. In spite of essential differences, we still find parallel features. In both instances, the followers are dependent for their whole existence upon their leader. And in both instances, this following includes the experience of miracles, of deliverance, and of preservation. Here as well as there, obedience is identical with following. There is only the pointing out of the way, and the one sin is that of divergence (John 6:61f.). The transmission of the wilderness wandering tradition was intended to leave open the possibility of a new call out of settled life. This possibility was indeed realized during the time of the exile. In the history of Christendom, too, such periods were of special significance, periods in which the calling returned into a following which drew in one's entire way of life.

There is no correspondence in the New Testament to what then follows in the Old Testament historical books from the transition to settled life onward. It is indeed alluded to in the later New Testament writings, but it takes place only in church history. That is why we find no direct correspondences between the largest portion of the historical books of the Old to the New Testament. Only in church history does what the Old Testament historical books treat take place. The people of God or the church develop various, changing relationships with the other spheres of existence, to the various community forms such as the state, the economic forms, culture, education, art, and so on. In some stages the Christian church became as closely connected with the power of the state as did Israel during the monarchy, and in other stages political wars of liberation were waged in the name of the God of Christendom just as the wars of liberation in Israel's early period were waged in the name of Yahweh.

From the post-Christ perspective, the Old Testament historical books then acquire the function of showing the way of the people of God in its relationship to the other spheres of historical occurrences. Even if these relationships for all practical purposes do not come up at all in the New Testament, the path of the church is unthinkable without them. One unique feature of the Old Testament historical books is that in them all the community forms essential to human history come up during the sojourn of the people of God through the history portrayed there: the family, tribe (and tribal confederation), the people in the form of state, and the cultic congregation in the province of a large empire. We encounter all of these in the history of the church as well as economic and cultural movements and changes, all of which influence this history. In view of this, it was one-sided when through the Middle Ages all the way to the present in Christian theology one only considered the relationship between the church and state. It was one-sided if in doing so one only referred to a few passages in the New Testament such as Romans 13, while at the same time one neglected the prehistory of the relationship of the people of God to the state in the Old Testament.

God's Activity in Blessing in the New Testament

The transition to secure a settled life in the Old Testament, and later the transition to the state, is theologically characterized by the fact that God's saving work is combined with his activity in blessing. Since this transition in the New Testament stands only on the periphery, no attention has been paid to God's blessing activity in Christ. One considered "Christology" to be identical with "Soteriology." In the Gospels, however, God's saving activity very definitely has its place. It comes to expression in the fact that Jesus worked not only among his disciples, but also among the people in the cities and villages through which he traveled. Not enough attention is usually paid to the fact that Jesus only called a very few to follow him. The rest, for whom he worked, to whom he spoke, and whom he healed, he sent back home to their former life. The Gospels tell of a Jesus who encouraged those he met in their normal lives while he walked among them as healer, protector of life, and spiritual guide. A large part of Jesus' words and deeds belong in the context of his activity in blessing. This is particularly clear in the case of the parables, which speak of the coming of the kingdom of God in organic images of growth and maturity. A conscious association of the eventful with the constant is revealed in the message of Jesus here. The kingdom of God comes not only in events such as saving or conversion, but also in a gradual process of quiet growth. The same thing is shown in the double commission of Jesus in Matthew 10: proclamation and healing. It is shown in a different fashion in the farewell speeches in the Gospel of John, which are characterized by this constant, enduring quality (John 13—17).

What is only alluded to in the New Testament comes to full and unmistakable expression in the history of the church: the transition to a settled form of existence. The church could not remain a missionary activity but had to become a settled institution. This is shown particularly by the worship service. With the sedentary inclination of the church, it, too, adapted to the fixed form of worship with the holy place, holy time, and the mediator of the holy, along with the festivals in the rhythm of the natural year. This is a repetition of what happened in a similar fashion in the history of Israel's worship.

The Prophetic Message and Christ

The Prophecy of Judgment and Christ

It was the traditional interpretation that the significance of prophecy for the coming of Christ was that the prophets had announced it, and the fulfillment that the New Testament announces confirms the promise of Christ in the prophets. However, if the significance of prophecy for the coming of Christ consisted only of that, then it would have nothing to do with the central task of the prophets—the announcement of God's judgment on his people Israel. If there is any relationship of prophecy to Christ, then it must be explained in the light of the central function of the prophets. The relationship is that prophecy explains how things proceeded from the deliverance at the beginning (Exodus) to God's saving act in Christ. We have established the contrast between the two above. Now, things are not such that the Old Testament reports a series of God's saving acts in which it is a matter of external goods (liberation from enemies, land, security), whereas the New Testament reports God's saving act which in contrast is concerned only with spiritual goods. We have seen on the contrary that God's saving acts in the Old Testament stand within a historical movement leading to the New Testament. From the settlement onward, the danger to Israel's existence is no longer primarily the threat from political enemies, but rather the threat of defection from Yahweh, Israel's God. The prophets stepped in against this threat and the announcement of judgment to which they were commissioned was concerned with this threat. This of necessity resulted in the fact that, after the arrival of the judgment announced by the prophets, any deliverance of the remnant was only possible if associated with forgiveness.

The prophets were mediators of the word who were powerless in their ministry. Not one prophet attempted to exercise power in either a direct or indirect sense. In their function as messengers they had to make accusations against the people, and on the basis of these accusations to announce the coming of judgment upon those people. The fact that they encountered resistance in this is understandable. None of the prophets met with complete and thoroughgoing success in his message. The word which they had to announce was rejected. This rejection caused the prophets of judgment to suffer, not only by persecution but also by the awareness of their lack of success (Isa. 49:4). It is this connection between the prophets' message of judgment and their subsequent suffering that points toward Christ. But if the prophets' message of judgment died away apparently without effect, the suffering of the messengers of judgment acquired significance. In the line of prophets, the suffering of the last in line, Jeremiah, stands out so prominently that his laments (in chs. 11—20) become a main part of his message.

These laments continue in the songs of the suffering servant in Deutero-Isaiah. They announce something which up till then was not present in the Old Testament: the possibility of a new existence through the atoning suffering of an individual (Isa. 53). Whether the event is in the past, present, or future remains undecided. The redemption of the sins of the people through God's servant points to an event which cannot be fixed unequivocally in the Old Testament. When the title "Servant of the Lord" is applied to Christ in the New Testament, this justifiably corresponds to our present-day scientific understanding of these texts. The portrayal of Jesus in the New Testament has its closest contact with the Old in this correspondence. It exists between, on the one hand, the working of God's servant solely through the word, his suffering until death, his confirmation by God despite death or through and beyond death, and, on the other, the suffering, death, and resurrection of Jesus. In Isaiah 53, the chorus of those affected by the suffering and death of God's servant confesses that they at first falsely interpreted this new act of God as God's punishment (Isa. 53:4). This shows that even this new act demanded a complete change in thinking.

But the songs of the servant are not a random prophecy in the Old Testament pointing to Christ, but are rather the final stage of the history of pre-exilic prophecy and can be understood only within the context of this history. This context is expressly alluded to in one of the servant songs, Isaiah 49:1-6. In this song, the servant complains that he has striven in vain to bring Israel back to God. This complaint points back to the apparently fruitless work of the prophets of judgment before the exile. The servant of the Lord sees himself in the line of the prophets, even if he himself has another task. In spite of this complaint, however, his task is even further extended: "I will give you as a light to the nations" (Isa. 49:6). The servant's task is no longer limited to Israel. This corresponds, on the one hand, to the largely unrecognized fact that, outside the servant songs, Deutero-Isaiah has already announced an extension of Israel's salvation to the other nations. It corresponds, on the other hand, to the message of the New Testament that the work of Christ is valid for all of humanity.

The Prophecy of Salvation and Christ

In the prophecy of salvation, no such unequivocal relationship to the person and work of Christ can be recognized. The prophetic announcement of salvation heralds an event which must stand in a relationship to the situation in which the announcement is made. For this reason, the Immanuel prophecy in Isaiah 7:14 cannot refer to the birth of Christ: "A young woman shall conceive and bear a son and shall call his name Immanuel." What Isaiah announces here is protection from the approaching enemy. The birth of the child is a sign which is supposed to confirm the fulfillment of this announcement.

A distant allusion to Christ can be found in those oracles of salvation which announce something new that extends beyond the history of the people of God in the Old Testament. Thus Isaiah announces in an oracle of judgment a different future act of God dealing with the "scoffers who rule this people in Jerusalem": "Behold, I lay for a foundation in Zion a stone, a precious cornerstone . . . he who believes shall not be defeated" (Isa. 28:14-22, author's translation). Following the judgment, obedience to God will be grounded in faith, as in 1 Peter 2:4-6. Jeremiah 31:31-34 also points beyond the history of the people of the Old Covenant: God proclaims that he will make a new covenant with his people which will be completely different from the one broken by Israel. Even though with the coming of Christ not everything was fulfilled which is described here as the new covenant, one can still say that this message about the new covenant points to Christ. Nevertheless, neither of these two passages acts as a direct announcement of the coming of Christ.

Among the descriptions of future salvation in the post-exilic period, the messianic prophecies, about which we have already spoken within the context of kingship, require special mention. They acquired special significance in the New Testament and in the history of Christianity. Because Jesus received the title of messiah, the prophecies of a king for the salvation period were fulfilled in him. But what is said in these prophecies has little connection with Christ. Suffering has no significance for the king of the salvation period, and there is no mention of salvation through forgiveness. Here the king is much more a dispenser of blessing than of salvation. The songs of the suffering servant in Deutero-Isaiah point more directly to Jesus of Nazareth than do the messianic prophecies.

The main center of gravity in the relation between salvation prophecy and Jesus Christ lies in the history of the promise as a whole, not in individual sayings which may or may not point to Christ. The way of the promise through the Old Testament begins with the promises to the patriarchs and continues with the oracles of salvation spoken by prophets, known and unknown, through the time of the exile and later on. Understood in this way, the manifold promises with manifold content are signposts on the way pointing to a future expected from the mercy of God. It is essential for this way of the promise through the Old Testament that it meets the other way, that of the oracles of judgment or of judgment prophecy, at a certain point: in the prophecy of Deutero-Isaiah, who is a salvation prophet himself but who can be understood only in the line of the preceding judgment prophecy.

Three stages can now be recognized in the history of God's saving acts: the rescue in the beginning, founded upon the mercy of God toward his suffering people; the deliverance from the Babylonian exile, based on forgiveness in light of the preceding history of apostasy; the deliverance from sin and death in Christ, which introduces the history of the new people of God and which took place for the benefit of all humanity. With the liberation of Israel from exile, God's deliverance was already divorced from political power. Israel was saved, but did not regain its power as a state. Only these three stages can present what the Bible says about God as the savior. The message of Christ as savior is based on that which the Old Testament says about God as savior. What the New Testament says about the deliverance from sin and death through the work of Christ would be incomprehensible without the experience of physical deliverance from the threat of death. There would be no confession to Christ as the savior from sin and death if there were no thanksgiving offered by those delivered from the threat of death. That is why God in the New Testament still remains the savior from the physical threat of death, as shown in the Gospel narratives, and in the life of Christendom, as shown by the hymns which offer thanksgiving for the deliverance from the threat of death.

Christ and the Response of God's People

The Response in Words in Its Relationship to Christ

The history recounted in the Old Testament is a history of interaction between God and humanity. The response of those for whom God acts and to whom God speaks is an integral part of this history. For this reason the Psalms are an essential part of the Old Testament, and one should perhaps ask whether in them, too, any relation can be found to what the New Testament says about Christ.

The New Testament portrayal of the Passion of Jesus shows an especially marked correspondence to Psalm 22. The frequency of quotations from this Psalm shows that the early Christian congregations had observed a striking similarity between the two. If this was regarded in the New Testament and in early Christianity in the sense of a prophecy, it must nevertheless be asked whether, regardless of this view, an agreement still exists when the Psalm is understood not as a prophecy but rather as was really intended, as a prayer. In any case, this original meaning of the Psalm is implied by Jesus' cry from the cross, which is definitely a call of prayer (Ps. 22:2 = Mark 15:34; Matt. 27:46). In the Psalms the lament of being forsaken by God is an expression of grievous, inescapable suffering. The accusation of God very frequently expresses in the Psalms of lamentation what we, in secular language, call despair, the experience of the abyss of meaninglessness.

When Jesus employs these words on the cross, he enters into the manifold experience of suffering among his people. Thus, he is no more than a sufferer among sufferers. Representative suffering is also suffering *with* those who suffer. Jesus takes up in his lament the same language of pain which was shaped by many individuals over many generations. He not only died for sinners but died for sufferers as well. His work, all the way to this abyss of meaninglessness, was done for the sake of human suffering. The work and suffering of Jesus are not only a part of the history of the mediator, as we have seen in the context of prophecy. They are equally a part of the long line of anonymous human suffering.

In addition to this, we encounter a whole host of quotations from Psalm 22 in the Passion narrative. This makes it clear that the entire Psalm is being referred by these individual quotations. Among the many Psalms of lamentation, this one is distinctive in that, in its second part, it develops into a Psalm of praise. The turning point in the suffering of the lamenting person finds expression in a praise of God which looks back upon the deliverance from impending death. If, however, the Psalm is meant in the quotations from Psalm 22 in the Passion narrative of Jesus, then the sequence of suffering, death, and resurrection is also meant as *one* context. If, however, the structure of Psalm 22 underlies the Passion narrative, then Jesus' resurrection must have belonged together with the suffering and death. Hence, there never was a tradition of the suffering and death of Jesus without any indication of this turning point. The fourth servant song has the same structure. Here, too, God's Yes to the servant, even beyond death, follows the report of his suffering and death.

Jesus' adoption of the lament of the suffering, however, also brought about a change. Christ also died for his enemies, and from the cross he also pleaded for forgiveness for them. The request concerning the enemies, the request for the destruction of the unrighteous, which was an integral part of the Psalms of lamentation, are thus done away with. With Christ we no longer have the possibility of the righteous being saved by the ruin of the unrighteous.

In the *Psalms of praise* one can recognize a relationship in form and content to what the New Testament says about Christ. A more formal relationship can be found in the Psalms of thanksgiving or narrative Psalms of praise. The experience of rescue has the same sequence of events in both cases. This is manifest in the structure of the Psalms. After the announcement (e.g., "I will praise you . . . ") and an introductory summary comes the retrospective view of distress, and the report of rescue is in three steps: I called out—he heard—he saved me. The Psalm closes with renewed vows of praise and/or praise of God (e.g., Pss. 18; 30; 40; 66:13-20). The songs of praise in Luke 1:28-75 and 2:29-32, in which God is praised as the one who sent the savior of his people, are similar to this structure. The equivalent in the hymns of the church is even clearer, as in Luther's Reformation hymn: "Now Rejoice, All Ye Christian People" which corresponds point for point to the narrative of praise, or in the fourth verse of the song by J. J. Schütz, "Sing Praise to God Who Reigns Above." This equivalence confirms that, in the Old Testament as in the New, God's saving act receives the same response.

An equivalence to the structure of the narrative Psalm of praise can also be seen in the structure of the letter to the Romans, although it must naturally be taken into consideration that this letter is characterized by theological reflection. It deals with God's saving act in Christ. After the announcement in 1:14f. comes the introductory statement in 1:16f., the retrospective view of distress in 1:18—3:20, and the report of saving in 3:21—8:39. The three elements of this report, I called—he heard—he saved, characterize the seventh chapter. The similarity to the Psalms of praise is also shown in the final call of praise to God in the eighth chapter. The beginning of the section of exhortation, chapters 12:1f., echoes the renewed vow of praise.

A correspondence based more on content is presented by the descriptive Psalms of praise or hymns. They summarize what the Old Testament says about God's compassion. It is not a timeless quality of God but rather what a person experiences in relation to God. Amazed and moved, the congregation praises the God who turns in compassion towards them from his distant majesty: "Who is like the LORD our God, in the heavens and upon the earth, who is seated on high, who looks far down . . . ?" (Ps. 113:5f., author's translation). It is this amazing joy at God's bending down to the depths of human suffering and human sin which finds similar expression in the New Testament in reference to the coming of Christ: "Blessed be the Lord God of Israel, for he has visited and redeemed his people" (Luke 1:68). The Christ hymn in Philippians 2 may also be compared with this. Once again, it is the hymns of the church in which this note is taken up, especially the songs of the incarnation, the Christmas hymns: "God gives, to prevent our suffering, his son from the throne of his power and glory." Christianity sees in the incarnation the ultimate revelation of God, who came down from the majesty of his divine being into the depths of human suffering and sin.

A totally different relation appears in the imperative call of praise which either introduces the Psalm of praise or permeates it. It has the tendency to expand. At first, only the worshiping congregation is called to praise. Then, however, all the kings of the earth, all nations and parts of the earth, and indeed all creatures are called. God's work is so marvelous and so powerful that it must resound to the limits of all creation. God's act in Christ is spoken of in the same way in the book of Acts, and the missionary impulse is the same: to spread God's mighty acts over the whole earth.

From what has been said regarding the relationship between Psalms of lament and praise to Christ, we can now draw a conclusion concerning prayer. If in contrast to the Old Testament the New Testament contains no collection of prayers (or songs), one reason is that there was not enough time for an equivalent collection to develop. Another is that the Psalter at first remained the prayer book of young Christianity, just as was the case for Christ. A certain type of prayer, however, then gradually emerged in the Christian church which was essentially different from the prayer of the Psalms. The Psalm prayer continued to be used in worship. We need to ask, however, whether this juxtaposition, to a large extent still unexplained, should not be studied anew and a greater significance attributed, as regards the Christian prayer as well, to the Psalm prayers with their more intense immediacy of calling to God in the polarity of lament and praise.

The Response in Action in Its Relationship to Christ

This element of the Old Testament has been seen as decisive for the relationship of the Old Testament to Christ, particularly in Paul and after him in Christian theology. Indeed, it functions as a contrast. It was rooted in Jewish theology in the centuries before Christ, this theology being the "spiritual homeland" of Paul, but it was not actually present in the Old Testament itself. Paul's contrast between the two ways of salvation, through works of the Law and through the saving work of Christ, has no foundation in the Old Testament. There is not a single context in the Old Testament in which the Law is depicted as a means of salvation. Usually Deuteronomy is cited in this connection; the obedience of the people to the commandments, rules, and laws is made the condition of Israel's welfare in the promised land. But observance of the Law in Dueteronomy is not tied to salvation, but rather to the people's well-being, namely the blessing in the promised land. The commandments and laws belong to another theological context in the Old Testament, that of reaction, of obedience. The fulfillment of the commandments and laws is not an action which will achieve deliverance or salvation, but is rather the action of those who have experienced God's salvation, as the structure of the book of Exodus points out.

There is yet another point at which the Pauline doctrine of the Law does not correspond to the Old Testament. Paul includes both commandment and law under the concept of "Law." He took this over from his Jewish teachers, and it corresponds to the latest usage of *torah* in the Old Testament. Prior to this, however, the Old Testament distinguishes quite clearly between commandments and laws (see above pp. 175ff.). They also have a quite different theological significance. From this perspective we must also make a distinction between what Paul calls "Law" and Jesus' commandment. The church drew this distinction in practice between commandment and law and this is shown by the fact that the Ten Commandments remained indisputably valid. As important as this juxtaposition of law and gospel is for Paul's theological situation, it cannot be decisive for the definition of the relationship of the Old Testament to Christ on the whole. The existence of God's people rests, in the Old Testament as well as in the New, on the saving act of God. Likewise, in both cases obedience to the commandments of God and of Christ, respectively, is part of the reaction of those who have experienced salvation.

The New Testament says very little about worship. None of the Christian forms of worship has developed solely on the basis of the New Testament, since they all belong to the settled church. The act of worship in Christianity can only be based on the whole Bible, the Bible of the Old and of the New Testaments. However, if this is acknowledged, then it necessarily follows that one can also understand the act of worship only from its history. There is no such thing as a totally unchangeable act of worship, since it cannot be extracted from the history of God's people and the church. To be sure, the constant elements are determinative in the cult of all religions, but it must also contain variable elements which are dependent upon historical changes. If this is seen, then the act of worship, in its constant elements which are common to many forms of worship, could have a function which links more strongly than it separates.

Conclusion: The Question of a Biblical Theology

What we have found in investigating the relationship of the Old Testament to Christ are not conceptual relations and contrasts but rather correspondences or contrasts which relate to a sequence of events, a history between God and humanity. This history, with which both the Old and New Testaments deal, occurs in two circles: the wider, which stretches from the creation to the end of the world, and the more limited one, which is the history of God with a specific section of humanity, the people of God. The Old and New Testaments deal with the history of the wider circle. Both speak about the God who created heaven and earth and who ultimately leads the world and humanity to a final goal. And both deal with the narrower circle which has two sections, the first treated in the Old Testament, the second treated in the New. The history of God's people in the Old Testament leads away from power and toward salvation on the basis of forgiveness. The new people of God can no longer preserve its existence by means of victories over other peoples, but rather only through its existence *for* the rest of humanity, as was already suggested by the servant songs in Deutero-Isaiah. The same transformation occurs in the case of the saving of the individual through God. Because Christ died on the cross even for his enemies, the charge of the pious against their enemies is dismissed. The saving of the faithful no longer implies death for nonbelievers. This also removes the curse from the suffering of believers. The book of Job already allows the new insight emerge that human suffering does not have to be God's curse or punishment. It acquires a positive meaning through the suffering of Christ.

In the history recounted by the Old Testament we can thus see a movement toward a goal which points to what the New Testament says about Christ. In the light of Christ a Yes and Amen are spoken to the Old Testament as the way which leads to this goal. At the same time, with Christ a No is spoken to that which, through the work of Christ, is overcome and now ended: the association of God's salvation with power which is also the power of destruction, and the association of the salvation of the individual with the request against the unrighteous which aims at his destruction.

This Yes to the Old Testament from the perspective of Christ, and this No to the Old Testament from the perspective of Christ, however, are not dogmatic and not theoretical, but are rather historical. One cannot say that what the New Testament says about God is correct, and what the Old Testament says false. That part of what the Old Testament says about God which has come to an end is done away with by the historical event of the coming of Christ as God's final word and final act.

Then the history of the church or the history of the Christian churches becomes a section of the whole history of God with his people between the coming of Christ and his return, which must be seen in the light of the *entire* Bible. From the perspective of the whole Bible, we then need to ask whether the period in church history in which the church once again became associated with power is not a regression behind the extraction of the people of God from political power, as already shown in Deutero-Isaiah. The question should then be directed to New Testament theologians whether it is not possible to return from an intellectual and conceptual structure of New Testament theology to a verb-dominated or historical structure to present what happens in the New Testament between God and humanity. The first step toward this would be the recognition that what happened is more important than what was thought about it. What the New Testament says about Christ also has essentially the form of a report or story: first in the Gospels, which lead up to the death and resurrection of Christ, and then in the Book of Acts, which starts from the death and resurrection of Christ and is directed toward Christ's return, with which Revelation also deals. Here, too, there is a correspondence to the Old Testament which should not be overlooked. While the Old Testament points from creation beyond the history of God's people to the "center of time," the New points from the center of time to the end of time. Thus Old and New Testaments belong together so that, side by side, they can report the history of God with his people and can place this history into the broader horizon of the history of God with humanity and with the world.

If this basic historical structure of what the Old and New Testaments say about God were recognized in Old as well as in New Testament studies, we could return to a biblical theology which included the Old as well as the New Testament and which was based upon both. A biblical theology is necessary for the incipient ecumenical era of the Christian churches.

Abbreviations

AnBibl	*Analecta Biblica*
ATANT	*Abhandlungen zur Theologie des Alten und Neuen Testaments*
ATD	*Das Alte Testament Deutsch*
AzTh	*Arbeiten zur Theologie*
BBB	*Bonner Biblische Beiträge*
BEvTh	*Beiträge zur Evangelischen Theologie*
BHHW	*Biblisch-Historisches Handwörterbuch*
BK	*Biblischer Kommentar* (Neukirchen)
BSt	*Biblische Studien* (Münster)
BWANT	*Beiträge zur Wissenschaft vom Alten und Neuen Testament*
BWMANT	*Wissenschaftliche Monographien zum Alten und Neuen Testament, Beiheft*
BZAW	*Beihefte zur Zeitschrift für die alttestamentliche Wissenschaft*
EvTH	*Evangelische Theologie*
Festschr.	*Festschrift*
FRLANT	*Forschungen zur Religion und Literatur des Alten und Neuen Testaments*
Ges. Aufs.	*Gesammelte Aufsätze*
Ges. Stud.	*Gesammelte Studien*
HAT	*Handbuch zum Alten Testament* (Hg. O. Eißfeldt)
IDB	*The Interpreter's Dictionary of the Bible* (1962)
Interp	*Interpretation*
KD	Karl Barth, *Die kirchliche Dogmatik*
KlSchr.	*Kleine Schriften*
KuD	*Kerygma und Dogma*
NKZ	*Neue Kirchliche Zeitschrift*
RGG	*Die Religion in Geschichte und Gegenwart*
SBS	*Stuttgarter Bibelstudien*
SKG	*Schriften der Königsberger Gelehrten Gesellschaft*. Geisteswissenschaftliche Klasse
StBTh	*Studies in Biblical Theology*
THAT	*Theologisches Handwörterbuch zum Alten Testament* (Jenni/Westermann)
ThB	*Theologische Bücherei*
TheolEx	*Theolgische Existenz heute*
ThR	*Theologische Rundschau*
ThSt	*Theologische Studien*
ThZ	*Theologische Zeitschrift* (Basel)

TTKi	*Tidsskrift for Teologi og Kirke*
WR	*Wege der Forschung* (Darmstadt)
WMANT	*Wissenschaftliche Monographien zum Alten und Neuen Testament*
ZAW	*Zeitschrift für die Alttestamentliche Wissenschaft*
ZDPV	*Zeitschrift des Deutschen Palästina-Vereins*
ZThK	*Zeitschrift für Theologie und Kirche*

Notes

Part I

1. G. von Rad, *Old Testament Theology*, p. 127f.; R. Smend, ThSt 101; G. F. Hasel, ZAW 86; W. Zimmerli, EvTh 35.
2. B. S. Childs points to the significance of the canon for OT theology; see also G. W. Coats–B. O. Long.
3. The history of OT theology can show how difficult it is to present the variety of Old Testament talk about God as a whole. E. Würthwein gives an overview, ThR NF 36, 3.
4. See pp. 85f.; cf. C. Westermann, BK I/1, pp. 436-467 concerning Genesis 4:17-26, and ThB 55, pp. 149-161; similarly: W. Zimmerli, *Old Testament Theology in Outline*, p. 141f.
5. M. Buber, *I and Thou* and *Schriften über das dialogische Prinzip:* also H. H. Schrey, *Erträge der Forschung* 1.
6. F. Hesse, KuD 4; same author, ZThK 57 and G. von Rad, introduction to the fourth edition of his *Old Testament Theology*.
7. A. Alt, Josua, K1Schr. I, pp. 176-192; M. Noth, RGG³ II, pp. 1498-1501.
8. The classic presentation is by K. von Hofmann. F. Delitzsch gives a good explanation in brief form in *Gen. Komm.,* pp. 277-284.
9. This understanding of the word is shown with particular clarity in the Proverbs which deal with the word, as e.g.: "A word spoken at the proper time is like golden apples in a silver husk," as well as Prov. 12:18; 15:23; 16:24; 24:26; 25:12; and others.
10. Concerning this tradition, see pp. 206f.
11. C. Westermann, ed., *Probleme alttestamentlicher Hermeneutik.* ThB 11 (1960); cf. there particularly R. Bultmann, *Weissagung und Erfüllung*, pp. 28-53, and W. Zimmerli, *Verheißung und Erfüllung*, pp. 69-101. In addition, A. H. J. Gunneweg, *Understanding the Old Testament: A Study in Hermeneutics.*
12. As regards the termini *nir'ah* and *niglah,* cf. the article in THAT II.
13. Gerhard von Rad's theology also takes into consideration the fact that human response belongs to what the Old Testament says about God, Vol. I, concerning Israel's Response; see also W. Zimmerli IV, *Life Before God,* section 16 "The Response of Obedience," and section 17 "Praise of Yahweh and Cry for Help."
14. It is significant that L. Köhler writes the following in the foreword of his *Old Testament Theology:* "Only one chapter, that on the cult, was difficult to place." There is no independent section on the cult in the theology of von Rad and W.

Zimmerli; in G. Fohrer as well as in L. Köhler it is viewed negatively as human work.

15. This corresponds to the same distinction in the word of God; see pp. 15ff.

Part II

1. Cf. the listing in M. Noth (1972), pp. 47-50.
2. Particularly *nṣl* and *jš'* both hi. Concerning this, cf. the appropriate articles in THAT I, pp. 785-790 and II, pp. 96-99.
3. C. Westermann, ThB 24, pp. 306-335.
4. It is precisely this state of affairs which has been obscured by the ordinary concepts. If one speaks of redemption *(Heil)* then the distinction is evident: The redemption *(Heil)* of which the Old Testament speaks is something other than the redemption of which the New Testament speaks. But when one speaks of the salvation of God *(Retten Gottes)* then it is evident what both have in common, that the Old Testament like the New Testament speaks of salvation *(Retten)* or of the saving acts *(rettenden Handeln)* of God.
5. Amos 3:2: "You only have I known *(jada'ti)* of all the families of the earth; therefore I will punish you for all your iniquities." *Jada'ti* should be translated as "elected" (L. Köhler had already objected to this); "known" is to be understood in the sense of recognition in the encounter.
6. This occurred particularly in the Old Testament theology of W. Eichrodt, which was extremely influential. A revitalization of "Covenant Theology" was prompted by the archaeological discovery of the Hittite contract formulations, which were viewed as the religious-historical background for the OT references to a covenant between God and the people. D. J. McCarthy has reviewed the profusion of literature concerning this (see bibliography). Among others, the dissertation of D. G. Spriggs (1974) shows the influence on OT theology.
7. Concerning the meaning of the word *berit*, cf. A. Jepsen, *Festschrift W. Rudolph,* who renders the word as "solemn pledge, promise, obligation," and a series of works by E. Kutsch, collected in THAT I, 339-352, which renders it as "obligation." Additional bibliography included.
8. Concerning this L. Perlitt, pp. 55-77 and C. Westermann, BK I/2 concerning Genesis 15 (in preparation); further bibliography in both instances.
9. R. Smend, ThSt 68; R. Kraetzschmar, L. Perlitt, pp. 101-115, Deut. 26:16-19 and the Covenant Formulation, also further bibliography.
10. "They recapitulate the main events of the saving history from the time of the patriarch . . . down to the conquest," *Old Testament Theology,* Vol. I, p. 122. Neither could I say with M. Noth that the great themes of the Pentateuch tradition are summarized here (1972, pp. 46-47).
11. Concerning this text, see G. von Rad, *The Problem of the Hexateuch* and L. Rost (1965).
12. L. Rost, ZDPV 66 = 1965, pp. 101-112.
13. A. Alt, "Josua" (1936).
14. W. Richter, BBB 21.

15. L. Rost, BWANT 42; G. v. Rad, NKZ 31.
16. Concerning the terms, cf. R. Albertz' article on *pl'* in THAT I, pp. 413-420; concerning the complex as a whole, cf. G. Quell, *Festschrift W. Rudolph*, further bibliography in both.
17. Concerning this, J. Jeremias, WMANT 10; C. Westermann, *The Praise of God in the Psalms*, pp. 93-101.
18. S. Hermann, BWANT 5, 5; W. Zimmerli, ThB 11.
19. Cf. C. Westermann, ThB 55, pp. 230-249.
20. G. von Rad, ThB 8, pp. 87-100.
21. For further discussion, C. Westermann, *The Promises to the Fathers*.
22. G. von Rad, *Genesis*, concerning this passage, and H. W. Wolff, ThB22.
23. G. v. Rad (1951) and R. Smend, FRLANT 84.
24. R. Albertz (1978).
25. H. D. Preuβ, ZAW 80; D. Vetter, AzTh 1, p. 45, 1971.
26. BK I/1, pp. 606-614 concerning Genesis 8:20-22.
27. H. Wildberger, article about *'mm* in THAT I, pp. 177-209; further bibliography there.
28. The figure of Joshua was formed as the successor to Moses though that is an undertaking from a later perspective.
29. Cf. the varying evaluation of the historicity of Moses in Israel's history by M. Noth and S. Hermann; also R. Smend (1959).
30. K. Koch, KuD 8.
31. W. Zimmerli, ThB 19, pp. 11-40.
32. R. Albertz-C. Westermann, article about *ruah* (spirit), THAT II, pp. 726-753; further bibliography there.
33. C. Westermann, ThB 55, pp. 291-308.
34. Among many others, M. Buber, *The Prophetic Faith*.
35. Concerning the preliminary history of prophecy, see C. Westermann, "Propheten" BHHW III (1966), pp. 1496-1512; further bibliography there.
36. Concerning this text, see C. Westermann, *Isaiah 40–66* regarding the various passages; S. Mowinckel (1959), pp. 187-260; G. von Rad, *Old Testament Theology*, Vol. II, p. 238f.

Part III

1. C. Westermann BK I/1, Genesis 1—11, further bibliography there for Genesis 1—11 as a whole and concerning specific sections; a report on the status of scholarship can be found in "Erträge der Forschung" 7 and ThB 55, pp. 96-114.
2. W. Beyerlin, ed., *Near Eastern Religious Texts Relating to the Old Testament*, particularly pp. 3-11 and 74-84.
3. R. Albertz, Weltschöpfung und Menschenschöpfung (1974).
4. This is discussed more thoroughly in ThB 55, pp. 96-114. The parallels are discussed in Beyerlin, *Near Eastern Religious Texts*, pp. 85-97.
5. BK I/1, Introduction, pp. 26-65.

6. My supporting arguments for what follows can be found in my commentary BK I/1; further bibliography there.

7. BK I/1, pp. 52-57; K. Koch, ZThK 62.

8. Concerning this see C. Westermann, *Festschrift für W. Zimmerli,* pp. 479-497.

9. In O. Loretz, SBS 32, pp. 20-30; also D. Ritschl, Ges. Aufs I, pp. 102-122.

10. Concerning this, see J. Bauer, ed. (1977); in the same collection: C. Westermann, pp. 5-18.

11. The same view in Job 31:38-40.

12. Concerning *dominium terrae* see G. Liedke, *Stud. zur Friedensforschung* 8, pp. 40-56.

13. Concerning the form and subject of wisdom oracles see ThB 55, pp. 149-161.

14. So also W. Zimmerli, ThB 19, pp. 300-315.

15. The relationship between greeting and blessing is also shown in the fact that both have universal character.

16. BK I/2 concerning Gen. 12:1-3; further bibliography there.

17. G. von Rad also suggests this, BWANT 47.

18. One should not underestimate the significance of the annually recurring festivals; as such, they point to God's perpetual action. The worship services recurring annually have a stronger affinity with God's perpetual action, even though one-time events are celebrated there.

19. Concerning this, cf. S. Mowinckel, *He That Cometh* (1952); 2nd ed. 1959, pp. 155-186.

20. Cf. G. Gerlemann, article on *ślm,* "having enough," THAT II, pp. 919-935; further bibliography p. 921.

21. M. Saeboe, article on *ṣlḥ,* THAT II, pp. 551-556.

22. ThB 55, pp. 191-196 and M. Saeboe's article *'pr pi.,* "to praise joyfully," THAT I, pp. 257-260.

23. Cf. the bibliography given in my commentary (note 1), and also Beyerlin, *Near Eastern Religious Texts* pp. 3-11 and pp. 74-84; key word "creation."

Part IV

1. Cf. R. Knierim (1965) and by the same author the article in THAT I, pp. 541-549: *ḥṭ'* "to err" and THAT II, pp. 243-249: *'awon* "folly," pp. 488-495: *paša'* "crime."

2. *Theological Dictionary of the New Testament,* Vol. I (1933), pp. 267-335, Quell, Grundmann, Rengstorf.

3. C. Westermann, KuD 13.

4. C. Westermann, BK I/1, pp. 66-77.

5. We encounter it as an argument in the dialogue section of the book of Job 4:12-21; 9:2; 15:14-16; 25:4-6, which the friends present and Job agrees with. As a motif in the Psalm of lament Ps. 143:2, cf. C. Westermann, Hiob . . . , 2nd ed. (1977), pp. 102-104.

6. Only for this reason is forgiveness possible for the entire people, as announced by Deutero-Isaiah.

7. BK I/2, *Die Religion der Patriarchen*, pp. 116-128.

8. K. Koch, ed., WF 125.

9. The relationship between sin and punishment is also shown by the fact that the word *awon* (folly, sin) can mean punishment in certain contexts.

10. J. J. Stamm, article on *slḥ*, "to forgive" in THAT II, pp. 150-160.

11. G. von Rad, *Old Testament Theology*, Vol. II, "Theology of Israel's Prophetic Tradition."

12. ThB 24, pp. 171-188.

13. Article "Propheten," BHHW, pp. 1496-1512.

14. Discussed more thoroughly in *Basic Forms of Prophetic Speech.*

15. ThB 55, pp. 291-308, particularly pp. 298-311.

16. In the comparison between the accusations directed to Israel and those directed against the nations we see the difference between sins common to all people and the sins of Israel, which presuppose the relationship to Yahweh. The accusations against the nations all correspond to the narratives of guilt and punishment in Genesis 1—11.

17. The most important transcending context in which the talk of God's compassion has its place is the descriptive Psalm of praise (hymnos), in which God is praised in his majesty and goodness after the Psalm's imperative introduction; see Part V. Concerning the terms, see H. J. Stoebe, THAT I, pp. 587-597, pp. 600-621; II, pp. 761-768.

18. Cf. the article by H. J. Stoebe (note 17), *ḥnn* "to be merciful" and *ḥaesaed* "goodness" and the bibliography there.

19. Concerning God's "wrath" see G. Sauer's article *qṣp* "to be wrathful," THAT II, pp. 663-666 and the same author *af* "wrath," THAT I, pp. 220-224 and the bibliography there. We cannot understand what the Old Testament means when it speaks of God's wrath if we are thinking of the mood changes of a transcendent being. God's wrath in the Old Testament is the experience of a destructive, annihilating power whose activity is a necessary part of reality. In his wrath, God reacts to evil, corruption, and mortal threats of all sorts. The energy and passion expressed in the word "wrath" serves life. Even in destruction, it is a power securing and preserving life. This is seen in the recurring emphasis on the preponderance of God's compassion as compared to his wrath (Ps. 30:5): "For his anger is but for a moment, and his favor is for a lifetime." Even when the destructive activity of God's wrath cannot be understood rationally, it remains the wrath of the God which wants life. A God which was only goodness would not correspond to reality.

20. BK I/2, pp. 116-128.

21. R. Albertz (1978).

22. See the bibliography concerning Part I, and also the bibliography concerning Part II, "God's Mercy with His People."

23. I refer here to S. Herrmann (1965) and C. Westermann, ThB 55, pp. 230-249, as well as the history of promises sketched above (pp. 51f.) in the context of the saving activity.

24. H. W. Wolff, BK XIV/2 concerning Amos 9:11-15.

25. G. von Rad, EvTh 8 (1948/49).

26. Concerning cult prophecy see J. Jeremias, WMANT 35.

27. W. Zimmerli, ZAW 66 (1954) and BK XIII/1.2 (1955-56).

28. H. H. Rowley (1944), bibliography up to that time; G. von Rad, *Theology* Vol. II, pp. 301-315, "Daniel and Apocalyptic."

Part V

1. Cf. the article "Gebet im Alten Testament," BHHW I (1962), pp. 519-522.

2. A. Wendel (1931).

3. Concerning names of praise in name-giving ceremonies, see M. Noth, BWANT 46, pp. 169-194; R. Albertz (1978).

4. Concerning this, see Ch. Barth (1947).

5. Concerning the Egyptian and Babylonian hymns, see Beyerlin, *Near Eastern Religious Texts,* pp. 12-15 and pp. 99–118.

6. F. Crüsemann, WMANT 32, pp. 83-104.

7. C. Westermann, ZAW 66.

8. H. Jahnow, BZAW 36 and the article on "Mourning" in IDB III, pp. 452-454.

9. A precise presentation in the *Einleitung in die Psalmen* by H. Gunkel-J. Begrich, p. 117 and p. 172f.

10. *Lob und Klage in den Psalmen,* C. Westermann, p. 52.

11. C. Westermann, *Der Aufbau des Buches Hiob* (1956; 2nd ed. 1977) with recent bibliography.

12. L. Perlitt, Festschr. G. von Rad, pp. 367-382.

13. F. Ahuis, diss. Heidelberg; U. Eichler (1978).

14. C. Westermann, Interp. 28, pp. 20-38.

15. M. Noth, SKG 17, p. 2.

16. J. J. Stamm (1958).

17. M. Noth, *Josua,* HAT I, pp. 105-110.

18. Concerning this see G. Liedke, WMANT 39.

19. G. von Rad gives a convincing presentation of the commandments (in contrast to the laws) in *Old Testament Theology,* Vol. I, pp. 190-203.

20. Cf. J. J. Stamm, Note 15.

21. A. Alt, *Essays,* pp. 88ff., and also G. Liedke, Note 18.

22. A. Alt (Note 21) has particularly emphasized this.

23. G. v. Rad, BWANT 47; R. P. Merendino, BBB 31.

24. H. Graf Reventlow, WMANT 6.

25. K. Koch, FRLANT NF 53.

26. Concerning this, I refer especially to the presentation by W. Zimmerli, *Old Testament Theology,* p. 120f. Concerning the first commandment see W. H. Schmidt, Theol Ex 165.

27. Beyerlin, *Near Eastern Religious Texts,* pp. 3-11; pp. 74-98; pp. 151-165; pp. 190-221.

28. It can therefore hardly be an accident that the turn away from history went hand in hand with early Christian theology's turn toward inner-divine problems in christology and the doctrine of the trinity. No longer did what happen between God (Christ) and humanity stand in the foreground, but rather what happened within the inner-divine realm. Thus also did the Old Testament increasingly lose significance.

29. Article on *'aebaed* "servant," THAT II, pp. 182-200; C. Westermann and the same author, article on *śrt* "to serve," THAT II, pp. 1019-1022.

30. Concerning this, BK I/1, pp. 381-435.

31. Concerning this, BK I/1, pp. 606-614.

32. Concerning this, BK I/2, pp. 123-125.

33. L. Rost, ZDPV 66 = Das kleine Credo, pp. 101-112.

34. Concerning the following, C. Westermann, *Festschr. E. Eichrodt*, pp. 227-249.

35. Concerning this, ThB 55, pp. 128-133 and the article on *kbd* "to be difficult," THAT I, pp. 794-812.

36. The question of how one is to imagine God's presence in the temple is of secondary significance. One spoke of God's dwelling in the sanctuary, which corresponds simply to the designation "the house of God." Or, if that seemed too massive, one spoke of the house above which Yahweh's name is named (e.g., Jer. 7:10), or of the glory *(kabod)* of God which descends on the sanctuary, as in the Priestly Writing.

37. Concerning this, H. J. Kraus, *Worship in Israel*, pp. 26-92; H. H. Rowley (1967), pp. 87-95; R. Martin-Achard (1974).

38. Cf. R. Albertz (1978).

39. Cf. R. de Vaux, *Ancient Israel: Its Life and Institutions*, p. 345f.

40. Cf. R. de Vaux, *op. cit.*, pp. 447f.; R. Rendtorff, WMANT 24.

41. G. v. Rad, BWANT 4 = ThB 8, pp. 9-86; H. W. Wolff, EvTh 24 = ThB 22, pp. 345-373.

42. G. v. Rad, *Old Testament Theology*, Vol. II, pp. 99-125.

43. B. Albrektson (1967).

44. J. Barr, *Old and New in Interpretation*.

45. M. Noth, *Überlieferungsgeschichtliche Studien I;* H. W. Wolff, ZAW 73 = ThB 22, 2nd ed. (1973), pp. 308-324.

46. K. Elliger, ThB 32, pp. 174-198 and see Note 25.

47. C. Westermann, see Note 34.

48. BK I/1, pp. 230-244.

Part VI

1. Concerning this section, let us refer particularly to A. H. J. Gunneweg, *Understanding the Old Testament;* in that, particularly Ch. II, and Ch. VII.

Bibliography

Theology of the Old Testament

E. Sellin, *Theologie des Alten Testaments* (1923; ²1933).

W. Eichrodt, *Theology of the Old Testament,* tr. J. A. Baker (Philadelphia: Westminster, 1961-67.

L. Köhler, *Old Testament Theology,* tr. A. S. Todd (Philadelphia: Westminster, 1957).

O. Procksch, *Theolgie des Alten Testaments* (1950).

Th. C. Vriezen, *An Outline of Old Testament Theology* (Newton, Mass.: Branford, 1962).

E. Jacob, *Theology of the Old Testament,* tr. A. W. Heathcote and P. J. Allcock (New York: Harper, 1958).

G. von Rad, *Old Testament Theology,* tr. D. M. G. Stalker (New York: Harper and Row, 1962, 1965).

G. Fohrer, *Theologische Grundstrukturen des Alten Testaments* (1972).

W. Zimmerli, *Old Testament Theology in Outline,* tr. David E. Green (Atlanta: John Knox, 1978).

Part I: What Does the Old Testament Say About God?

Concerning the Preliminary Remarks

B. S. Childs, *Biblical Theology in Crisis* (1970).

R. Smend, *Die Mitte des Alten Testaments:* ThSt 101 (1970).

C. Westermann, "Weisheit im Sprichwort," in *Festschrift A. Jepsen* (1971), pp. 73-85 = ThB 55 (1974), pp. 149-161.

E. Würthwein, "Zur Theologie des Alten Testaments," ThR NF 36, 3 (1971), pp. 185-208.

G. F. Hasel, "The Problem of the Center in the Old Testament," ZAW 86 (1974), pp. 65-82.

C. Westermann, *Genesis:* BK I/1 (1974; ²1975).

W. Zimmerli, "Zum Problem der 'Mitte des Alten Testaments,' " EvTh 35 (1975), pp. 97-118.

G. W. Coats-B. O. Long, *Canon and Authority: Essays in Old Testament Religion and Theology* (1977).

Concerning the History

K. v. Hofmann, *Weissagung und Erfüllung* (1841-1844).

F. Delitzsch, *Die Genesis:* KD (⁴1872).

M. Buber, *I and Thou,* 2nd ed., tr. R. G. Smith (New York: Scribner, 1958).

A. Alt, "Josua" (1936), in KlSchr. I (1953), pp. 176-192.

————, *Essays on Old Testament History and Religion,* tr. R. A. Wilson (Oxford: Basil Blackwell, 1966).

M. Buber, *Schriften über das dialogische Prinzip* (1954).

F. Hesse, "Die Erforschung der Geschichte Israels als theologische Aufgabe," KuD 4 (1958), pp. 1-19.

M. Noth, "Geschichtsschreibung im Alten Testament," RGG³ II (1958), pp. 1458-1501.

F. Hesse, "Kerygma oder geschichtliche Wirklichkeit," ZThK 57 (1960), pp. 17-26.

Concerning the Word of God in the Old Testament

W. Pannenberg, *Revelation as History,* tr. D. Grankskou (New York: Macmillan, 1968).

R. Rendtorff, "The Concept of Revelation in Ancient Israel," in W. Pannenberg (1968).

Part II: The Saving God and History

Concerning the Meaning of God's Saving Activity in the Old Testament

R. Kraetzschmar, *Die Bundesvorstellung im Alten Testament in ihrer geschichtlichen Entwicklung* (1896).

K. Galling, *Die Erwählungstraditionen Israels,* BZAW 48 (1928).

G. von Rad, *The Problem of the Hexateuch* (New York: McGraw Hill, 1966); German original: ThB 8 (1958), pp. 9-81.

M. Noth, *A History of Pentateuch Traditions,* tr. B. W. Anderson (Englewood Cliffs, N. J.: Prentice Hall, 1972).

H. H. Rowley, *The Biblical Doctrine of Election* (1950).

Th. C. Vriezen, *Die Erwählung Israels nach dem Alten Testament* (1953).

K. Koch, "Zur Geschichte der Erwählungsvorstellung Israels," ZAW 67 (1955), pp. 205-226.

K. Baltzer, *The Covenant Formulary,* tr. D. E. Green (Philadelphia: Fortress, 1971).

R. Martin-Achard, "La signification théologique de l'élection d'Israël," ThZ 16 (1960), pp. 333-341.

G. E. Mendenhall, *Recht und Bund in Israel und dem Alten Vorderen Orient,* ThSt 64 (1960).

H. Wildberger, *Jahwes Eigentumsvolk: Eine Studie zur Traditionsgeschichte und Theologie des Erwählungsgedankens,* ATANT 37 (1960).

A. Jepsen, "Berith. Ein Beitrag zur Theologie der Exilszeit," *Festschrift W. Rudolph* (1961), pp. 161-179.

D. J. McCarthy, *Treaty and Covenant. A Study in Form in the Ancient Oriental Documents and in the Old Testament,* AnBibl 21 (1963).

R. Smend, *Die Bundesformel,* ThSt 68 (1963).

C. Westermann, "Vergegenwärtigung der Geschichte in den Psalmen," ThB 24 (1964), pp. 306-353 = *Lob und Klage in den Psalmen* (1977), pp. 165-194.

D. J. McCarthy, *Old Testament Covenant: A Survey of Current Opinions* (Richmond: John Knox, 1972).

N. Lohfink, *Die Landverheißung als Eid. Eine Studie zu Genesis 15*, SBS 28 (1967).

L. Perlitt, *Bundestheologie im Alten Testament*, WMANT 36 (1969).

D. G. Spriggs, *Two Old Testament Theologies*, StBTh (1974).

Concerning the Activity of Saving and History

L. Rost, *Die Überlieferung von der Thronnachfolge Davids*, BWANT 42 NF 3 (1926) = *Das kleine Credo* (1965), pp. 119-253.

G. von Rad, "Zelt und Lade," NKZ 31 (1931), pp. 476-498 = ThB 8 (1958), pp. 109-129; see bibliography concerning I.

A. Alt, "Josua," see bibliography concerning Part I.

L. Rost, "Weidewechsel und altisraelitischer Festkalender," ZDPV 66 (1943), pp. 205-215 = *Das kleine Credo* (1965), pp. 101-112.

W. Richter, *Die Bearbeitung des "Retterbuches" in der deuteronomischen Epoche*, BBB 21 (1964).

L. Rost, *Das kleine Credo und andere Studien zum Alten Testament* (1965).

Concerning the Elements of Saving Activity

J. Begrich, "Das priesterliche Heilsorakel," ZAW 52 (1934), pp. 81-92.

G. von Rad, "Verheißenes Land und Jahwes Land," ZDPV 66 (1943), pp. 191-204 = ThB 8 (1958), pp. 87-100.

———, *Genesis*, tr. J. H. Marks (Philadelphia: Westminster, 1961).

M. Buber, *The Prophetic Faith*, tr. C. Witton-Davies (New York: Macmillan, 1949).

G. von Rad, *Der heilige Krieg im alten Israel* (1951).

S. Mowinckel, *He That Cometh. The Messianic Hope in the Old Testament and in the Time of Jesus* (1952; ²1959).

W. Zimmerli, "Ich bin Jahweh," *Festschrift A. Alt* (1953), pp. 179-209 = ThB 19 (1963), pp. 11-40.

C. Westermann, *The Praise of God in the Psalms*, tr. K. Crim (Richmond: John Knox, 1965).

R. Smend, *Das Mosebild von Heinrich Ewald bis Martin Noth* (1959).

G. Quell, "Das Panomen des Wunders im Alten Testament," *Festschrift W. Rudolph* (1961), pp. 253-300.

K. Koch, "Der Tod des Religionsstifters," KuD 8 (1962), pp. 100-123.

R. Smend, *Jahwekrieg und Stämmebund. Erwägungen zur ältesten Geschichte Israels*, FRLANT 84 (1963).

H. W. Wolff, "Das Kerygma des Jahwisten," EvTh 24 (1964), pp. 73-98 = ThB 22 (1964), pp. 345-373.

S. Hermann, *Die prophetischen Heilserwartungen im alten Testament. Ursprung und Gestaltwandel*, BWANT 5, 5 (85) (1965).

J. Jeremias, *Theophanie, Die Geschichte einer alttestamentlichen Gattung*, WMANT 10 (1965).

C. Westermann, *Isaiah 40-66: A Commentary*, tr. D. M. G. Stalker (Philadelphia: Westminster, 1969).

H. D. Preuβ, ". . . ich will mit dir sein!" ZAW 80 (1968), pp. 139-173.

D. Vetter, *Jahwes Mit-Sein, ein Ausdruck des Segens*, AzTh 1, 45 (1971).

S. Herrmann, *A History of Israel in Old Testament Times* (Philadelphia: Fortress, 1975).

C. Westermann, "Das sakrale Königtum in seinen Erscheinungsformen und seiner Geschichte," ThB 55 (1974), pp. 291-308.

———, *The Promises to the Fathers: Studies on the Patriarchal Narratives*, tr. D. E. Green (Philadelphia: Fortress, 1979).

R. Albertz, *Persönliche Frömmigkeit und offizielle Religion*, Calwer Monographien (1978).

Part III: The Blessing God and Creation

Concerning the Creator and Creation

K. Budde, *Die biblische Urgeschichte (Gen. 1-12:5) untersucht* (1883).

H. Gunkel, *Schöpfung und Chaos in Urzeit und Endzeit. Eine religionsgeschichtliche Untersuchung über Gen. 1 und ApJoh 12* (1895; [2]1921).

G. von Rad, "Das theologische Problem des alttestamentlichen Schöpfungsglaubens," BZAW 66 (1936), pp. 138-147 = ThB 8 ([3]1965), pp. 136-147.

K. Barth, *Church Dogmatics* III, 1 (1958).

W. Zimmerli, "Ort und Grenze der Weisheit im Rahmen der alttestamentlichen Theologie," ThB 19 (1963), pp. 300-315.

W. H. Schmidt, *Die Schöpfungsgeschichte der Priesterschrift*, WMANT 17 (1964; [2]1967).

K. Koch, "Wort und Einheit des Schöpfergottes in Memphis und Jerusalem," ZThK 62 (1965), pp. 251-293.

H. J. Hermisson, *Studien zur Spruchweisheit*, WMANT 28 (1968).

O. Loretz, *Schöpfung und Mythos, Mensch und Welt nach den Anfangskapiteln der Genesis*, SBS 32 (1968).

G. von Rad, *Wisdom in Israel*, (Nashville: Abingdon, 1972).

O. Steck, *Die Paradieserzählung*, BSt 60 (1970).

R. B. Y. Scott, *The Way of Wisdom* (1971).

C. Westermann, *Creation*, tr. J. J. Scullion (Philadelphia: Fortress, 1974).

G. Liedke, "Von der Ausbeutung zur Kooperation," *Studien zur Friedensforschung* 8 (1972), pp. 36-65.

C. Westermann, *Genesis 1-11*, Erträge der Forschung 7 (1972).

———, "Die theologische Bedeutung der Urgeschichte," TTKi 44 (1973), pp. 161-176 = ThB 55 (1974), pp. 96-114.

H. W. Wolff, *Anthropology of the Old Testament*, tr. M. Kohl (Philadelphia: Fortress, 1974).

R. Albertz, *Weltschöpfung und Menschenschöpfung untersuch bei Deuterojesaja, Hiob und in den Psalmen*, Calwer Theol. Monographien 3 (1974).

D. Ritschl, "Die Last des augustinischen Erbes," *Konzepte, Ges. Aufs.* I (1976), pp. 102-122.

J. Baur, ed., *Zum Thema Menschenrechte* (1977).

C. Westermann, "Das Alte Testament und die Menschenrechte," in J. Baur (1977), pp. 5-18.

Concerning the Blessing

J. Pederson, *Israel, Its Life and Culture* I-II (1926; [2]1946); "Blessing," pp. 182-212.

G. von Rad, *Das Gottesvolk im Deuteronomium*, BWANT 47 (1929).

S. Mowinckel, *He That Cometh* (1952; [2]1959).

H. W. Wolff, "Das Kerygma des Jahwisten," EvTh 24 (1964) pp. 73-98 = ThB 22 (1964; [3]1973), pp. 345-373.

C. Westermann, *Blessing in the Bible and the Life of the Church*, tr. K. R. Crim (Philadelphia: Fortress, 1978).

G. Wehmeier, *Der Segen im Alten Testament. Eine semasiologische Untersuchung der Wurzel brk*, theol. diss. 6 (1970).

Concerning Creation and Blessing in the History of Religions and in the Old Testament.

W. Beyerlin, ed., *Near Eastern Religious Texts Relating to the Old Testament*, tr. J. Bowden (Philadelphia: Westerminster, 1978).

Part IV: God's Judgment and God's Mercy

Concerning Sin and Judgment

C. Westermann, *Der Aufbau des Buches Hiob* (1956; [2]1977).

R. Knierim, *Die Hauptbegriffe für Sünde im Alten Testament* (1965; [2]1967).

C. Westermann, "Der Mensch im Urgeschehen," KuD 13 (1967), pp. 231-246.

K. Koch, ed., *Um das Prinzip der Vergeltung in Religion und Recht des Alten Testaments*, WF 125 (1972).

Concerning the Prophecy of Judgment

G. Hölscher, *Die Propheten* (1914).

H. Gunkel, *Die Propheten* (1917).

H. W. Wolff, "Hauptprobleme alttestamentlicher Prophetie," EvTh 15 (1955), pp. 116-168 = ThB 22 (1964; [3]1973), pp. 206-231.

C. Westermann, *Basic Forms of Prophetic Speech*, tr. H. C. White (London: Lutterworth Press, 1967).

———, "Propheten," BHHW III (1966), pp. 1496-1512.

G. Fohrer, *Die Propheten des Alten Testaments* I-IV (1974-77).

Concerning God's Mercy with His People; Salvation Prophecy

G. von Rad, "Die Stadt auf dem Berge," EvTh8 (1948-49), pp. 439-447 = ThB 8 (1958; [3]1965), pp. 214-224.

W. Zimmerli, "Die Eigenart der prophetischen Rede des Propheten Ezechiel," ZAW 66 (1954), pp. 1-26 = ThB 19 (1963), pp. 148-177.

———, *Ezechiel*, BK XIII/1 (1955-56).

S. Mowinckel, *He That Cometh* (1952; [2]1959).

C. Westermann, "Der Weg der Verheißung durch das Alte Testament," in *The Old Testament and Christian Faith*, ed. B. W. Anderson (1963), pp. 200-224 = ThB 55 (1974), pp. 230-249.

——, "Das Heilswort bei Deuterojesaja," EvTh 24 (1964), pp. 355-373.

S. Hermann, *Die prophetischen Heilserwartungen im Alten Testament* (1965).

C. Westermann, *Isaiah 40-66: A Commentary*, tr. D. M. G. Stalker (Philadelphia: Westerminster, 1969).

J. Jeremias, *Kultprophetie und Gerichtsverkündigung in der späten Königszeit*, WMANT 35 (1970).

R. Albertz, *Persönliche Frömmigkeit und offizielle Religion* (1978).

Concerning God's Judgment and God's Mercy at the End: Apocalyptic

H. H. Rowley, *The Relevance of Apocalyptics: A Study of Jewish and Christian Apocalypses from Daniel to the Revelation* (1944; [2]1947).

K. Löwith, *Weltgeschehen und Heilsgeschichte* (1953; [3]1956).

D. Rössler, *Gesetz und Geschichte* (1960).

S. Aalen, "Apokalyptik," BHHW I (1962), pp. 107f.

M. Rist, "Apocalypticism," IDB I (1962), pp. 157-161.

O. Plöger, *Theocracy and Eschatology*, tr. S. Rudman (Richmond: John Knox, 1968).

P. von der Osten-Sacken, *Die Apokalyptik in ihrem Verhältnis zur Prophetie und Weisheit*, TheolEx 157 (1969).

Part V: The Response

Concerning the Response in Speech

H. Jahnow, *Das hebräische Leichenlied im Rahmen der Volksdichtung*, BZAW 36 (1923).

H. Gunkel-J. Begrich, *Einleitung in die Psalmen* (1928; [3]1966).

M. Noth, *Die israelitschen Personennamen im Rahmen der gemeinsemitischen Namengebung*, BWANT 46 (1928) = Ges. Stud. (1966), pp. 66-101.

U. Eichler, *Der Klagende Jeremia*, Diss. Heidelberg (1978).

A. Wendel, *Das freie Laiengebet im vorexilischen Israel* I-III (1931).

Ch. Barth, *Die Errettung vom Tode in den individuellen Klage- und Dankliedern des Alten Testaments* (1947).

C. Westermann, "Struktur und Geschichte der Klage im Alten Testament," ZAW 66 (1954), pp. 44-80 = ThB 24 (1964), pp. 266-305 = *Lob und Klage in den Psalmen* (1977), pp. 125-164.

——, *Der Aufbau des Buches Hiob* (1956; [2]1977).

S. Mowinckel, *The Psalms in Israel's Worship* (1972).

F. Crüsemann, *Studien zur Formgeschichte von Hymnos und Danklied in Israel*, WMANT 32 (1969).

F. Ahuis, *Der leidende Gerichtsprophet*, diss. Heidelberg (1971).

L. Perlitt, "Die Verborgenheit Gottes," *Festschrift G. von Rad* (1971), pp. 367-382.

E. Gerstenberger, "Psalms," in *Old Testament Form Criticism*, ed. J. H. Hayes (1974), pp. 179-224.

C. Westermann, "The Role of the Lament in the Theology of the Old Testament," Interp. 28, 1 (1974), pp. 20-38.

————, "Anthropologische und theologische Aspekte des Gebets in den Psalmen," *Zur neuen Psalmen-Forschung,* ed. P. Neumann (1976), pp. 452-468.

R. Albertz, see above concerning Part IV, *("God's Mercy . . . ")* (1978).

Concerning Commandment and Law in the Old Testament

G. von Rad, *Das Gottesvolk im Deuteronomium,* BWANT 47 (1929).

A. Alt, *Die Ursprünge des israelitischen Rechts* (1934) = K1Schr. I (1953), pp. 278-332.

J. Hempel, *Das Ethos des Alten Testaments,* BZAW 67 (1938; ²1964).

M. Noth, *Das Buch Josua,* HAT I, 7 (1938; ²1953).

————, *The Laws in the Pentateuch and other Studies,* tr. D. R. Ap-Thomas (Philadelphia: Fortress, 1967).

W. Zimmerli, "Das zweite Gebot (Exod. 20:4-6)," in *Festschrift A. Bertholet* (1950), pp. 550-563 = ThB 19 (1963; ²1969), pp. 234-248.

J. J. Stamm, *Der Dekalog im Lichte der neueren Forschung* (1958; ²1962).

K. Koch, *Die Priesterschrift von Ex. 25 bis Lev. 16. Eine überlieferungsgeschichtliche Untersuchung,* FRLANT NF 53 (1959).

H. Graf Reventlow, *Das Heiligkeitsgeset, formgeschichtlich untersucht,* WMANT 6 (1961).

R. P. Merendino, *Das deuteronomische Gesetz,* BBB 31 (1969).

W. H. Schmidt, *Das erste Gebot. Seine Bedeutung für das Alte Testament,* TheolEx 165 (1969).

G. Liedke, *Gestalt und Bezeichung alttestamentlicher Rechtssätze. Eine formgeschichtlich-terminologische Studie,* WMANT 39 (1971).

A. H. J. Gunneweg, *Understanding the Old Testament: A Study in Hermeneutics* (Philadelphia: Westminster, 1978), chapter 4.

W. M. Clark, "Law," in *Old Testament Form Criticism,* ed. J. H. Hayes (1974), pp. 99-140.

Concerning Worship

L. Rost, "Weidewechsel und Altisraelitischer Festkalender," ZDPV 66 (1943), pp. 205-216 = *Das kleine Credo* (1965), pp. 101-112.

H. J. Kraus, *Worship in Israel,* tr. G. Buswell (Richmond: John Knox, 1966).

R. de Vaux, *Ancient Israel: Its Life and Institutions,* tr. J. McHugh (New York: McGraw-Hill, 1961).

R. Rendtorff, *Studien zur Geschichte des Opfers im alten Israel,* WMANT 24 (1967).

H. H. Rowley, *Worship in Ancient Israel: Its Form and Meaning* (1967).

C. Westermann, "Die Herrlichkeit Gottes in der Priesterschrift," in *Festschrift W. Eichrodt* (1971), pp. 227-249 = ThB 55 (1974), pp. 115-137.

R. Martin-Achard, *Essai biblique sur les fêtes d'Israël* (1974).

Concerning the Response of Contemplation or Reflection

G. von Rad, *The Problem of the Hexateuch* (New York: McGraw-Hill, 1966).

M. Noth, *Überlieferungsgeschichtliche Studien* I (1943; ²1957).

K. Elliger, "Sinn und Ursprung der priesterlichen Geschichtserzählung," ZThK 49 (1952) = ThB 32 (1966), pp. 174-198.

H. W. Wolff, "Das Kerygma des deuteronomischen Geschichtswerkes," ZAW 73 (1961), pp. 171-186 = ThB 22 (1964; ²1973), pp. 308-324.

————, "Das Kerygma des Jahwisten," EvTh 24 (1964), pp. 73-98 = ThB 22 (1964; ²1973), pp. 345-373.

B. Albrektson, *History and the Gods: An Essay of the Idea of Historical Events as Divine Manifestations in the Ancient Near East and in Israel,* Coniectanea Biblica, OT Ser. I (1967).

J. Barr, *Old and New in Interpretation: A Study of the Two Testaments* (London: SCM, 1966).

Part VI: The Old Testament and Jesus Christ

G. Ebeling, "What Is Biblical Theology," in *Word and Faith,* tr. J. W. Leitch (London: SCM, 1963).

G. von Rad, *Old Testament Theology,* Vol. II (1965).

H. Gese, "Erwägungen zur Einheit der biblischen Theologie," ZThK 67 (1970), pp. 417-436.

H. J. Kraus, *Die biblische Theologie, ihre Geschichte und Problematik* (1970).

J. Barr. "Trends and Prospects in Biblical Theology," JThSt 24 (1974), pp. 265-282.

B. W. Anderson, "The New Crisis in Biblical Theology," in *C. Michalson: The Drew Gateway* (1974/75), pp. 159-174.

P. Stuhlmacher, "Schriftauslegung auf dem Wege zur biblischen Theologie," ZThK 72 (1975), pp. 128-166.

H. Seebass, "Zur Ermöglichung biblischer Theologie," EvTh 37 (1977), pp. 591-600.

A. H. J. Gunneweg, *Understanding the Old Testament: A Study in Hermenuetics* (Philadelphia: Westminster, 1978).

Scripture Index

Subject Index